'Don We Now Our Gay Apparel'

Dress, Body, Culture

Series Editor **Joanne B. Eicher**, *Regents' Professor, University of Minnesota*

Advisory Board:

Ruth Barnes, *Ashmolean Museum, University of Oxford*
Helen Callaway, *CCCRW, University of Oxford*
James Hall, *University of Illinois at Chicago*
Beatrice Medicine, *California State University, Northridge*
Ted Polhemus, *Curator, "Street Style" Exhibition, Victoria & Albert Museum*
Griselda Pollock, *University of Leeds*
Valerie Steele, *The Museum at the Fashion Institute of Technology*
Lou Taylor, *University of Brighton*
John Wright, *University of Minnesota*

Books in this provocative series seek to articulate the connections between culture and dress which is defined here in its broadest possible sense as any modification or supplement to the body. Interdisciplinary in approach, the series highlights the dialogue between identity and dress, cosmetics, coiffure, and body alterations as manifested in practices as varied as plastic surgery, tattooing, and ritual scarification. The series aims, in particular, to analyze the meaning of dress in relation to popular culture and gender issues and will include works grounded in anthropology, sociology, history, art history, literature, and folklore.

ISSN: 1360-466X

Previously published titles in the Series

'Don We Now Our Gay Apparel'

Gay Men's Dress in the Twentieth Century

Shaun Cole

BERG

Oxford • New York

First published in 2000 by
Berg
Editorial offices:
150 Cowley Road, Oxford, OX4 1JJ, UK
838 Broadway, Third Floor, New York, NY 10003-4812, USA

Berg is an imprint of Oxford International Publishers Ltd.

Library of Congress Cataloging-in-Publication Data
A catalogue record for this book is available from the Library of Congress.

British Library Cataloguing-in-Publication Data
A catalogue record for this book is available from the British Library.

ISBN   1 85973 415 4 (Cloth)
       1 85973 420 0 (Paper)

Typeset by JS Typesetting, Wellingborough, Northants.
Printed in the United Kingdom by Biddles Ltd, Guildford and King's Lynn.

For Andrew
Falala Lalala La La La

Contents

Acknowledgements

I would firstly like to thank all the men that I interviewed (and this includes those who may not have been aware that I was gleaning information from them as we chatted). Without their time and memories this book could never have been written. Even where I have not directly quoted from our conversations I am grateful for the thoughts, ideas and further leads that they offered. Particular thanks go to John Hardy, Jonathan Jackson, Joe Pop and Ray Weller. I am also grateful to those who have allowed me to publish their photographs.

I am indebted to the staff of the libraries that hold archives that I have used in the course of my research: the National Art Library, the New York Public Library, San Francisco Public Library, the Hall Carpenter Archive, the Mass-Observation Archive, The Gay and Lesbian Historical Society of Northern California Archive (especially Willie Walker), The Lesbian and Gay Community Services Center, the National Archive of Lesbian and Gay History in New York (Rich Wandell), the National Sound Archive (Rob Perks) and the BBC Sound Archive.

Quotations from the Mass-Observation archive are reproduced with the permission of Curtis Brown Ltd, London, Copyright the Trustees of the Mass-Observation Archive at the University of Sussex. The Tom of Finland drawing is reproduced with the permission of the Tom of Finland Foundation, Los Angeles.

I would like to acknowledge the work others before me have done into the recording of gay history, particularly George Chauncey and the Brighton Ourstory Project, whose research and publications have been of great importance and guidance to me and I'm sure to many others working in this field.

I am extremely grateful to Amy de la Haye and Andrew Tomlin for taking the time to read drafts of this book in its various forms. Their comments, thoughts and suggestions were invaluable.

I would like to thank all my friends (especially John), family and colleagues (notably Cath and Katie) who have supported me through this project, listening and offering encouragement and advice, tea and cake when they were needed.

Acknowledgements

I would also like to thank Berg for giving me the opportunity to pursue this project, from its initial thoughts to the book you see today.

And finally I would like to acknowledge all gay men for having the courage to be true to themselves, and having such fabulous dress sense; without you there would be no book!

Shaun Cole
London

Preface

When I began this project I soon realised that one of the most important elements would be real gay men's experiences. Many of the best books dealing with gay histories have utilised an oral history approach, and some of the first references I discovered to gay men's dress were included in such accounts. In order to present these 'real' memories and experiences I conducted a series of twenty-four interviews with gay men, whose ages ranged from thirty to eighty-nine. Most conversations were recorded and took between one and three hours. The three earliest interviews I conducted were for a report I was asked to produced for the Victoria and Albert Museum's exhibition *Streetstyle: From Sidewalk to Catwalk*. I interviewed one of these men a second time, as he had touched on experiences in the first interview that were not relevant for the exhibition yet that I felt would be vital to the research for the book. All the men interviewed gave their permission to be quoted in this book. Six of the interviewees asked me to use only their first names, and two preferred to be known by pseudonyms.

I gathered my interviewees by a number of methods. Some responded to advertisements in the British gay press. Others were introduced to me by colleagues researching related fields of interest. Three, who had published books, I approached directly, asking permission to interview them. Four were friends who had discussed their experiences once they were aware of this project. At first I hesitated to conduct formal interviews with these men, but later realised that they were an important and valuable source. All the interviews provided me with information and thoughts for this book, even where the men have not been directly quoted.

Introduction

The Clothes! The Ralph Lauren polo shirts, the Halston suits, the Ultrasuede jackets, T-shirts of every hue, bleached fatigues and painters jeans, plaid shirts, transparent plastic belts, denim jackets and bomber jackets, combat fatigues and old corduroys, hooded sweatshirts, baseball caps, and shoes lined up under a forest of shoe trees on the floor; someone had once left the house and all he could tell his friends was that Malone had forty-four shoe trees in his closet. There were drawers and drawers of jump suits, shirts by Ronald Kolodzie, Estee Lauder lotions and astringents, and drawers and drawers of bathing suits, of which he had twenty eight, in racing and boxer styles. And then there were the clothes that Malone really wore: The old clothes he had kept since his days at boarding school in Vermont – the old khaki pants, button down shirts with small collars (for someone who ran around with the trendiest designers, he loathed changes in style), a pair of rotten tennis sneakers, an old tweed jacket. There was one drawer filled with nothing but thirty-seven T-shirts in different colors, colors he had bleached them or dyed them, soft plum and faded shrimp and celery green and all shades of yellow, his best color. He had scoured the army–navy surplus stores in lower Manhattan looking for T-shirts, for underwear, plaid shirts and old faded jeans. There was a closet hung with thirty-two plaid shirts, and a bureau filled entirely with jeans faded to various shades of blue. I finally stood up, depressed at all these things – for what were they but emblems of Malone's innocent heart, his inexhaustible desire to be liked?[1]

This passage appears just a few pages into Andrew Holleran's 1978 novel, *Dancer From The Dance*, which describes the lives of two gay men living in New York in the 1970s and their (and by implication other gay men's) obsession with clothes. Many gay novels or novels dealing with a gay subject have utilised descriptions of dress to form a picture of the physical appearance and also the personality of gay characters (this is, of course, a device that is also utilised by authors for heterosexual characters). Within this book the importance of descriptions of dress in such novels is highlighted because clothing, along with adornment and demeanour, has been a primary method of identification for and of gay men. In his book, *Men in Black*, the literary historian John Harvey notes the importance of commentary on dress in novels (something he himself utilises to the full extent). But even though he stresses the value of remarks on dress, he admits that there is 'some redundancy in the ordinary run of clothing-comment in novels', most notably because 'what is often said is that an interest in dress is frivolous, and that this interest is especially a feminine frivolity'.[2]

The issue of ephemerality, and particularly the characterisation of an active interest in clothing as feminine and frivolous, has been a prevalent, and an active, issue for debate in studies of twentieth-century men's clothing. For example, in *The Face of Fashion* Jennifer Craik notes that the 'rhetoric of men's fashion takes the form of a set of denials', one of which is that 'men who dress up are peculiar (one way or another)'.[3] Implied in this 'peculiarity' is homosexuality. The notion of a man's interest in clothing, acting as a signifier of his homosexuality, is mentioned in most works on twentieth-century fashion, but usually in the form of a denial that all men interested in clothes and fashion[4] were or are homosexual. What many of these commentaries do offer is an opinion that (for various reasons, the most notable being their status as 'outsiders' and the self-association of some gay men with the feminine), gay men were ahead of 'fashion' and influenced changes in men's fashion through their challenge to the hegemony of men's dress codes.

It would be incorrect to assume that all gay men have shown a developed interest in what they wear and have made efforts to define their dress choices through, or as a marker of, their sexual orientation. However, there have been a considerable number of gay men who have made conscious efforts to utilise their clothing to express this important facet of their identity. Apparel and adornment had provided an indication of homosexuality or of a tendency toward same-sex sexual activity since the seventeenth century. Contemporary accounts of eighteenth-century homosexuals or 'mollies'[5] concentrate on the effeminate appearance and dress choice of these men: 'There was a particular Gang of Sodomiticall Wretches in Town who call themselves Mollies and are so far degenerated from all Masculine Deportment . . . that they rather fancy themselves as Women, imitating all the little Vanities . . . of the Female Sex.'[6] Scholars whose work has concentrated on this period concur that molly culture amounted to the development of a same-sex subculture. 'There was now a continuing culture to be fixed on', Alan Bray identified, 'and an extension of the area in which homosexuality could be expressed and therefore recognised; clothes, gestures, language, particular buildings and particular public places.'[7]

Professor Elizabeth Wilson has argued that dress serves to 'stabilize identity' and that the identity that dress makes firm is both single and shared: 'The way which we dress may assuage that fear [of not sustaining the autonomy of the self] by stabilizing our individual identity.'[8] For many men growing up gay, experimentation with clothing offered a means of exploring that sense of difference. 'Straight men never [have to] question their identity', stated

John, 'but growing up gay and realising that one is different means a constant questioning of who you are. Experimenting with clothes is a way of exploring this difference, a way of showing or accepting your difference.'[9]

Just as important as identifying and 'stabilising' an individual identity is the need to define oneself as part of a group. Gay men are, as the historian Dennis Altman has argued, 'by necessity far more conscious of the symbols of identity than people who are part of an ethnic group from birth on'.[10] Altman identifies that whether or not people are 'born' disposed to homosexuality, 'the adoption of a homosexual identity involves a series of choices'.[11] Drawing on the work of George Herbert Mead, Fred Davis notes the importance of (ambivalence surrounding self-) identity, highlighting the questions one frequently asks concerning what clothes say about the self.[12]

Various strategies were developed by gay men to 'manage' their identities in worlds where they were seen as 'immoral and ill, pathetic and dangerous' (to quote the title of an essay by Frank Pearce).[13] These were reflected in behaviour, demeanour and, most importantly for this study, dress. The sociologist Martin P. Levine has identified three such strategies: 'passing, minstrelization and capitulation'.[14] Passing involved dressing and behaving in such a way as to become 'invisible' as a gay man, to be able to negotiate the wider world under a disguise of heterosexuality. Minstrelization was the adoption of cross-gendered behaviour through feminine dress, behaviour and speech, described by many (observers and participants, both gay and straight) as 'camp'. Capitulation arose from the sense of guilt and self-hatred about one's homosexuality resulting from the belief that homosexuality was a form of gender deviance. These three strategies were, however, not exclusive. Gay men moved through the three states as they passed through the different spheres of their lives. In his seminal work *The Presentation of Self in Everyday Life* (1959), Erving Goffman used the notion of the theatre to describe the social processes through which actors execute different performances in front of different audiences. He proposes that the self is constantly created and recreated through interactions with other actors. Thus the gay man is playing to his heterosexual or homosexual audiences on differently defined stages, as 'those before whom [he] plays one of his parts won't be the same individuals before whom he plays a different part in another setting'.[15] Pre-Liberation observational accounts of gay life noted the inconstancy of gay men's behaviour (and dress) in different settings, reflecting their presenting different parts on different stages. In his pseudo-psychological account, *The Sixth Man* (1962), Jess Stearn observed 'They have a different face for different occasions. In conversations with each other, they often undergo a subtle change. I have seen men who appeared to be normal suddenly smile roguishly, soften their voices and simper as they greeted homosexual friends.'[16] Despite the many changes brought about by gay liberation, allowing gay men the freedom and (legal) rights to live their lives openly, such tactics were (and still are) necessary, as Andrew Holleran identified: 'How to integrate our homosexuality with the rest of our selves, our lives ... Most of us just kept everything in compartments. Most of us led double, triple, quadruple lives, changing costumes as actors do.'[17]

Symbols or signs of identity are, the literary theorist Harold Beaver has argued, of primary importance to gay men: 'For to be homosexual in Western society entails a state of mind in which all credentials, however petty, are under increasing scrutiny. The homosexual is beset by signs, by the urge to interpret whatever transpires, or fails to transpire between himself and every chance acquaintance. He is a prodigious consumer of signs – hidden meanings, hidden systems, hidden potentiality. Exclusion from the common code impels the frenzied quest: in the momentary glimpse, the scrambled figure, the sporadic gesture, the chance encounter, the reverse image, the sudden slippage, the lowered guard.'[18] Gay men had 'developed a semiotics for identification and/or invisibility within the larger culture, as well as communication among themselves'.[19]

Since the late nineteenth century gay men had imbued certain elements of dress with symbolism, using them as means of attracting other men or revealing their secret identity to one another. Oscar Wilde and his circle had worn green carnations as an indicator of their sexuality. Some symbols had been intended entirely to identify men as gay, either to society at large or each other. Other symbols were intended purely to be used within a gay space to indicate sexual preference: active or passive, available or spoken for, or type of activity. Codes or signs are of course not just important for gay men; indeed, they play a part in every aspect of every life, and even the most presumed phenomena can function as signs. Stuart Hall has argued that codes 'cover the face of social life and render it classifiable, intelligible, meaningful'.[20] But codes and signs can be interpreted in a variety of ways, and readings are dependent upon the familiarity of the reader with the contexts in which the sign is created and utilised. Signs, of course, need not be intentional. Umberto Eco wrote that 'not only the expressly intended communicative object ... but every object may be viewed as a sign'.[21] Gay codes also allowed men to see themselves as participants in the dominant culture by enabling them to see themselves in the interstices of that culture. Gay men, like everyone else, constructed their images and presentational style from the materials of the broader culture. Neither masculine nor feminine styles, Martin P. Levine affirms, are innate in gay physiology; neither is genetically encoded.[22] But these styles represent the construction of a gay male identity from the artefacts and materials that gay men find in their culture.

If codification was intended as a means of distinguishing gay men from the majority of the population, it was important for those codes to retain their exclusivity. In 1977, D. J. West identified that 'they must change in order to keep ahead, to maintain the identity of the group, for straight society tends to pick up and often to take over what was once almost exclusively the prerogative of a sexual minority'.[23] This is, of course an argument that could be levelled at the fashion industry's appropriation of any subcultural dress code.[24] For many gay men, the adoption of gay dress styles by heterosexual men marks the importance and the relevance of gay culture: 'gay style actually sets trends. It's what people take fashion from', Tony asserts. Joe Pop confirms this opinion, stating: 'apart from a few things gay culture is basically what becomes straight culture six months later'. It is not just gay men (who, it could be argued, have a vested interest in promoting the importance and the trend-setting nature of their culture) who have noted the importance of gay culture and dress. Susan Sontag, in her influential essay 'Notes on Camp', wrote that 'Jews and homosexuals are the outstanding creative minorities in contemporary urban culture . . . The two pioneering forces of modern sensibility are Jewish moral seriousness and homosexual aesthetics and irony.'[25] The importance of gay dress is acknowledged by the dress historian Amy de la Haye, who stated that 'gay and lesbian dress is crucial to the study of subculture'.[26]

Fashionability and the importance of remaining at the forefront of fashion runs parallel to the desire to remain outside or ahead of mainstream fashion. Toby Young believed that 'the pleasure we take from being *à la mode* consists in knowing about something which others do not'.[27] Fashionability has often, in critiques of or commentaries on gay lifestyles, been presented in a negative fashion, equating it with a desire amongst gay men to extend or retain their youth. Stratton Ashley noted that 'young and fashionable attire' was 'essential' in New York gay bars, and that 'homosexuals in general tend to dress younger than their years'.[28] Martin Hoffmann echoed this fact four years later pointing out that 'In the gay world there is a tremendous accent on youth . . . Along with the younger men, there are somewhat older men who are trying to look young. They attempt to accomplish this primarily by dress.'[29] The primacy of youth on the gay scene is one that has continued. Michelangelo Signorile's 1997 book *Life Outside* offers many testimonies to the currency of youth or perceived youth on the contemporary gay 'circuit', where men spend hours at the gym, take steroids and undergo cosmetic surgery to retain the illusion of youth.[30]

Gay men's clothing has frequently been 'ahead of fashion, attention-seeking and meant to be sexy, all of which helps when out hunting for a sexual partner'.[31] Sexiness and sexual attractiveness have been one of the primary focuses for the adoption of certain items of clothing or dress styles for gay men. In *Fashion as Communication* (1996), Malcolm Barnard discusses the various theories proposed about clothing and fashion serving as indicators of immodesty versus attraction. He notes how some theorists and comment-ators (such as Elizabeth Rouse) have claimed that men dress for social status and women for sexual attraction in order to attract men, while others (particularly Valerie Steele) have contended that men have dressed in erotic and exotic ways, but that no one has charted women's erotic interest in male anatomy. He concludes his thoughts on this subject by noting that these accounts 'seem to be firmly heterosexualist, in the sense that none of them conceive of the possibility that men and women might wear some clothing to attract sexual partners of the same sex'.[32] *Don We Now Our Gay Apparel* will attempt, in part, to redress this balance by assessing how gay men have used their clothing specifically to attract sexual partners.

Ideas of what is sexually attractive have fluctuated over the decades, reflecting social attitudes towards masculinity.[33] It has been argued that gay men's being attracted by masculine images is a reflection of the wider culture's demands for displays of masculinity.[34] In the first quarter of the twentieth century a 'real' form of working-class masculinity was seen as sexually attractive, and reflected a tradition of middle-class men's being attracted by the working classes. Running alongside this was a tendency for working-class gay men to advertise their sexual availability through the adoption of female dress or feminine-associated items of clothing and accessories. This allowed for sexual interactions to occur between men, as one of the pair was very much a pseudo-woman. With the development of ideas about homo-sexuality through the twentieth century the idea of homosexuality as a character trait as opposed to a sexual activity gained currency. As men began to label themselves as homosexual or gay, so they began to question the position of fairies and queers having sexual relations with 'normal' men. Alongside the examination of sexual roles came a questioning of the notion of appropriate dress.

This work grew initially from my involvement in the Victoria and Albert Museum's exhibition *Streetstyle: From Sidewalk to Catwalk*, staged in 1994–5. I was asked to prepare a paper on gay men's and lesbians' dress choices, and to argue whether gay men and lesbians constituted a specific subcultural group within the parameters defined for the exhibition. My research revealed that much work had been done on lesbian dress, most notably by Joan Nestle, Madeline D. Davis and Elizabeth Lapovsky Kennedy, and Judith Schuyf,[35] but very little had been written directly addressing the issue of gay men's dress choices. The resulting section of the exhibition presented an idea of the wide-ranging forms and styles of clothing adopted by gay men and lesbians and the place they took in influencing, adopting and adapting subcultural dress. The inclusion of gay and lesbian dress in the exhibition marked a significant point in the study of [youth] subcultures, indicating that gay men (and lesbians) were active in these other recognised and recorded groups, as well as forming their own distinct homosexual subcultural groups. This was a fact that had been largely ignored, as Michael Brake noted: 'Subcultural studies of youth never mention homosexuals, and this is hardly surprising given the masculinist emphasis on practically all youth subcultures. Young gay people are swamped by the heterosexism emphasis they find in peer groups and subcultures.'[36] Daniel Harris approaches this point from a different angle, noting that in the past there has been no separate youth gay culture, highlighting the 1970s, when 'the gay community was then far more unified, linked together by the shared exhilaration of being part of a new movement whose followers listened to the same Donna Summer songs, wore the same bomber jackets, danced the same dances, and exchanged copious amounts of the same bodily fluids in the orgy rooms of the same baths and action bars'.[37] In the light of these two opinions I continue the thoughts opened by the Streetstyle exhibition (one that was furthered by the inclusion of gay men's clothes in sections other than the gay and lesbian section), and look at the role of gay men in recognised subcultures and the role that those subcultures have played in those gay men's clothing choices and in their formation of an identity.

It is pertinent to define the word 'subculture' in this book. The *Concise English Dictionary* states that a subculture is 'a cultural group within a larger culture, often having beliefs or interests at variance with those of the larger community'. Within this book the term subculture is used with reference to a group that has an identifiable reason for being or a set of beliefs that set them outside the main or dominant culture, the hegemony. Therefore, gay men are set outside society (in one way) by the fact that culturally, morally and legally their sexual activities have been deemed wrong, immoral, illegal.[38] The term subculture is often used to refer specifically to youth or delinquent subcultures;[39] but within the context of a gay history, the word does not refer specifically or exclusively to youth. Taking Phil Cohen's definition of a subculture as a '. . . compromise solution between two contradictory needs: the needs to create and express autonomy and difference from parents . . . and the need to maintain the parental institutions'[40] places gay men both within and outside a subculture; essential to the premise of this work is the belief that the dress choice of many gay men was an attempt to '. . . express and resolve, albeit magically, the contradiction[s] which remain hidden or unresolved in the parent [i.e. heterosexual] culture.'

This book presents a series of thematic chapters addressing the major elements of importance in gay men's dress, and is not intended to be a full chronological history charting every trend and nuance of gay men's clothing and fashions. Britain and the United States are the primary locations for this study, with particular emphasis placed upon metropolitan areas with large gay communities, such as London, New York and San Francisco.[41] Drawing on an oral history tradition it utilises individuals' testimonies and experiences to illustrate significant points and elements of gay dress. The lives of gay people had until fairly recently been shrouded in secrecy, or particular aspects of those lives had been avoided or denied, for a variety of legal, moral and social reasons. Where gay lives were noted they were often viewed in terms of medical or social problems. As a result of gay liberation gay people began to take a more active interest in their place in society, in gay histories and gay individuals' lives. In order to redress the balance against the existing, often homophobic, commentaries or against the 'symbolic annihilation'[42] of gay people, personal testimonies began to be taken. This has resulted in a large volume of works that give voice to a previously 'hidden history'.[43] There will be aspects of this book that readers will agree and disagree with, and points where experiences differed and may even appear contradictory to the histories detailed in this book. Some points in the book concentrate on clothing that was exclusively or initially gay; others highlight styles of dress that, while not exclusively or predominantly gay, were worn by significant numbers of gay men and assimilated into the rhetoric of gay dress.

One of the major themes that arises from a study of gay dress and flows throughout this book is the importance of gender-appropriate or gender-inappropriate clothing, and the associated opposition between masculinity and femininity. In the earlier parts of the century these two forms of dress were seen as contrary strategies. However, with the rise of exaggerated male styles theorists began to note the similarity in their constructedness. 'Gay masculinity is not,' Jamie Gough argued, 'in any simple way, "real" masculinity, any more than "camp" is femininity. It is more self-conscious than the real thing, more theatrical, and often more ironic.'[44] Judith Butler progressed this theory, declaring that gender is performative, that is, something that we do. Dress, therefore, is a visible and conscious marker of this constructed or performed gender.[45]

Chapter 1 of this book discusses middle- and upper-class men's attraction to working-class imagery and the role the aesthete played in forming a role model for gay men throughout the first half of the twentieth century. Subsequent chapters continue the theme of working-class influenced dress that developed over the century as gay men adopted increasingly masculine styles of dress, *becoming* the objects of their own sexual desire, which culminated in the hyper-masculinity of the clones in the 1970s.[46] The second and third chapters look at the adoption of traditionally female-associated clothing and accessories as a point of identification for men who were perceived (by themselves and others) as other than 'real men'. In contrast, other chapters look at the reliance by some men on markers of masculinity and the ways in which these were used initially as a means of concealing a 'deviant' sexuality or nature, but later as a means of announcing and celebrating that nature. Chapters 6, 11, 12 and 13 address the roles gay men have played in the formation and development of recognised (youth) cultures, such as hippies and punks.

This book offers an insight into some of the dress choices available to gay men, and begins to address the role that clothing has played in gay men's changing identities and self-presentational strategies throughout the twentieth century.

Notes

1. Andrew Holleran (1980 [1978]), *Dancer From the Dance*, London, pp. 20–1.

2. John Harvey (1995), *Men in Black*, London, p. 197

3. Jennifer Craik (1994), *The Face of Fashion: Cultural Studies in Fashion*, London, p. 176. Contemporary historians and commentators are now exploding this notion. See for example the work of Christopher Breward and Frank Mort.

4. Chapter 1 of Malcolm Bernard (1996), *Fashion as Communication*, London and New York presents an etymology of both of these words (as well as the associated dress and adornment) and goes some way to defining the differences and potential uses of each.

5. For more details on eighteenth-century homosexual subculture and 'mollies' see Richter Norton (1992), *Mother Clap's Molly House: The Gay Subculture in England 1700–1830*, London and Alan Bray (1982), *Homosexuality in Renaissance England*, London.

6. Ned Ward, *The London Spy*, c.1700, quoted in Colin Spencer (1995), *Homosexuality: A History*, London: 'Some were completely rigged in gowns, petticoats, head-cloths, fine laced shoes, furbelowed scarves, and masks; some had riding hoods; some were dressed like milk maids, others like shepherdesses with green hats, waistcoats, and petticoats; and others had their faces patched and painted and wore very expensive hoop petticoats, which had been very lately introduced.' Quoted in Norton, *Mother Clap's Molly House*. Originally from *Murders, Rapes, Sodomy, Coining, Frauds and Other Offenses at the Session-House in the Old Bailey*, 3 vols, 1742.

7. Bray, *Homosexuality in Renaissance England*, pp. 92, 104. These are the same types of signifiers and sites that are recognisable right up to the present day. See also Norton, *Mother Clap's Molly House;* and Randolph Trumbach (1989), 'Gender and the Homosexual Role in Modern Western Culture: The 18th and 19th Centuries Compared', in Dennis Altman, Carole Vance, Martha Vicinus and others, *Homosexuality, Which Homosexuality?*, London.

8. Elizabeth Wilson (1985), *Adorned in Dreams: Fashion and Modernity*, London, p. 12.

9. Cole interview with John, 7 June 1997.

10. Dennis Altman (1982), *The Homosexualization of America: The Americanization of the Homosexual*, New York, p. 156.

11. Ibid. In his travel journal *States of Desire*, Edmund White identifies the same point, that 'once one discovers one is gay one must choose everything, from how to walk, dress and talk to where to live, with whom and on what terms' (Edmund White (1986), *States of Desire: Travels in Gay America*, London, p. 16).

12. Fred Davis (1992), *Fashion, Culture, Identity*, Chicago, p. 24.

13. Frank Pearce (1973), 'How to be Immoral and Ill, Pathetic and Dangerous, All at the Same Time: Mass Media and the Homosexual', in Stanley Cohen and Jock Young (eds), *The Manufacture of News: Social Problems, Deviance and the Mass Media*, London.

14. Martin P. Levine (1998), *Gay Macho: The Life and Death of the Homosexual Clone*, New York and London, p. 21.

15. Erving Goffman (1959), *The Presentation of Self in Everyday Life*, New York, p. 57.

16. Jess Stearn (1962), *The Sixth Man*, New York, p. 29.

17. Andrew Holleran (1988), *Ground Zero*, New York, p. 178.

18. Harold Beaver, 'Homosexual Signs (in Memory of Roland Barthes)', *Critical Inquiry*, Autumn 1981, pp. 104–5.

19. Hal Fischer (1977), *Gay Semiotics*, San Francisco, p. 22.

20. Stuart Hall (1977), 'Culture, the Media and the "Ideological Effect"', in James Curran, Michael Gurevitch, and Janet Wollacott (eds), *Mass Communication and Society*, London, p. 330.

21. Umberto Eco (1973), 'Social Life as a Sign System', in D. Robert (ed.), *Structuralism: The Wolfson College Lectures 1972*, New York.

22. Levine, *Gay Macho*, p. 56.

23. D. J. West (1977), *Homosexuality Re-Examined*, Minneapolis, p. 150.

24. The 'bubble up' theory of the development of fashion was one on which the Victoria and Albert Museum's *Streetstyle* exhibition was based. See Amy de la Haye and Cathie Dingwall (1996), *Surfers, Soulies, Skinheads and Skaters: Subcultural Style From the Forties to The Nineties*, London and Ted Polhemus (1994), *Streetstyle: From Sidewalk to Catwalk*, London.

25. Susan Sontag (1969), 'Notes on Camp', in *Against Interpretation*, New York, pp. 291–2.

26. Quoted in James Collard (1994), 'No Style on Queer Street?' *Attitude*, October, p. 14.

27. Toby Young (1986), 'The Fashion Victims', *New Society*, 14 March, p. 456

28. Stratton Ashley (1964), 'The "Other" Homosexuals', *One*, vol. VII, no. 2.

29. Martin Hoffman (1968), *The Gay World: Male Homosexuality and the Social Creation of Evil*, New York, p. 54.

30. Michelangelo Signorile (1997), *Life Outside*, New York.

31. West, *Homosexuality Re-Examined*, p. 150.

32. Malcolm Barnard (1996), *Fashion as Communication*, London and New York, p. 56.

33. Writing in *Gay News* in 1973, Iain T. Finlayson identified the progression of erotic interest up men's legs from 'a well-turned calf to the swell of thighs . . . [to] the buttocks and hips': Iain T. Finlayson (1973), 'The Shifting Erogenous Zone', *Gay News*, no. 28, p. 6.

34. See Signorile, *Life Outside*, Chapter 2.

35. Joan Nestle (1987), *A Restricted Country: Essays & Short Stories*, London; Madeline D. Davis and Elizabeth Lapovsky Kennedy (1993), *Boots of Leather, Slippers of Gold: The History of a Lesbian Community*, New York and London; Judith Schuyf (1993), '"Trousers with Flies!!" The Clothing and Subculture of Lesbians', *Textile History*, 24 (1), pp. 61–73.

36. Michael Brake (1985), *Comparative Youth Culture*, London, p. 11.

37. Daniel Harris (1997) *The Rise and Fall of Gay Culture*, New York, p. 71.

38. Essays in Routledge's 1996 *Subcultures Reader*, ed. Ken Gelder and Sarah Thornton, particularly those in section one by Milton Gordon and John Irwin, take steps to further define subculture(s).

39. The latter adjective is especially applicable to early work defining subcultures, and work on delinquency often defined delinquents as moving within or belonging to specified 'subcultures'. Albert Cohen, for example, defined (delinquent) subculture as 'not only a set of rules, a design for living which is indifferent to or even in conflict with the norms of "respectable" adult society', but 'defined by its "negative polarity" to these terms' (Albert Cohen (1976), 'The Delinquency Subculture', in Rose Giallombardo (ed.), *Juvenile Delinquency*, New York, p. 108).

40. Phil Cohen (1972), 'Subcultural Conflict and Working Class Community', *W.P.C.S.*, 2, Birmingham.

41. For a view of general world-wide gay life see Neil Miller (1992), *Out in the World: Gay and Lesbian Life from Buenos Aires to Bangkok*, New York. For Europe see Antony Copley (1989), *Sexual Moralities in France, 1780–1980: New Ideas on the Family, Divorce and Homosexuality*, London; John Fout (1992), *Male Homosexuals, Lesbians and Homosexuality in Germany: From the Kaiserreich Through the Third Reich, 1871–1945*, Chicago and London; Doug Ireland (1988–9), 'Gays in Eastern Europe', in *Peace and Democracy News*, Winter 1988–89; D. Tuller (1991), 'Gay Activism in Eastern Europe', *The Advocate*, 18 June; Simon Karlinsky (1989), 'Russia's Gay Literature and Culture: The Impact of the October Revolution', in Martin Baum Duberman, Martha Vicinus and George Chauncey Jr (eds), *Hidden From History: Reclaiming the Gay and Lesbian Past*, London; Harry Oosterhuis (ed.) (1991), *Homosexuality and Male Bonding in Pre-Nazi Germany: The Youth Movement, the Gay Movement and Male Bonding Before Hitler's Rise (Original Manuscripts from Der Eigene, the First Gay Journal in the World)*, trans. Hubert Kennedy, New York and London; James Steakley (1975), *The Homosexual Emancipation Movement in Germany*, New York; A. X. van Naerssen (ed.) (1987), *Gay Life in Dutch Society*, New York. For Australia and New Zealand see Robert

Aldrich and Garry Wotherspoon (eds) (1998), *Gay and Lesbian Perspectives IV: Essays in Australian Culture*, Sydney; Nigel Gearing (1997*)*, *Emerging Tribe: Gay Culture in New Zealand in the 1990s*, Auckland and London; Garry Wotherspoon (1991), *'City of the Plain': History of a Gay Sub-Culture*, Sydney. For Asia see Bret Hinsch (1990), *Passions of the Cut Sleeve: The Male Homosexual Tradition in China*, Berkeley and Los Angeles; Peter A. Jackson (1989), *Male Homosexuality in Thailand: An Interpretation of Contemporary Thai Sources*, Elmhurst, NY; Tsueo Watanabe and Junichi Iwata (1989), *The Love of the Samurai: A Thousand Years of Japanese Homosexuality*, London. For Africa see Gordon Isaacs and Brian McKendrick (1992), *Male Homosexuality in South Africa: Identity Formation, Culture and Crisis*, Cape Town and Oxford; Cary Alan Johnson (1986), 'Inside Gay Africa', *The New York Native*, 3 March 1986; Gill Shepherd (1987), 'Rank, Gender and Homosexuality: Mombasa as a Key to Understanding Sexual Options', in Pat Caplan (ed.), *The Cultural Construction of Sexuality*, London. For South and Latin America see Lordes Aguelles and B. Ruby Rich (1989), 'Homosexuality, Homophobia and Revolution: Notes Toward an Understanding of the Cuban Lesbian and Gay Male Experience', in Martin Baum Duberman, Martha Vicinus and George Chauncey Jr (eds), *Hidden From History: Reclaiming the Gay and Lesbian Past*, London; João Silvério Trevison (1986), *Perverts in Paradise*, London (Brazil); Allen Young (1981), *Gays Under the Cuban Revolution*, San Francisco.

42. Larry Gross uses this concept to mean the non-representation of minorities (including gay men and lesbians) by others in the mass media: Larry Gross (1991), 'Out of the Mainstream: Sexual Minorities and the Mass Media', *Journal of Homosexuality*, no. 21(1/2), pp. 19–46.

43. See for example Brighton Ourstory Project (1992), *Daring Hearts: Lesbian and Gay Lives of 50s and 60s Brighton*, Brighton; Eric Marcus (1992), *Making History: The Struggle for Gay and Lesbian Equal Rights, 1945–1990*, New York; Peter M. Nardi, David Sanders and Judd Marmor (1994), *Growing Up Before Stonewall: Life Stories of Some Gay Men*, London, 1994; Kevin Porter and Jeffrey Weeks (eds) (1991), *Between the Acts: Lives of Homosexual Men 1885–1967*, London. For commentary on oral history methodology see Madeline D. Davis and Elizabeth Lapovsky Kennedy (1993), *Boots of Leather, Slippers of Gold: The History of a Lesbian Community*, New York and London, 1993, Elizabeth Lapovsky Kennedy (1995), 'Telling Tales: Oral History and the Construction of Pre-Stonewall Lesbian History', *Radical History Review*, no. 62, pp. 58–79 and Esther Newton (1993), *Cherry Grove, Fire Island: Sixty Years In America's First Gay And Lesbian Town*, Boston.

44. Jamie Gough (1989), 'Theories of Sexual Identity and the Masculinisation of the Gay Man', in Simon Shepherd and Mick Wallis (eds), *Coming on Strong: Gay Politics and Culture*, London, p. 12.

45. See Judith Butler (1990), *Gender Trouble: Feminism and the Subversion of Identity*, London.

46. Andrew Holleran describes a clone as 'a male homosexual in his twenties or thirties (if there was any age limit at all) who – I'll give my version – travelled in

packs with other clones, had short dark hair, a short dark moustache, and wore Levi's, work shoes, plaid shirt, and bomber jacket over a hooded sweatshirt. The jeans were faded and sometimes frayed in strategic places. Dark glasses were aviator-style and occasionally mirrored . . . Clonestyle was not a soft look – especially when the dark glasses were mirrored – but it was more a middle-of-the-road version of the masculine homosexual style': Andrew Holleran (1982), 'The Petrification of Clonestyle' in *Christopher Street*, no. 69, p. 14.

Homosexuality, Class and Dress

1

In the last quarter of the nineteenth century a number of pioneering sexologists began to define what we now term homosexuality. Although there was a centuries-long history of same-sex relations between both men and women, definitions generally relied upon descriptions of physical acts rather than on any form of cultural or social identity.[1] Karl Heinrich Ulrichs's theory proposed that homosexuality was an inborn state and that male and female homosexuals constituted a third sex. He argued that male homosexuals had a female soul trapped inside a man's body, and therefore possessed the personality characteristics of women. Other sexologists such as Richard von Krafft-Ebing subscribed to the degeneracy theory, which contended that medical, psychiatric and social problems were transmitted from generation to generation. Like Ulrichs, von Krafft-Ebing resorted to gender stereotypes in his studies and descriptions of homosexuals.[2] It was this emphasis on binary gender division and the related theories of female souls trapped inside male bodies that were to have an overwhelming impact upon the development of homosexual identity and as a consequence dress choices in the first half of the twentieth century.

By the end of the nineteenth century there were recognisable gay subcultures in all major cities in Western Europe and the United States. A series of events in London at the end of the nineteenth century were to fix the idea and image of the male homosexual in the public mind. Two of these events, both legal trials, were to have an impact upon the public awareness and the self-identification of gay men for the next twenty-five years.[3] The first was the trial of two cross-dressing male prostitutes in 1871, and the second the now legendary trial of Oscar Wilde.

The trial and acquittal in 1871 of Ernest Boulton and Frederick Payne, two cross-dressing young men known as Fanny and Stella prompts the question: how visible was the homosexual subculture in London, and what role did men in drag play within that subculture?[4] The opening remarks of the Attorney General hinted that it was their transvestism, their soliciting men as *women,* which was the core of their crime; and Jeffrey Weeks believes that the reason they were not demonised and punished was due to 'concepts of homosexuality', as late as 1871, 'being extremely undeveloped'.[5] Neil

Bartlett believes that Fanny and Stella were all too visible, making 'determined efforts to use their frocks to create public space for themselves in London, in the separate but overlapping worlds of the actress, the prostitute and the demi-mondaine ... They were well aware that they were playing precise games with their appearance, and that an exact understanding of the rules was a prerequisite of survival.'[6] He argues that concepts of homosexuality were well enough developed in certain quarters, for example amongst the men who were involved in liaisons with the duo. The strategic skills of Fanny and Stella were designed to enable them to make the contacts they wished without attracting any unhelpful attention.[7] The experiences of Fanny and Stella have a parallel in the experiences of fairies in New York at around the same period.[8] Some people saw only what they wanted to see, women. Others saw men in women's clothes, and treated them in the same manner that they would have treated female prostitutes. For some men they offered a means of engaging in homosexual sexual activity while maintaining their masculinity: by their taking the active role the interaction remained one between a man and a (surrogate) woman.

In 1885 the Labouchère Amendment to the Criminal Law Amendment Act brought all forms of homosexuality between men within the scope of the criminal law, and made them illegal in Britain.[9] This clause, with its specification of 'public or private', played into the hands of the blackmailers, and became known as the 'blackmailers' charter'. It also equated homosexuality with prostitution, which Jeffrey Weeks points out was a common link in all Acts concerning homosexuality.[10] It was under this law that Oscar Wilde was sentenced to two years' hard labour in 1895, after three separate trials. The long-drawn-out trial process resulted from a libel suit Wilde brought against the Marquis of Queensberry, the father of his lover, Lord Alfred Douglas.[11] The effects of the Wilde trials were tremendous, not least because they created a public image for the homosexual. As a result, gay men who could afford to fled to the Continent, fearing a clampdown and exposure of their activities and lifestyles. Wilde became an object of revulsion in England, so much so that the word *Oscar* became a popular term of contempt[12] and was still in use over twenty years later, when E. M. Forster has the hero of his novel *Maurice* describe himself as 'an unspeakable of the Oscar Wilde sort'. Neil Miller notes that the trials also had an effect in America, where over one hundred sermons were preached against Wilde between 1895 and 1900; and by 1900 a set of pornographic photographs, entitled 'The Sins of Oscar Wilde', was being sold to undergraduates.[13]

Havelock Ellis wrote that the publicity surrounding the Wilde trials 'may have brought conviction of their perversion to many inverts who were before only vaguely conscious of their abnormality, and paradoxical though it may seem, have imparted greater courage to others'.[14] Alan Sinfield draws attention to the fact that at the time of the Oscar Wilde trials 'effeminacy was still flexible, with the potential to refute homosexuality, as well as to imply it'. When Henry Labouchère turned against Oscar Wilde in July 1883, he wrote of him as 'an effeminate phrase-maker'. This to an extent associated aestheticism with same-sex passion.[15] As a result aestheticism became a component in the image of the gay man as it emerged.[16] Despite the involvement of a wide range of socio-economic groups in the homosexual subculture of the late nineteenth century, it was the ideology of the upper classes that appears to have dominated, probably because there was a more clearly defined homosexual identity amongst those men (who would have had access to the works of the sexologists such as Krafft-Ebing, Havelock Ellis and Edward Carpenter) and the money and mobility to make homosexual contact.[17] Havelock Ellis had thought that the genuine invert was likely to belong to 'the professional and most cultured element of the middle class'.[18] George Chauncey draws a similar conclusion about the gay men in New York around the same period, while emphasising the distinctions made between working-class fairies and middle- or upper-class queers.[19] The issue of class and homosexuality was one that was to persist until well after the Second World War in both Britain and the USA, and plays an important role in the adoption of dress and demeanour for gay men.

Following in the aesthetic tradition set by Wilde and his followers at Oxford University in the 1870s a new breed of aesthetes emerged when a number of gay young men, including Evelyn Waugh, John Betjeman and Stephen Spender, who came to be known, in deference to Waugh's novel, as 'The Brideshead Generation', enrolled at Oxford during the 1920s.[20] This predominantly male preserve was, in Anthony Powell's words, 'indifferent to homosexuality'. At Cambridge University, Cecil Beaton drew a similar crowd of aesthetes, including Stephen Tennant. Beaton, who described himself as 'really a terrible, terrible homosexualist and [I] try so hard not to be',[21] was often to be seen on the streets of Cambridge wearing 'an evening jacket, red shoes, black-and-white trousers, and a huge blue cravat'; and as the weather got colder 'he brightened the Cambridge scene with an outfit comprising fur gauntlet gloves, a cloth-of-gold tie, a scarlet jersey and Oxford bags'. In his novel *Brideshead Revisited* (1945), Evelyn Waugh describes the clothes of an out gay man who, because he is not English, is already marked out as different. The effete and openly homosexual Anthony Blanche, a thinly disguised portrait of Waugh's 'incorrigible homosexual' friend Brian Christian de Claiborne Howard, wears 'a smooth chocolate-brown suit with loud white stripes, suede shoes, a large bow-tie and he drew off yellow, wash-leather gloves as he came into the room; part Gallic, part Yankee, part, perhaps Jew; wholly exotic'[22]

The image of the queer aesthete was still prevalent as late as the 1950s. 'Pussy' Wilkinson in Jocelyn Brooke's *Orchid Trilogy* (1950) was cultured and leisured, and was 'a perfect period-piece a man of the nineties who had managed to preserve the authentic aroma of that (to me) still fascinating decade. He had known Robbie Ross and Reggie Turner, and had even, on one memorable occasion, been introduced (at Dieppe) to none other than "Sebastian Melmoth" himself' [i.e. Wilde]; he 'had never married'.[23] The signals that are given, while not especially explicit about Pussy's queerness, were plain enough indications to anyone reading the book in 1950, when it was published, of homosexuality, or at least of the 'Wildean unspeakable'. Through the representations of queer characters such as Pussy Wilkinson and Anthony Blanche, queers were generally assumed to be leisure-class. Conversely, leisure-class men might fall under suspicion, regardless of their actual preferences. Some indicators, such as pinkie rings, could be seen to represent either class or homosexuality or indeed both.[24] Alan Sinfield has concluded that

> the queer manner was immensely convenient for leisure-class men, who only had to inflect a mode to which they had been bred. If they wished, they might pass even *at the same time* as signalling the queer image to those they wished to reach. They could move conveniently into a 'dissolute' milieu which might include bohemians and prostitutes, and they had the resources to secure privacy.[25]

In both Britain and America Noel Coward came to personify an image of the homosexual that transcended sex and the physical aspects of homosexuality. This 'sophisticated' figure with a cigarette-holder and a dry martini signified something that society did not wish to consider or embrace. This led to the emergence of an effete, almost sexless, caricature 'queer', of a 'certain type' of British man. This was to remain the stereotype for many years, usually associated in the mind of 'the public' with hairdressers, antiques dealers and ballet-dancers.[26] The association with theatre and artistic circles was one that permeated many perceptions of homosexuality. The men in the aforementioned circles at Oxford and Cambridge were writers or artists, and it was in the bohemian enclaves of major cities that homosexuality was accepted and even contributed to the 'alternative' images of those societies.[27] In her book *Greenwich Village, 1920–1930*, the sociologist Caroline Ware emphasised the extent to which becoming an artist or a writer made one a deviant in early-twentieth-century middle-class society.[28] The unconventional behaviour of many bohemian men – ranging from their long hair, colourful dress, and interest in art to their decided lack of interest in the manly pursuits of getting married and making money – often led outsiders to consider all of them as homosexual. Although not everyone thought their queer tastes extended to sexual matters, the bohemian men of the Village were often regarded as unmanly as well as un-American; and in some contexts calling a man 'artistic' became code for calling him homosexual. The particular forms of eccentricity allowed the 'artistic types' made it unusually easy for gay men and lesbians to fit into bohemian society, and also provided a cover for those who adopted flamboyant styles in their dress and demeanour.

From the working-class point of view, homosexuality was, for the most part, identified with leisure-class privilege, and was respected and despised accordingly. For John Shires

> Working-class culture, the majority experience in society, had no space and no role for the homosexual, except as an object of hatred and ridicule. Hence the even greater invisibility of working-class homosexuals (but not working-class homosexual activity) than amongst the minority whose wealth could buy themselves privacy, or men who were able to 'de-class' themselves by working in the effete occupations [such as hairdressing, catering and the theatre].[29]

While on the one hand 'The queer *bricolage*[30] of effeminacy, aestheticism and class' Alan Sinfield maintains, 'stood at an opposite extreme from mainstream working-class values' the association with 'posh' culture offered working-class gay men a step away from the confines of hegemonic working-class male behaviour and a new sense of worth. 'For me, growing up gay and getting into this sort of culture felt like the same process, namely a process of establishing an identity,' wrote Richard Dyer. 'Queerness brought with it artistic sensitivity . . . It was a compensation for having been born or made queer . . . It made you "doubly different" . . . How splendid to be different, even if you were awful.' Dyer elaborated on this thought, that 'Somehow to me cultural sensitivity was "feminine"; and being queer was not being a man – that was why the two went together.'[31] In the 1940s and 1950s, the most likely gay venues were 'some corner of a bar, usually in the "best" hotel', or in cities perhaps 'behind the facade of some "gentleman's club"': 'The small groups of gay men gravitated to the better hotels because it was there that people felt least prone to the prying curiosity of others, but it was an arrangement which served to reinforce the prevailing misconception that homosexuality was something alien to the working class.'[32] This was also the case in New York, where the most famous such bar was the one in the Astor Hotel, at the corner of Seventh Avenue and Forty-fifth Street. Gay men gathered on one side of the oval bar, where the management allowed them to congregate as long as they did not become too 'obvious'. It was important for them to remain 'invisible', so that the straight men among them would not realise they were surrounded by gay men; and to achieve this they used the signifiers they had developed in other contexts to alert each other to their identities: wearing clothes that were fashionable among gay men but not stereotypically associated with them, or casually using code words (such as *gay*) well known within the gay world but unremarkable to those outside it.[33]

For the majority of working- and middle-class homosexuals the first three decades of the twentieth century were ones in which they were the objects of scorn or pity, or else had to disguise their sexual inclinations. This did not however put a stop to homosexual sexual activity.[34] In fact, as Jeffrey Weeks identifies 'the most basic purpose of the homosexual subculture in the nineteenth and early twentieth centuries . . . was to provide ways to meet sexual partners'.[35] Whilst male prostitution is beyond the scope of this book, it is important to bear in mind the subject of solicitation for sex between men, whether money is involved or not, as it has implications for the dress choices of gay men. Patterns of behaviour in 'cruising' for sex are effected by societal climates and attitudes. The cross-dressing of men such as Fanny and Stella had acted as a signifier to other men that they were available for sexual contact. Richard Dellamora writes that 'in the nineteenth century, "effeminacy" as a term of personal abuse often connotes male–male desire'.[36] However, it would not be right to assume that these always correspond to men's desires. Much of the evidence available points towards an attraction to working- class masculinity, at least amongst the wealthier classes.[37] Given this evidence, it is important to view effeminacy as often a symbol of availability rather than of the object of desire.[38]

The works of men such as Walt Whitman, John Addington Symonds and Edward Carpenter in the late 1800s centre on the attraction of working-class men, of what was regarded as an authentic masculinity. They advocated love between 'men' as something special, often referring to classical works such as Plato's *Symposium*. This attraction to working-class men and what would later be termed 'rough trade' subsequently played a significant role in the development of gay men's self-presentation strategies. The photographs that Montague Glover took of his lovers and 'rough trade' in the 1920s and 1930s dressed in working-class clothes, such as 'shabby trousers, jacket, cloth cap and collar-less shirt'[39] and in various uniforms illustrate this fascination. Bobby Sillock, a character in the 1953 novel *The Heart in Exile*, recognises the attraction to working-class men: 'We don't like anyone like ourselves. We don't want anybody who shares our standards, I mean educated, middle class and so on. In fact, we want the very opposite. We want the primitive, the uneducated, the tough.'[40] He accepts that whilst some gay men could find happiness with men of the same class, for him this was impossible. There is an inherent problem in ascribing these working clothes and uniforms to gay men, as many of the working-class lovers of these upper-class men did not identify as homosexual and frequently went on to get married.[41] There is however a correlation: as the ideas of gay reform (in Britain and USA) were brought into the public domain, gay men began to see that their dress choices were not limited to effeminate stereotypes or the hegemonic dress confines of the day. They realised their wardrobes could reflect the types of men they wished to be and wished to 'have'.[42]

The Second World War marked a turning-point for gay men. Those joining up to fight for their country were liberated when they were thrown into same-sex environments. This did have an effect on the dress choices of gay men. Many were in military uniform, but sought ways of otherwise identifying themselves. John Alcock told of a foray to Leicester Square in 1944, where he found it fascinating to see 'young airforce men in uniform with make-up on'.[43] The wearing of military uniforms (often in a civilian context) was another style of dress that became popular amongst homosexuals. For many men these clothes were immediately available – they were doing or had done National Service and had retained their uniforms; but added a gay touch. '[Tyrell] Dighton was wearing his familiar grey demob suit and his Air Force tie, but I noticed he had on a pair of new shoes: brown box calf with crêpe soles . . . He lay down on the couch. I noticed he was wearing grey-blue Air Force socks.'[44] As a teenager at the end of the Second World War Peter Robins's dress choices were somewhat limited. The clothes that were most readily available were military uniforms. Peter was desperate to have a battledress jacket, but wasn't too keen on the available colours, so he took the ethos of Make-Do and Mend and customised a jacket himself.

> We begged, borrowed or almost stole our fathers', older brothers', cousins' battle dress tops – the tank tops, people would now say. But here the gay man started to stand out, or the young gay man. I wasn't content to have that dreary khaki or the even the civil defence or fire fighters' navy blue. I got the khaki, but you could at least have things dyed, and I had mine dyed a nice dark cherry red, burgundy.[45]

For other gay men uniforms offered a fantasy. Men in uniform were often the unavailable (or sometimes not so unavailable) objects of men's sexual fantasy.[46] Dressing up could go some way to fulfilling that fantasy. These dress choices were often limited to private spaces where homosexuals could be themselves, and so uniforms became a popular choice at the Arts and Drag Balls for men who did not want to drag up. John Hardy described the clothes his friend wore to the Vic-Wells Ball at the Lyceum in the mid-1950s. 'He went as an American sailor. That was one of the gay things at the time, because sailor's rig at that time was quite sexy: white bell bottoms, tight-fitting here around the waist and hips, tight-fitting cotton and the mess jacket and one of those little white cotton hats.'[47] Donald Webster Cory, eaves-dropping at a drag ball, heard the following conversation, which plays on the idea that gay men's dress choices were always a form of dressing up or drag:

> When I last attended a drag, not very long ago, I watched a sailor dancing with a young man. The sailor was in uniform, his companion in a tweed suit. They both talked loudly and vociferously. Their bodies were in exciting contact, their faces close upon one another's. They had no secrets from the world on this night; even their words must be shared. I could not help but be an eavesdropper. 'Ever come here in drag?' the sailor asked. 'Just once, never again,' came the reply. 'How about you?' 'What do you call this?'[48]

Soldiers and sailors had had an erotic appeal for gay men throughout the twentieth century, as one man's reminiscences of sailors' uniforms during the 1920s indicates:

> It was very flattering, quite unlike the uniform of recent times. The neck of their tunic was cut in a very rough square, which gave the wearer a very masculine appeal . . . The trousers must have been made to titillate. They were very tight around the waist and bottoms, but baggy around the ankles. If the sailor wore no underwear then very little was left to the imagination.[49]

Uniforms continued to play a role in the private (and sexually-related dress) choices of gay men throughout the century. Along with the appropriation of masculine working clothes, the clones adopted uniforms, continuing the fetishisation of 'masculine icons'. Elements of military uniform, such as jungle fatigues and bomber jackets, were incorporated into everyday wear, and authentic, full uniforms were worn to club nights opened specifically to cater for gay men interested in uniforms, such as London Blues at Heaven in London. Reading Jean Genet's homoerotic novel *Querelle de Brest* provided one young gay man with a 'sailor-look' fashion image for summer in the mid-1980s: 'You can wear baggy jeans, with a striped T-shirt and they look OK, sailorish, like Querelle.'[50]

One particular class-related style of dress that was associated with homosexuals during the late 1940s and early 1950s was the New Edwardian look. Styled by 'a London minority consisting of ex-Guards officers and interior decorators, some of whom turned out to be both'[51] it made a gesture towards the sartorial elegance of upper-class young men in the early part of the century. Indeed, both the guards and interior decorators are infamous for their homosexual proclivities, or at the very least their associations with homosexuality. The New Edwardians favoured a tailored look that was in complete contrast to the popular American Wide Boy look or the 'demob suit'. It drew heavily on the tailored look of the period immediately preceding the First World War – overcoats based on army greatcoats, tapered trousers that finished just above the ankle, and bowler hats, slightly too small, that sat forward on the head. While not all the New Edwardians were homosexual, the look was 'camp, that is to say it was equivocally witty and self-mocking, but at the same time affectionate about what was being lightly mocked'.[52] Alan Sinfield has noted that 'camp, as used in male homosexual subcultures, includes an allusion to leisure-class mannerisms, and may coincide, in effect or intent, with upward class mobility . . . the mode includes a recognition of its inappropriateness, of its impertinence'.[53] The adoption of New Edwardian dress by gay men mirrored the Teddy Boys' adoption, in that both were looking to an outdated upper-class model to express their desires to transcend their positions in society – by constructing an identity based on an older model of the dandy in the case of gay men, and in that of the Teds to display upward mobility, by dressing to display wealth.

New Edwardian clothing offered the homosexuals of the late 1940s and early 1950s an opportunity to look smart, while not quite conventional, with a distinct sartorial edge over the average man in the street. It was precisely this elitism that appealed to some gay men. John Hardy comments that the look was particularly favoured by

> all the piss elegant queens [who] used to go to The Rockingham and they all used to dress up in their three-piece pin-striped suits, starched collars and . . . they all preened themselves and . . . were all dressed a bit like Bunny Rogers . . . [who] used to walk up and down Bond Street in this terribly elegant sort of Edwardian fitted suit with waistcoat and lapels and a carnation or a rose in his buttonhole and chains and he always had a curly brimmed bowler sat on top of his head'.[54]

The look was taken to its camp extreme by [the dress designer, socialite and dandy] Bunny Roger, who burst forth 'in greens and gold and crimsons, pinks and purples: and he draped himself in accessories and trinkets'.[55] Nik Cohn, in *Today There Are No Gentlemen*, states that it was the homosexuals who killed off the New Edwardian look as an ordinary middle-class fashion.[56] What he does not consider is that homosexuals and 'ordinary' middle-class 'Edwardians' could quite easily have been the same men. In his assessment of the development of the New Edwardian into the Ted, Jon Savage identified a common ground between gay men and the working class (two groups that again could well have included the same men). 'Since they [gay men] were cut off from the mainstream anyway, both sexually and socially, they had nothing to lose by outrageousness in their clothes . . . Both homosexuals and Edwardians occupied a similar psychic space – "creatures of the moment, living in an everlasting present" – and attracted similar hatred.'[57] The adoption of this style of dress offered a meeting-point for different classes of gay men, who were either wearing the clothes as a marker of their leisured-class position or as statement of their aspiration to a higher class. However, Nik Cohn does point out that this style of dress lasted until 1954, by which time the Teddy Boys had taken it up and 'even homosexuals were embarrassed to wear it'.[58]

The impact of class on the dress choices of gay men was great, particularly in the first half of the twentieth century. For upper-class gay men, money and privilege could buy an acceptance of difference and the opportunities to move in bohemian circles that welcomed difference, or to create a safe private space. Georg Simmel's theory of fashion centred on the proposition that subordinates imitate superordinates, who for their part are anxious to differentiate themselves in a continual large-scale process of overtaking and dodging, which Simmel saw as occurring at every social level.[59] For middle- and working-class men, there was the possibility of social mobility through associating with higher classes, often through artistic or theatrical circles. Part of this process was to dress in an aspiration style based on that of the next class, a process that was to be reversed in the later part of the century, when many aspired to dress in clothes associated with the lower classes. Whilst the upper-class gay man could produce or find a model of homo-sexuality for himself, for many middle-class men invisibility was the safest route. And with little or no access to information on homosexuality, the predominant image available for working-class gay men was that of the ef-feminate 'fairy'.

Notes

1. See Richter Norton (1992), *Mother Clap's Molly House: The Gay Subculture in England 1700–1830*, London; Alan Bray (1982), *Homosexuality in Renaissance England*, London; Martin Bauml Duberman, Martha Vicinus and George Chauncey, Jr (eds) (1989), *Hidden From History: Reclaiming the Gay and Lesbian Past*, London; and Colin Spencer (1995), *Homosexuality: A History*, London, amongst others.

2. For more details on the pioneering sexologists see Neil Miller (1995), *Out of the Past: Gay and Lesbian History from 1869 to the Present*, London, Chap 2.

3. Details of other such trials in late nineteenth- and early twentieth-century Britain and America can be found in Jeffrey Weeks (1990), *Coming Out*, London and George Chauncey (1994), *Gay New York: Gender, Urban Culture and the Making of the Gay Male World, 1890–1940*, New York.

4. Fanny and Stella were arrested outside the Strand Theatre and tried the next day at Bow Street Court, London for conspiracy to commit a felony, still cross-dressed from the night before. They were acquitted after just fifty-three minutes. See Alan Sinfield (1994), *The Wilde Century*, London, pp. 6–7.

5. Jeffrey Weeks (1990), *Sex, Politics and Society*, London, p.101.

6. Neil Bartlett (1988), *Who Was That Man?*, London, pp. 138–9.

7. The condition for the homosexual/male prostitute subculture may have been that it was in many quarters unrecognisable. In the light of this view, Bartlett believes that the court may have been wilfully blind: Neil Bartlett (1988), *Who Was That Man?*, London, p.142.

8. See Chauncey, *Gay New York*, Chapter 2.

9. Up to this point only sodomy had been a punishable offence – by death, until 1861. The new law defined 'acts of gross indecency' between two men in public *or* private as 'misdemeanours', punishable by up to two years of hard labour.

10. Jeffrey Weeks (1989), 'Inverts, Perverts, and Mary-Annes: Male Prostitution and the Regulation of Homosexuality in England in the Nineteenth and Early Twentieth Centuries', in Duberman, Vicinus and Chauncey, *Hidden From History*, pp. 198–9.

11. For details of Wilde's trials see Richard Ellmann (1987), *Oscar Wilde*, London.

12. This is comparable to the use of the names Quentin and Jeremy as euphemisms for homosexuality in the late 1970s, which followed the television screening of the 'Naked Civil Servant', based on Quentin Crisp's autobiography and newspaper reports of Jeremy Thorpe's alleged activities as a communist spy and his homosexual relationship with Norman Scott.

13. Miller, *Out of the Past*, p. 50.

14. Quoted in Miller, *Out of the Past*, p. 51.

15. Sinfield, *The Wilde Century*, p. 93.

16. Despite his own inability to see Wilde as homosexual at the time, Frank Harris in 1916, thirty years after the event, linked Wilde's early success to 'a small minority of passionate admirers' who 'for the most part' were 'persons usually called "sexual inverts" '. As the use of the term 'sexual inverts' indicates, Harris is retrospectively consolidating the image of the gay man. Frank Harris (1918), *Oscar Wilde*, New York, pp. 106–7.

17. See Weeks , 'Inverts, Perverts, and Mary-Annes', pp. 202–3.

18. Havelock Ellis (1936), *Sexual Inversion, Studies in the Psychology of Sex*, vol.2, part 2, New York, pp. 21, 64. Even the middle-class gentleman, Eve Kosofsky Sedgwick has suggested, though he might have attended the same school and university as the leisure-class man, 'seems not to have had easy access to the alternative subculture, the stylized discourse, or the sense of immunity of the aristocratic/bohemian sexual minority': Eve Kosofsky Sedgwick (1985), *Between Men*, New York, pp. 207–13.

19. Chauncey, *Gay New York*, introduction and part one.

20. Humphrey Carpenter (1979), *The Brideshead Generation: Evelyn Waugh and His Friends*, London.

21. Cecil Beaton's diary, 9 October 1923 quoted in Hugo Vickers (1955), *Cecil Beaton*, London, p. 40.

22. Evelyn Waugh (1985), *Brideshead Revisited*, London, p. 34. Rodney Garland makes a similar description in 1953. Don Juan de Lavabos, a South American queer wears 'a dark grey suit with a discreet, embroidered overstripe, a cream silk shirt and a plain, ribbed, silk tie. Everything about him had the simplicity of a Rolls Royce': Rodney Garland (1995), *The Heart in Exile*, Brighton, p. 222. The television adaptation of *Brideshead Revisited* in 1981 provided the inspiration for a (short-lived) fashion for young gay men. 'I can remember being absolutely mesmerised by [Brideshead]', said Jonathan Jackson, 'And from then on everything was cricket trousers and cricket jumpers and suits and wanting to have a Brideshead look. And it was kind of, it did coincide with what was happening in Boulevard because everybody started wearing white suits – and baggy white suits and kind of, a little bit – ehm – Last Days of the Raj kind of look': Cole interview with Jonathan Jackson, 26 August 1997. The author and social commentator, Pickles, also noted the Brideshead-inspired look amongst young gay men, but highlighted the basis in class: '*Brideshead Revisited* has spawned a waxwork generation of look-alike English queens, playing with vowels, wearing cricket sweaters like social emblems … They are mostly lower-middle-class pretenders, enchanted by the idea that commoners … will swoon if they upper-middle their classy appeal': Pickles (1984), *Queens*, London, p. 107. This reflects the history of gay men's aspiring to a leisured-class ideal and a queer role model. For a similar account of gay lower-middle-class aspirations see Garland, *The Heart In Exile*, pp. 223–4.

23. Jocelyn Brooke (1950), *Orchid Trilogy*, London, pp. 371–2.

24. According to Dudley Cave, 'pinkie rings were normally worn by anyone who had been to university, at least a proper university, and then have a signet ring on the little finger of the left hand. And that really indicated, if it indicated anything, that they went to university and been given that for their 21st birthday or something. So that was quite meaningless, and if you look around at politicians nearly all of then have a signet ring on their little fingers': Cole interview with Dudley Cave, 21 May 1997; Daniel recalled that that pinkie rings could identify the wearer as gay, but that this wasn't a given: 'Pinkie rings were around, but I mean pinkie rings weren't really [for] your ordinary, everyday person. I mean you'd probably see them in the theatre group, … Yes they identified them as possible gay, but if you went up to someone with a pinkie ring, you might get a smack in the eye. So, they didn't identify you' (Cole interview with Daniel, 20 May 1997).

25. Sinfield, *The Wilde Century*, p. 138; 'Bill Miller, designer for and part owner of the Village Squire, which caters to a clientele that includes many homosexuals agrees with Weitz [that it is the rich who set fashions] "If you ask me who influences fashion most, I would say the jet set. The homosexual is one of the few people who can cross social lines. He mixes with, is inspired by, and inspires the jet set dresser"': Robert J. Lukey (1970), 'Homosexuality in Menswear', *Menswear*, February, p. 73.

26. Hugh David looks at this 'stereotype' in far more detail: Hugh David (1997), *On Queer Street: A Social History of British Homosexuality 1895–1995*, London, Chap 4.

27. For more details of gay and lesbian life and acceptance in bohemian quarters see Miller, *Out of the Past*, Chapters 9–13.

28. Caroline Ware (1935), *Greenwich Village, 1920–1930*, New York, p. 239.

29. Quoted in Bob Cant and Susan Hemmings (eds) (1988), *Radical Records: Thirty Years of Lesbian and Gay History*, London, p. 234.

30. John Clarke has stressed the way in which prominent forms of discourse (particularly fashion) are radically adapted, subverted and extended by the subcultural *bricoleur*: 'Together, object and meaning constitute a sign, and, within any one culture, such signs are assembled, repeatedly, into characteristic forms of discourse. However, when the bricoleur re-locates the significant object in a different position within that discourse, using the same overall repertoire of signs, or when that object is placed within a different total ensemble, a new discourse is constituted, a different message conveyed': John Clarke (1976), 'The Skinheads and the Magical Recovery of Working Class Community', in Stuart Hall and T. Jefferson (eds), *Resistance Through Rituals*, London.

31. Derek Cohen and Richard Dyer (1980), 'The Politics of Gay Culture', in Gay Left Collective (eds), *Homosexuality: Power and Politics*, London, pp.176–8.

32. Allan Horsfall (1988), 'Battling for Wolfenden', in Bob Cant and Susan Hemmings (eds), *Radical Records: Thirty Years of Lesbian and Gay History*, London, p.15.

33. See Chapter 4 and Chauncey, *Gay New York*, p. 350.

34. See the many oral history accounts of gay life such as Kevin Porter and Jeffrey Weeks (eds) (1991), *Between the Acts: Lives of Homosexual Men 1885–1967*, London and Peter M. Nardi, David Sanders and Judd Marmor (1994), *Growing Up Before Stonewall: Life Stories of Some Gay Men*, London.

35. Weeks (1989), 'Inverts, Perverts, and Mary-Annes', p. 202. This was also true of other early homosexual subcultures, such as Molly culture.

36. Richard Dellamora (1990), *Masculine Desire*, Chapel Hill, NC, p. 199.

37. Many of the witnesses in the Wilde trials and the earlier Cleveland Street scandal of 1889–90 were young working-class men who worked as, amongst other things, post office workers and guardsmen.

38. Richter Norton remarked that 'first and foremost, effeminacy is a form of self-advertisement': Norton, *Mother Clap's Mollyhouse*, p.104. Jeffrey Weeks, in his discussion of male prostitution, recognised that 'effeminate behaviour can be as much an adopted role as inherent': Weeks, 'Inverts, Perverts and Mary-Annes', pp. 205–6. It is worth bearing this point in mind when considering effeminacy in Chapter 2.

39. Montague Glover was a British Army Officer and architect, born in 1897. His photographs are reproduced in James Gardiner (1992), *A Class Apart: The Private Pictures of Montague Glover*, London; Hugh David illustrates this attraction to working- class 'rough' through a description of Reggie Kray's and Brian Epstein's fascinations with such men: see David, *On Queer Street*, pp. 205–9.

40. Garland, *The Heart In Exile*, pp. 67–8. Other novels worth noting for their view of the interactions between upper-, middle- and working-class gay men are Anonymous (1958), *A Room in Chelsea Square*, London; André Tellier (1948),

Twilight Men, New York; Charles Ford and Parker Tyler (1933), *The Young and Evil*, New York; Mary Renault (1959), *The Charioteer*, London; and Angus Wilson (1952) *Hemlock and After*, London.

41. For a fictional account see J. R. Ackerley (1960), *We Think the World of You*, London.

42. See the description of Michael Brown's cruising outfit in Chapter 7.

43. Hall Carpenter Archives Gay Men's Oral History Group (1989), *Walking after Midnight: Gay Men's Life Stories*, London, p. 44. For an account of the lives of British gay men during the Second World War see Alkarim Jivani (1997), *It's Not Unusual: A History of Lesbian and Gay Britain in the Twentieth Century*, London; for an account of the lives of American gay men see Alan Bérubé (1990), *Coming Out under Fire: The History of Gay Men and Women in World War Two*, New York. Gay men in Germany during this period had a very different experience: see Günter Grau (ed.) (1995), *Hidden Holocaust?: Gay and Lesbian Persecution in Germany 1933–45*, trans. Patrick Camiller, London.

44. Garland, *The Heart In Exile*, p. 135.

45. Cole interview with Peter Robins, 4 August 1997.

46. There are a number of works that refer to the 'availability' of uniformed members of the armed forces for sexual liaisons: see for example Quentin Crisp (1985), *The Naked Civil Servant*, London.

47. Cole interview with John Hardy, 12 June 1995.

48. Donald Webster Cory (1951), *The Homosexual in America: A Subjective Approach*, New York, p. 130.

49. From a memoir of gay life during the 1920s, quoted in Patrick Higgins (ed.) (1993), *A Queer Reader*, London.

50. Quoted in Frank Mort (1996), *Cultures of Consumption: Masculinities and Social Space in Late Twentieth-Century Britain*, London, p. 195. Both Richard and Simon recalled wearing sailors' tops during the mid-1980s, as they drew on an erotic masculine appeal and because they could be easily obtained from army surplus stores: Cole interviews with Richard, 19 August 1998 and Simon, 12 May 1999.

51. Letter from Geoffrey Squire to the author.

52. Ibid.

53. Alan Sinfield quoted in Murray Healy (1996), *Gay Skins: Class, Masculinity and Queer Appropriation*, London, p. 30.

54. Cole interview with John Hardy, 12 June 1995. During the 1950s police raids and prosecutions became facts of life for established gay venues such as the Rockingham Club – 'piss-elegant and full of queens who thought they were in the Athenaeum' – where Tom Driberg, E. M. Forster and J. R. Ackerley were occasionally to be observed among the regular clientele: Simon Raven, interview with Peter Parker, quoted in David, *On Queer Street*, p. 165.

55. Nik Cohn (1971), *Today There Are No Gentlemen: The Changes in Englishmen's Clothes Since the War*, London, p. 27.

56. Ibid.

57. Jon Savage (1988), 'The Enemy Within: Sex, Rock and Identity', in Simon Frith (ed.), *Facing the Music: Essays on Pop, Rock and Culture*, London, p. 148. A similar interaction and adoption between gay men and skinheads and rockabillies is assessed in Chapter 13.

58. Cohn (1971), *Today There Are No Gentlemen*, p. 27.

59. Georg Simmel (1904) 'Fashion', *International Quarterly* reprinted in *American Journal of Sociology* 62 (May 1957) pp. 541–58. Dighton, one of the characters in Garland's *The Heart in Exile*, recounted that before he met him his upper-class lover, Nigel, he 'seldom wore suits as I do now. And I never wore blazers. Now I always wear dark grey flannel trousers with a blazer. I also took to wearing Air Force ties . . .': Garland, *The Heart In Exile*, p. 150.

2

Fairies and Queens: The Role of Effeminate Stereotypes

Effeminacy and effeminate styles of dressing have been associated with homosexuality for as long as homosexuality has had a name. In the late nineteenth century and the early part of the twentieth the image of the 'fairy' was the only one that was publicly recognised as homosexual. This effeminacy was viewed in a different way from the effeminacy of the aesthetes, although with the trials of Oscar Wilde in England in 1895 the public had begun to associate aestheticism with homosexuality.[1] The effeminate homosexual continued to remain visible throughout the twentieth century, and offered a primary role model for men who were beginning to form a gay identity right up until the 1980s. However, not all gay men saw themselves as 'flaming faggots' or 'screaming mary's', nor did all of them adapt a highly visible, effeminate style of dress. Some men adopted this image and these behavioural attributes only as a first step into the gay world, but quickly moved on once they became aware of alternatives. While the culture created by overtly effeminate homosexuals provided support for men who rejected the gender persona and sexual roles prescribed them by the dominant culture, it also alienated many, who were repelled by the flamboyant style and the consequential loss of manly status.[2]

Many gay men accepted the equation of homosexuality with effeminacy, and thus viewed feminine presentational strategies as a means of expressing their identity as gay men: hence they feminised their presentational imagery by adopting womanly mannerisms and interests. Leo says that 'Back in the early twenties, people had to be quite effeminate to be identified, at least that was true in my case.'[3] Another man who was not naturally effeminate confirms Leo's statement: 'If not naturally, we tried to walk very effeminately, to talk effeminately, look effeminate, use rouge and make-up etc., to impersonate a female.'[4] In 1920s New York effeminacy was used predominantly by gay men to make themselves visible and attractive to potential 'straight' partners. Effeminacy attracted 'men' by utilising an established 'cultural script'. They were adopting characteristics of the opposite gender, and thus could be treated as surrogate females. The behaviour, and particularly the sexual behaviour, followed very strict gendered rules. The 'normal' men were active/male, while the 'queen' was passive/female.[5] As such effeminate men were tolerated to a degree, but were almost certainly not respected. One gay man observed that heterosexual men responded positively to effeminate homosexuals on some occasions:

> It is a well known fact that the secret of a woman's appeal to a man is not so much her sex as her effeminacy . . . The attitude of the average man to the homosexual is determined by the degree of effeminacy in the homosexual . . . Of course, they seek the eternal feminine in the homosexual . . . [and] feminine homosexuals naturally have the greater number of admirers.[6]

This was a widely held belief amongst gay men in the mid-1920s. While on certain occasions gay men were tolerated, on others they were the subject of physical and verbal abuse. Despite this lack of respect, many gay men felt that they had to adopt such strategies in order to proclaim who they were and allow 'normal' men to approach them. One man interviewed by Samuel Khan commented that the men he knew 'talk and act like women, have feminine ways . . . use rouge and powder . . . *in order to attract men*'.[7]

Although such men were often known as 'female impersonators', relatively few wore women's clothes or cross-dressed except in secure private environments. They were much more likely to use a single item of feminine or unconventional clothing to signify their identity. In the 1890s, Ralph Werther 'proclaimed [him]self' as a 'fairy' to working-class youth on 14th street by wearing 'white kids [gloves] and [a] large red neck-bow with fringed ends hanging down over my lapels'.[8] In attracting sexual partners male prostitutes usually adopted an effeminate appearance. In 1892 the Reverend Charles Parkhurst discovered the Golden Rule Pleasure Club on West Third Street, a brothel where the basement was divided into cubicles, each occupied by 'a youth, whose face was painted, eye-brows blackened, and whose airs were those of a young girl, . . . [who] talked in a high falsetto voice, and called the others by women's names'.[9]

A red necktie was one of the better known signifiers of homosexuality, particularly of a fairy, in America before the Second World War. In his now famous work on homosexuality of 1915, *Sexual Inversion*, Havelock Ellis quotes an 'invert' who told him that 'to wear a red necktie on the street is to invite remarks from newsboys and others'.[10] James Kiernan reiterated this fact a year later, when he declared in a scientific journal that 'male perverts in New York . . . are known as "fairies" and wear a red neck tie'.[11] However, red neckties were known as a sign of homosexuality only in certain circles.

They were understood far better in certain contexts than in others, and this is certainly true of all gay signifiers. For example, on a well-known New York cruising street such as Riverside Drive or 14th Street a man in a red necktie was likely to be labelled a fairy, whereas in a less alert social setting he would just be considered odd. In an era of conservative clothes a red tie inevitably announced unorthodox tastes, but unorthodox tastes of a particular sort only to those in the know. In a diary entry for Tuesday, 12 April 1927 Jeb Alexander recounts the tale of his friend Isador's encounter with the travel writer Richard Halliburton: 'Isador, who had been wearing a royal-purple tie, asked Richard Halliburton, who was wearing a red tie, for his autograph. Halliburton remarked, "Our ties speak a language." In Isador's autograph album Halliburton wrote: "To Isador, a good boy, from Dick Halliburton, another one."'[12] The painter Paul Cadmus used the red tie (along with bleached hair and tweezed eyebrows) in paintings, such as *The Fleet's In*, to signify a character's homosexuality. As with all fashions and codes, the red tie eventually lost its significance, and by the Second World War was no longer a recognisable sign.[13]

By the 1930s, effeminacy was widely believed to equate with homosexuality. At the core of his account of the appearance of the homosexual, Foucault writes of 'a certain way of inverting the masculine and the feminine in oneself. Homosexuality appeared as one of the forms of sexuality when it transposed from the practice of sodomy onto a kind of interior androgyny, a hermaphroditism of the soul.'[14] Based on the formulation of sexologists at the turn of the century, the dominant notion was that of a female soul in a male body. In her 1931 novel, *Strange Brother*, Blair Niles has one of her characters explain his preferred effeminate appearance: 'I'm happier so, your honor. Since I was a child I'm happier so. There were five older brothers at home and mother wanted me to be a girl. She let me dress in girl's things when I was small.'[15] These men paid particular attention to gendering their appearance by moulding their bodies in the ways favoured by women, and as a result the most obvious indicators of a fairy were 'plucked eyebrows, rouged lips, powdered face and marcelled blondined hair'.[16] Blair Niles gives a vivid description of effeminate homosexuals at a nightclub in Greenwich Village: 'the five young men had carefully marcelled hair, all had their eyebrows plucked to a finely pencilled line, all had carmined lips, all were powdered and rouged, all had meticulously manicured nails, stained dark red, all had high voices and little trilling laughs, and all expressed themselves in feminine affectations and gestures'.[17]

Along with the physical attributes that were altered to signify their sexuality, these men also used their bearing. A reporter in the 1930s observed that 'The most striking feature [of homosexuals] would be that the fact that although they represent and are dressed as one sex they act and impersonate the opposite sex . . . by gesture, voice inflection, manner or mode of speech, or walk, and in general [they] impersonate all of the other characteristics of a female that they can possibly assume.'[18] Seymour Kleinberg believes that gay men 'imitated women because they understood that they were victims in sisterhood of the same masculine ideas about sexuality. Generations of women defined themselves entirely in men's terms, and homosexual men often seemed to accept the same values ... It was not a particularly effective means of ending oppression, but it was a covert defiance of a society that humiliated them.'[19] Quentin Crisp's view is that homosexuals are excessively effeminate because, whereas women know they are feminine, homosexuals 'must, with every breath they draw, with every step they take, demonstrate that they are feminine'.[20]

Only a proportion of the men who engaged in same-sex practices identified themselves with this effeminate image. Peter Robins noted that while the effeminate homosexual may have become a popular stereotype and did offer a valid style of dress and self-identification for men such as Quentin Crisp, it was not desirable or possible for others to adopt this image.

> Of course people now hear an awful lot about Quentin, and I'm not knocking him, I met him four or five times and like him as a person, but he had the assurance of the English middle-class background, you know, which counts for something, and did more so then. If you were a lad from south of the river or east of Aldgate pub you would never have had the nerve to do the things that Quentin did; and again, he had a well-worn beaten track from the Kings Road, Chelsea, which was always, well not always but from the beginning of the century, was liberal, if you like, through to Soho. He was beaten up, poor soul, as we know, two or three times; but he would have been crucified in Dukesford or Gateshead. And so you shouldn't run away with the idea that we were all like that, even if we wanted to be, because there is – again it's anthropological: if you want to attract your east London lad you try to look like your east London lad.[21]

In a self-fulfilling process, those who could identify as such, felt themselves drawn purposefully towards such vivid manifestations, thus both consolidating the stereotype and making it appear more daunting to the faint-hearted.

For many gay men effeminacy was a way in to a gay lifestyle, and many embraced an overtly effeminate style before later rejecting it. Becoming a 'fairy' was the first step many men took in the process of making sense of their apparent sexual and gender difference and reconstructing their image of themselves. As the 'screaming queen' was the most visible manifestation of homosexuality, dressing in this way was, for many young men, a means of identification, of becoming part of a recognisable group:

When I really found out about this life, I was about fourteen . . . I met somebody about my own age and they just took me into town and then I went really effeminate. I let my hair grow long and I dyed it, shaved my eyebrows off and put eye mascara on and all sorts and I went really effeminate. In fact I used to say . . . 'she's a screaming queen'. Well, that's what I was, and I thought, marvellous . . . you know, there's somebody else like me after all.[22]

Many gay men felt no sexual interest in effeminate homosexuals; but associating with them was often the only way gay men could find an entry into the predominantly hidden subculture: 'The people everyone assumed to be gay were not my type. They were too camp, too effeminate; they just weren't the kind of people I was attracted to. I rather wanted to get to know them, though, simply because I wanted to meet some gay people'.[23]

These obvious homosexuals were often frowned upon by more conventionally dressed gay men as giving all homosexuals a bad name. 'Unfortunately, the obvious type is the one we're typed with, you know. A lot of people assume we're bitchy and effeminate and go around jangling bracelets, you know, 'cause they're the obvious ones which normal people mostly see and assume practically the whole homosexual world is like that.'[24] The resentment many gay men felt toward these effeminate men may have resulted as much from the affinity they felt with them as from the difference in their styles:

[Effeminacy] is one thing that I do not like in a man. Of course I am not narrow-minded about it in any way. I realize that effeminacy was born with [some men] and sympathize with [their] handicap. I like gentleness, love it in a youth or man; but effeminacy repels me. Thank God I have been spared that. Homosexuality may be curse enough (though it has wonderful compensations and noble joys) but it is a double curse when one has effeminate ways of walking, talking or acting.[25]

The fact that so many men referred to them suggests the extent to which they saw themselves as part of a continuum linking them to a public stereotype, where they represented a less extreme form of the fairy. Gene S. maintained that 'I don't object to being known as homosexual but I detest the obvious, blatant, made-up boys whose public appearance and behaviour provoke onerous criticism . . . I don't begrudge normal people their feelings against homosexuals.'[26]

As they grew older many gay men moved away from effeminate styles. Some did so because they discovered there were other ways of being gay; others realised their professional advancement depended on giving up such ways, or at least restricting their expression to gay environments. 'I was a gawky sissy boy with plucked eyebrows and loud clothes' said one man of his youth in the 1920s. A 'teacher took pity on me, taught me how to dress, warned me against any appearance of effeminacy'.[27] Most men in the straight middle-class world sought to pass by dressing 'invisibly' and displaying their homosexuality only in more private settings or by using signals that were less easily recognised by outsiders.

The life of an effeminate homosexual was not an easy one. These men were not only subjected to abuse by their contemporaries but were also liable to be arrested. In New York a 1923 amendment to state legislation that allowed men to be arrested for 'degeneracy' was used primarily to prosecute men for trying to pick up other men (cruising). However, it was sometimes interpreted loosely enough to encompass the prosecution of men marked as both gay and disorderly on the basis of some gender-inflected sign: campy or effeminate behaviour, the use of rouge or lipstick, the practice of calling each other by camp or women's names, or other aspects of their dress and carriage.[28] The same was true in London. Quentin Crisp was stopped by police because of his feminine appearance. On one occasion a policeman accosted Crisp at a bus-stop and, suspecting him to be soliciting, accused him of wearing women's clothing.[29] Daniel, who dressed relatively conventionally but was by his own admission effeminate and wore make-up, confirms that it was necessary to be careful. You could be arrested for wearing items of women's clothing or make-up, and Daniel quickly disposed of his powder compact on many occasions before being stopped by the police.

Despite these difficulties, men did continue to accentuate their feminine characteristics. Grant remembers that in Brighton, a south-coast resort in England, in the 1950s the more outrageous

> queans [*sic*] all wore terribly flared trousers and terribly Hawaiian shirts with all sorts of tulle at the neck. Hairdos were rather flamboyant, it was all out of a bottle. Handkerchiefs, kerchiefs round their neck for scarves ... they loved jewellery; they used to have not one bracelet but about *four* ... Colourwise it was a bit grotesque. Pink velvet trousers with a green shirt.[30]

The hero[ine] of William Talsman's 1958 novel dresses in a similar fashion to the Brighton queens:

> She sneaks her legs into a pair of slacks. She doesn't forget her underwear. She deliberately omits it. She wiggles into the sheerest of her sheer silk shirts, the light, high blue one which she calls "a vaporous blue." Then she slips her feet into sandals which are really moccasins of soft, white leather. Since she got them on sale, they are too big for her, but they don't flop, for she curls her toes in a gesture of narcissism which she does not understand but which holds them securely on her feet. When she uncurls her toes, she creates a flap, a little noise which announces her approach or adds a flounce to her attire'.[31]

In New York in the early 1960s signs of effeminacy were limited to 'wearing eyeliner and mascara, and sometimes "doe eyes," with dark black lines on the top, and bottom lids filled in to a point'.[32] Anything more, such as jewellery, teased hair, or drag, would not only would have invited arrest, but would have meant debarment from many of the gay clubs. However, some of the bars such as The Stonewall did allow the 'flame' queens to use their back bars, at the risk of losing their licences for serving alcohol to homosexuals. These flame queens wore eye make-up and teased hair, but essentially dressed in male clothes – if an effeminate version of it, with fluffy sweaters and Tom Jones shirts.[33] In Los Angeles flamboyant queens also continued to be visible. John Rechy noted that 'later at night, you'll find, when the shadows will shelter them – queens in colourful shirt-blouses – dressed as much like women as The Law allows that particular moment – will dish each other like jealous bitchy women, commenting on the desirability or otherwise of the youngmen they may offer a place for the night'.[34]

Effeminacy remained a potent dress- and behavioural-based form of identification for young gay men in Britain through the 1960s and into the 1970s. Richard Cawley dressed in an overtly camp manner, wearing skin-tight baby-blue velvet trousers tucked into riding boots, with a jacket and hair in an afro style. He recalled that rather than inciting violence his clothes caused him to 'get whistled at a lot and builders and labourers used to say "Hello Ducky"'.[35] The changes in men's fashions in the 1960s, the feminisation of styles and the adoption of colour, the increasing visibility of long hair for straight men also meant that these markers no longer pointed straight to homosexuality.[36] As a result of this gay men were often inclined to take to a more exaggerated from of fashionable (feminised) dress. Tony recalled that this was the time 'when everything went really wild . . . I would wear some very outrageous clothes because that was the era'. Tony would wear:

> flared trousers, in check, a very bold check, with 23-inch bottoms . . . [or] . . . full yellow trousers, like a canary, beautiful yellow french trousers and they had buttons all the way down [the side] so that you could actually undo the buttons, so that you could get more of a flare . . . [with] . . . black lace shirts . . . [or] a dress shirt, I used to wear it a lot but I never used to wear it with a bow tie, you used to want to show off your chest in those days and medallions.[37]

Tony also emphasised that with flares he liked to wear 'very high heels, the thick, thick ones . . . which made me about six foot [tall], which was great when I went out. I had a pair with hearts on, which were black [with purple hearts].' Tony had very little trouble and abuse for being dressed in such an outrageous way. 'You would go out in those days but no one bothered you', he remembered, 'they knew but no one bothered you in that respect.' [38]

Despite the lack of trouble that dressing in such outrageous styles caused gay men, some like to dress in that way purely for the shock value, for the upset it would cause straight neighbours. '[A] favourite drug outing would be to go and outrage the folk of Glossop on speed and things like Mandrax,' Desmond recalled. 'My favourite outfit at the time was a pair of wide Oxford bags and a shaggy fun-fur coat with long fluorescent hair, and both David and Ron had enormous Afros, so we must have looked eccentric.'[39]

With the adoption of more masculine self-presentation strategies (see Chapter 7) the effeminate image was derided within much of the gay community by the late 1970s. However, a less masculine image or dress style did continue to play a role in the lives of many gay men. John Campbell stressed that there were two options for gay men in the late 1970s:

It was quite well defined; you were either queens or clones . . . On the gay scene you do have those that want to be in a uniform and those that are going to say 'I am me', and at times you get the clones that are going 'Oh no, you are being outrageous, you're not meant to, you're meant to be wearing the uniform, if you don't wear the uniform you're not gay.' So we always tend to have variations of various outfits.[40]

John had realised quite early that he was a queen; although he often wore what he described as a queeny version of clone, on the whole he went for the more feminine, 'camp' choice:

a fur jacket with a satin shirt, which brings back memories of college where I was mistaken for a member of Heatwave with a friend. It was '77: I had a brown satin shirt, brown trousers with laces criss-cross, white laces criss-crossed on the side. Brown flared trousers with criss-cross laces. Now only a queen would wear those . . . [or] . . . white boots with cut-off shorts, but those were satin cut-off shorts and just an Adidas singlet, because I didn't like Haines, they were very cloney, and I don't want to look like a clone, even though I didn't have a moustache. I tended to get something similar but more unique.[41]

The resistance to and resentment of effeminately dressed gay men or 'queens' that had been evident throughout the twentieth century became more evident in the late 1980s, when masculine images dominated the commercial gay scene. Indeed, there was even a classification of roles within the broad band of effeminacy from full drag through to minor enhancements, such as tweezed eyebrows. Gary used his dress to confront assumptions, to:

'deliberately play off tensions' through his dress. He would wear what he described as 'feminine hard' mixing a leatherman's hat and mini-skirts, but stressed that what he wore was not drag 'drag is drag: dress, high heels, and a wig – a "man" dressed in women's clothes. I'm *not* a queen slapped up to the eyeballs with a bad taste frock on.'[42]

Debates raged in the gay press on both sides of the Atlantic about the bad name that 'effeminate' men gave gay men, resorting to the argument that they were re-emphasising the stereotypes that had been fought against. For many the adoption of an effeminate dress style was a political statement. For them it confirmed the diversity of gay culture and the belief that it was not necessary to be bound by conventions of dress and behaviour, that being gay should allow one to step outside those confines.

Notes

1. George Chauncey asserts 'The effeminate fairy was the most visible incarnation of homosexuality in New York' during the first third of the twentieth century: George Chauncey (1994), *Gay New York: Gender, Urban Culture and the Making of the Gay Male World, 1890–1940*, New York. For a British perspective see Alan Sinfield (1994), *The Wilde Century*, London.

2. Edward Carpenter, in his account of men with same-sex preferences, grants that there are 'extreme specimens' – the 'distinctly effeminate type, sentimental, lackadaisical, mincing in gait and manners, something of a chatterbox, skilful at the needle and in woman's work, sometimes taking pleasure in dressing in woman's clothes'. But these are not 'the more normal and perfect types': Edward Carpenter (1906), *Love's Coming of Age*, London, pp. 126–30.

3. Quoted in Chauncey (1994), *Gay New York*, p. 55.

4. Samuel Khan (1937), *Mentality of Homosexuality*, Boston, p. 127.

5. The place and role of the effeminate gay man in black working-class culture was captured by the blues. The blues did not go so far as to celebrate such men, but recognised them as a part of black working-class culture, and acknowledged 'normal' men's potential sexual attraction to them. The female blues singers sang about 'sissies' and men who turned to sissies in place of their wives, and a number of male singers recorded 'Sissy Man Blues', in which they demanded 'If you can't bring me a woman, bring me a sissy man'. For more information on the place of gay men in black culture see Eric Garber (1982), "Tain't Nobody's Business: Homosexuality in Harlem in the 1920s', *Advocate*, May 13 and Chauncey, *Gay New York*, Chapter 9.

6. Khan, *Mentality of Homosexuality*, p. 155.

7. Ibid., p. 124.

8. Ralph Werther (1922), *The Female Impersonators*, New York, p. 104.

9. Charles W. Gardner (1894), *The Doctor and the Devil; or the Midnight Adventures of Dr Parkhurst*, New York, p. 52. London had a comparable subculture in the 1890s, in which effeminate men and male prostitutes used elements of female

clothing to a greater or lesser degree depending upon the safety and privacy of the location. Chapter 1 deals with this in more detail.

10. Havelock Ellis (1936), *Sexual Inversion, Studies in the Psychology of Sex*, vol. 2, part 2, New York, pp. 299–300.

11. James Kiernan (1916), 'Classification of Homosexuality', *Urological and Cutaneous Review*, no. 20, p. 350.

12. Ina Russell (ed.) (1983), *Jeb and Dash: A Diary of a Gay Life 1918–1945*, Boston and London, p. 94. Richard Halliburton (1909–39) was a writer who travelled around the world in his own aircraft, tracing Cortés's conquest of Mexico.

13. According to Roger Smith red ties were still being worn at the Astor bar in the late 1930s, but by the beginning of the Second World War had generally lost their currency as a homosexual sign: see Chauncey, *Gay New York*, p. 52.

14. Michel Foucault (1978), *The History of Sexuality*, vol. 1, *An Introduction*, trans. Robert Hurley, New York, p. 43.

15. Blair Niles (1991), *Strange Brother*, London, p. 98.

16. Dr La Forest Potter (1933), *Strange Loves: A Study in Sexual Abnormalities*, New York, p. 184. Bleached or blondined hair was a typical indicator of homosexuality. So much so, that a blond-haired gay protagonist gave one novel its name: *Goldie*. Goldie constantly feared policemen would recognise him as 'degenerate [because of] the unusual hue of his hair', and consequently wore a cap taking it off 'only to attract the attention of his prospect', who presumably was equally aware of the colouring's significance: Bruce Kennilworth (1933), *Goldie*, New York, pp. 102, 119.

17. Niles, *Strange Brother*, pp. 49–50.

18. *Gloria Bar and Grill, Inc. v. Bruckman, et al.*, 259 A.D. 706 (1st Dep't 1940), testimony of Walter R. Van Wagner in Record on Review, 229, 232, quoted in Chauncey, *Gay New York*, p. 55.

19. Seymour Kleinberg (1978), 'Where Have All the Sissies Gone?' *Christopher Street*, March, pp. 8–9.

20. Quentin Crisp (1985 [1977]), *Naked Civil Servant*, London, p. 26. In his 1953 novel about gay life Rodney Garland espoused the following viewpoint: 'On the whole I think they belong to a group of people who are stunted if not destroyed by inversion . . . They are more feminine than most women, the "modern" woman in particular. I can't laugh at them, perhaps because I am not normal, and I am painfully aware that, since they are conspicuous, the whole of the underground is associated with them. For that matter, they don't mind ridicule; in fact, they realise it is a protective armour – to laugh is partly to forgive. Nature has been unkind to them and they try to restore the balance through the easier and less efficient of two ways. Instead of physical exercise, which could help, they resort to plucked eyebrows and excessive application of the wrong shade of rouge': Rodney Garland (1995), *The Heart in Exile*, Brighton, pp. 62–3. William J. Helmer, writing in 1963, noted that 'Many psychiatrists trace effeminacy to a deep-seated identification with the female sex, pointing out that effeminate mannerisms are not necessarily an indication of homosexuality. Effeminate homosexuals often believe they are "just born that

way" but I heard other theories advanced. One was that mannerisms sometimes are acquired, perhaps unconsciously by young men who try to find acceptance in gay life by adopting what they believe to be its conventions . . . Blatant effeminism seems to be more prevalent among homosexuals of the lower socio-economic classes; if so, it may be that such men are more distressed by their loss of masculinity and less able to reach an intelligent understanding of it, and thus are more inclined to exhibit abnormal behaviour': William J. Helmer (1963), 'New York's "Middle-class" Homosexuals', *Harpers* vol. 226, pp. 85–92.

21. Cole interview with Peter Robins, 4 August 1997.

22. Quoted in the BBC Radio programme 'Male Homosexual', broadcast 6 January 1964. Growing up in Surrey, England in the 1960s, Daffydd Jenkins had believed that, 'if you weren't a screaming Mary, you weren't a proper queen. The few that were not overtly faggot were oddities in a way' – hence his surprise when a gang of gay skinheads first walked into the Union Tavern in 1969 (quoted in Murray Healy (1996), *Gay Skins: Class, Masculinity and Queer Appropriation*, London, p.149). The public and media image of the stereotyped effeminate homosexual played an increasing role in this process. As Stuart Hall has argued: 'As social groups and classes live, if not in their productive then in their 'social' relations, increasingly fragmented and more sectionally differentiated lives, the mass media are more responsible (a) for providing the basis on which groups and classes construct an image of the lives, meanings, practices and values of *other* groups and classes; (b) for providing the images representations and ideas around which the social totality composed of all these separate and fragmented pieces can be coherently grasped': Stuart Hall (1977), 'Culture, the Media and the "Ideological Effect"', in J. Curran *et al.* (eds), *Mass Communication and Society*, quoted in Dick Hebdige (1987 [1979]), *Subculture: The Meaning of Style*, London, p. 85.

23. 'Nicholas' quoted in Hugh David (1997), *On Queer Street: A Social History of British Homosexuality 1895–1995*, London, p. 160.

24. Quoted in the BBC Radio programme 'Male Homosexual', broadcast 6 January 1964.

25. Russell (ed.), *Jeb and Dash*, pp. 90–1.

26. George W. Henry (1941), *Sex Variants*, New York, p. 255. 'On *Easter Sunday*, Arthur, Michael, Peter, Inv. and Frank (a rich young man of 35 with a car – a recent addition to this group) went to Brighton by Frank's car. Michael insisted that all wear shorts, it was a particularly hot day and Arthur and Inv arrived at the flat in sports clothes, there changing into shorts. C was also in shorts [line through this sentence]. Peter in flannels as he wasn't able to obtain any shorts and Frank a lounge suit, collar and tie as he didn't realize the weather was going to be so warm, having left early. Frank is the clandestine type of homosexual and essentially an active type. He heartily disapproves of all varieties of 'camp' (i.e. flaunting the fact that one is queer see below in the pub) and unless he was known to be as such, would never be identified as a homosexual, except perhaps by being in the company of a more overt type of homosexual. (This was really one of the major reasons why Frank did not dress in a similar manner to the rest). Peter wore white shirt and flannels and sandals.

Arthur, Michael and Inv. white shirts, shorts (rolled high to expose as much thigh as possible) and sandals. Michael had a powdered face, and powdered hair tightly curled which he would continually pat into place and curl on his fingertips. . . . Early evening was spent in strolling up and down the promenade in the vicinity of the "Men Only" beach – which is a notorious haunt of homosexuals – and from which several were observed to leave. This strutting along the prom in white sandals rolled up shorts, white short sleeved shirts and sunglasses was a suggestively "camp" action and objected to by F who nevertheless accompanied the others': Mass-Observation, sex survey article 1 sexual behaviour, box 4, file e, Appendix 1, Abnormality, 6.7.49. Mass-Observation was founded in 1937 as a study of the everyday lives of ordinary people in Britain. The peak of its activities occurred during the Second World War, and during part of this time it was employed by the Ministry of Information to monitor civilian morale. By the late 1940s its focus had become primarily commercial. It employed two distinct methods of data collection. In the first a team of paid investigators recorded people's behaviour in a variety of public situations, and in the second a team of volunteer observers kept diaries and responded to questionnaires.

27. Henry C. in Henry, *Sex Variants*, p. 309.

28. See Chauncey, *Gay New York*, Chapter 12.

29. Crisp, *Naked Civil Servant*, p. 29.

30. Brighton Ourstory Project (1992), *Daring Hearts: Lesbian and Gay Lives of 50s and 60s Brighton*, p. 51. Godfrey Winn recounted the clothes worn by a friend of Somerset Maugham's (whose home he visited at Cap Ferrat in the 1920s) and his immediate response to that man's clothes: 'I glanced at the man in candy-pink beach-clothes, who was handing round the drinks, and instinctively something in me revolted. *I don't want to look like you. To resemble you in any way, ever*' (Godfrey Winn (1967), *The Infirm Glory*, London, pp. 262–3).

31. William Talsman (1966), *The Gaudy Image*, Great Britain, p. 9.

32. Martin Duberman (1994), *Stonewall*, New York, p. 82.

33. Ibid., p. 34.

34. John Rechy (1964), *City of Night*, New York, p. 92.

35. Quoted in Alkarim Jivani (1997), *It's Not Unusual: A History of Lesbian and Gay Britain in the Twentieth Century*, London, p. 145. Andrew Tomlin recalled 'watching Dick Emery [as his effeminate gay character, Clarence] on T.V. and being worried that I'd grow into that': Cole interview with Andrew Tomlin, 10 May 1999.

36. The rise of men's clothes shops in and around London's Carnaby Street will be discussed in more detail in Chapter 5.

37. Cole interview with Tony, 30 November 1993.

38. Ibid.

39. Brighton Ourstory Project (1995), 'Anyone Who Had a Heart', *Gay Times*, February, p. 68.

40. Cole interview with John Campbell, 31 July 1997.

41. Ibid. John Campbell felt that his racial origin had an effect upon his choice to dress as a queen rather than a clone: 'Being black means you can get away with so much more clothes-wise. Black gay men always, even within the gay community, do

have discrimination, and so black gay men have to change their look in a completely different way, because if they start to looking like clones, in certain ways it can look ridiculous, moustaches and all that. It just didn't come off. So as a result we tended to be . . . although we do, we do it different ways. Being black we can wear much brighter colours, so we tend to wear brighter colours, much better designs sometimes.'

42. Tony Reed (1984), 'Reclaiming Effeminacy – A Starting Point?', *Square Peg*, no. 5, p. 10.

3

You're Born Naked and the Rest Is Drag!

In the first half of the twentieth century gay men could project an overtly visible presence by adopting an effeminate appearance. Those who could not or did not want to adopt such an image in public restricted their gay identity to small signifiers or overt behaviour only in 'safe' gay spaces. In his portrait of gay life in New York up to 1940, George Chauncey devotes much attention to the creation and appropriation of spaces in which gay men were free to be themselves, discussing the gay enclaves in both Greenwich Village and Harlem, both of which became tourist attractions, through the pansy craze[1] and the Harlem renaissance. Perhaps the most notorious of these appropriated spaces were the drag balls. By the mid-1920s they were attracting thousands of participants and observers. Chauncey notes that with the advent of legislation and the after-effects of the depression the drag balls ceased to be such a major event in the eye of the public. However, gay men have continued to hold drag balls and to use drag as a means of expression right up to the present day. The use of drag has evolved, waxing and waning in popularity over the century. As such, it has played an important, but controversial, role in the dress choices of gay men. As we have seen, the effeminate stereotype played a significant role in gay men's processes of self-identification. Drag was, for some, an extension of these modes of identification; but it was also (and this is a more important aspect later in the century) a fun pursuit used by gay men to celebrate the holidays and important days in the gay calendar, such as Halloween.[2]

Masquerade balls had a long tradition and were common events at the turn of the century. In 1893 Charles H. Hughes wrote of 'an annual convocation of negro men called the drag dance' in Washington DC. It was, he said, 'an orgie [*sic*] of lascivious debauchery beyond pen power of description'. He does, of course, go on to describe the ball, noting that:

'in this able performance of sexual perversion all of these men are lasciviously dressed in womanly attire, short sleeves, low-necked dresses and the usual ballroom decorations and ornaments of women, feathered and ribboned head-dresses, garters, frills, flowers, ruffles etc., and deport themselves as women. Standing or seated on a pedestal, but accessible to all the rest, is the naked queen (a male), whose phallic member, decorated with a ribbon, is subject to the gaze and osculations in turn, of all the members of this lecherous gang of sexual perverts and phallic fornicators.[3]

This is perhaps an exceptional occasion, and differs from many of the better-known balls in other cities such as New York.

Masquerade balls did not usually begin life as gay occasions, but were frequently attended by gay men and lesbians, as they offered the opportunity to be themselves in an atmosphere that encouraged the transgression of normative social behaviours. 'Like most practices of [early twentieth-century] gay subculture', George Chauncey tells us 'they were patterned on – but gave new meaning to – the practices of the dominant culture that gay men had observed and participated in'.[4] By the late 1920s, however, annual gay drag balls were occurring, the best-known in New York being the Hamilton Lodge Ball held every February in Harlem. These drag balls, where both men and women could dress as they pleased and dance with whom they wished, were not only socially acceptable, they were officially sanctioned.[5] State legislation meant that normally the wearing of the clothing of the opposite sex was illegal. One provision of this law did permit people to appear in masquerade, so long as they were going to a masquerade ball licensed by the police. Gay men seized the opportunities provided by this exemption, and organisers of the balls went to great pains to obtain the necessary police permits to ensure participants could dress up. And dress up they did. One observer described how 'Many of the "effeminates" are elaborately coiffured, in the powdered head dresses of the period of Madame Pompadour. They wear the billowy, ballooning skirt of that picturesque pre-guillotine era . . . others wear the long, tight-fitting gowns which were a recent vogue . . . still others wear the long, trailing skirts and the constricting corsets of the 1880s.'[6] Blair Niles description in her 1931 novel, *Strange Brother*, notes the same range of costumes:

> Leaning over the railing [June] was absorbed in the pageant on the floor of the hall, the men dressed in what Harlem calls 'drag', men in the garb of women, as Mark had said, in all sorts of women's fancy dress, in elaborate wigs . . . from the towering curled and powdered head-dresses of the Marie Antoinette period to the close marcelled bobs of 1930. Men in the voluminous costumes which go with the powdered wigs and in the long sheath-like evening gowns of the mode of 1930. The grace and style with which these men carried themselves was a challenge to women, June thought.[7]

The drag queens on display at the balls embodied camp culture in their inversion (and often burlesque) of gender conventions.

The highlight of the balls was the beauty contest or 'parade of the pansies', in which the fashionably dressed 'drags' would vie for the title Queen of the Ball:

> Among the paraders were slim figures almost nude and often to all appearances as sexless as angels. There were feather costumes as gorgeous as those of the Magnolia Night Club (Harlem club where shows were put on for whites to experience a taste of decadent Harlem), feathers trailing in brilliant clouds back from the nearly naked bodies, while monstrous plumed headdresses waved like the undulating fronds of palm trees in the wind. Necklaces, ear-rings and bracelets glittered. Faces were powdered and rouged. There were figures perfectly straight and slender, figures with the curved development of young girls and figures with the rounded swinging hips and the soft flesh characteristic of women.[8]

But the drag balls had their disadvantages. A large percentage of those who attended the balls were heterosexual, there to observe rather than participate. According to Eric Garber it was not unusual to see the cream of Harlem society, as well as much of the white avant-garde set, on the ballroom's bandstand, craning their necks to see the drags.[9] Newspapers frequently reported on the spectacle of the drag balls, as they became more and more of a spectator attraction.

The balls were a particular source of pride for the fairies and drag queens who were ordinarily derided by 'normals' and 'normal'-looking gay men alike. One black gay man who frequented Harlem's balls in the twenties told George Chauncey that 'They admired us – they were *dazzled* by us.'[10] It was rumoured that the onlookers filling the balconies and crowding the entryways included numerous downtown fashion designers who had come up to see the gowns. 'What we wore to the ball one year,' Howard Raymond said, 'you'd see offered in the best shops the next season.'[11] Whether or not this was the case, his conviction that it was shows the pride with which he regarded these events.

In 1930s New York gay men did not restrict their wearing of drag to the balls. Some were brave enough to take to the streets. But it was in Harlem that more (black) gay men were willing to venture out in public in drag, and drag queens appeared regularly in Harlem's streets and clubs. In December 1930, Cyril Lightbody opened a cafe on Seventh Avenue. Baltimore's *Afro-American* reported 'Sunday afternoon was its opening and we saw erotics, neuretics [*sic*], perverts, inverts and other types of abnormalities, cavorting with wild and Wilde abandon to the patent gratification of the manager and owner . . . About two A.M., five horticultural gents came in "in drag" as the custom of appearing in feminine finery is known.'[12] The casual appearance of drag queens at Cyril's Cafe (7th Avenue) and the frequency of their appearance in Harlem's streets suggests a high degree of tolerance for them in the neighbourhood as a whole. It took a great deal of courage for men to appear in drag, since like the overtly effeminate, they risked harassment by other youths and arrest by the police. Some drag queens refused to cower before the police and defied them all the way to the courthouse. One Sunday morning in 1928 two policemen watched four young women, who 'seemed well lit up and out for a glorious morning promenade', until they realised the 'girls' were 'pansies on parade' and quickly arrested them. The next morning the men were sentenced to sixty days in the workhouse. Still defiant, the drag queens mocked the police officers, shouting 'Goodbye, dearie, thanks for the trip, as we'll have the time of our lives' as they were led out of the courtroom.[13]

Drag balls continued to play a part in gay culture in the 1950s. Donald Cory described a drag party in his 1951 insider's view of gay life:

> Perhaps three-quarters of the people at the drag are males and perhaps a third are in masquerade. Some can be spotted from afar. They trip over their skirts and their shoes. They are clumsy, gawky, uncomfortable. Others require close scrutiny, and a few can never be identified with certainty. . . The parade of the queens will take place. Every male in female attire who chooses may get in line. The gowns are mainly on the lavish side, with here and there some striking simplicity. But mostly one sees flowing skirts, flamboyant colors, an ostentatious overdressing. Many wear wigs; while others have scarves skilfully tied around their hair. There are no visible crew-cuts among them.[14]

Balls of this type were also an important event to gay men in Britain in the 1950s. Like the early masquerades in America, the Chelsea, Hampstead and Brighton Arts Balls were not primarily gay events. However, they did offer men a chance to dress up and behave in a manner they could not normally display in public. Daniel, a gay man who dressed in fashionable clothes of the day, describes the Arts Balls: 'In the late fifties, sixties the theatres and arts always had a ball on Christmas. I went to several of them, actually, and of course it was very theatrical. They had a fashion parade. It gave you a chance to dress [up] outside, to drag up, yes. All the people that went there was good with their needles; and the colours of the thing!'[15] The open-minded art-world environment allowed men to dress in whatever they chose and to dance together. In 1955, for a young homosexual, like John Hardy, it was a liberating experience to dance with another man in such a public place as Hampstead Town Hall. But being new to the homosexual 'scene', he was at first uneasy about it: this was not after all a private party, so when he 'saw this boy, girl, I thought it was a girl at first, I asked him to dance with me'.[16] John Hardy maintains that, although many of the people at these balls were from the arts or were artists, the 'majority were gay'. Emphasising the importance of the balls for homosexual men, he continues that 'if the gay community in London heard that a ball like this was going to happen then they would go and get tickets for it, because they knew they could be outrageous, dress in whatever [they] wanted'.[17]

The Aquarium, the Brighton venue for these Balls, was known all over England. The importance of the Arts Ball at the Aquarium is highlighted by Grant, who remembers 'a certain number of queans [who] used to spend the whole summer sitting on the Men's Beach [in Brighton] sewing sequins on the gowns . . . by the hundredweight'.[18] At first The Aquarium turned a blind eye to drag; but for the last two or three years before it shut, it would not permit it. The Hampstead Ball also caused quite an uproar. A reporter from the local paper tried to interview some of the partygoers on the night bus provided to get back to the centre of London, but after being teased and sent up he wrote a scathing report about 'a lot of fairies at the Town Hall' and called for the Balls to be banned.[19] Donald Cory noted that not all gay men had a favourable view of the drag balls. Their view was similar to that of the men who objected to overtly effeminate gay men. He does note the importance for the men who did attend:

For the homosexual minority, most of whom never attend the drags and are little interested in them, and many of whom are indignant at their very mention, these gatherings play a role which is not frequently understood. Anything of a semi-legal nature which aids in breaking down the veils of secrecy and in bringing the homosexual life into the open is desirable. It is necessary to compel recognition of the minority, to insist upon its right of assembly as well as publication and agitation, as a prelude to the struggle for civil rights, judicial rights, and finally social equality.[20]

Drag and cross-dressing were not by any means confined to the Arts Balls. 'There used to be drag parties which were often very grand, because these people usually had enormous flats and lots of money, and it was champagne and that sort of thing.'[21] Even in regional cities such as Bristol men were dragging up by the mid-1960s. Tony remembers that:

you used to get a lot of chaps [who] used to dress in drag and come to the pub in Victorian outfits. I had one friend who worked for a famous jeweller and he used to come out in Victorian fashion and it was perfect from head to toe and it was beautiful. It was a big thing for someone to do that, especially coming to a gay bar, dressed up like until one got to the club.[22]

The 1960s saw a continuation of drag balls and parties in America. San Francisco and other major cities saw regular drag balls. William Helmer, writing in *Harpers*, described them in the following way, 'About the only social event staged publicly for homosexuals is the "drag ball," at which so-called "drag queens" can legally impersonate women. These are held regularly in commercial halls and many draw a thousand or more persons, including a sizeable number of heterosexual curiosity seekers.'[23] Private parties offered a valuable location in which gay men could 'drag up' without too much fear of disclosure: 'A colorful – but not necessarily sexual event – in the gay world is the "drag party" to which guests may come dressed as women. Unlike genuine transvestism, such masquerading is often done as a titillating joke, the idea being to dress like a ridiculous parody of the female in order to humorously exaggerate one's "perversion".'[24] Debates amongst gay men around the rights of gay men to wear drag began during this period. Gradually these debates began to move towards a discussion of the importance of gender roles and dress as an important means of communication. R. W. Clark felt that 'Anyone should be able to dress anyway [*sic*] he wishes. Not only is it a right but an excellent means of communicating. "The clothes make the man." If those clothes happen to be women's clothes, then that's the image the man wants to project. Let him.'[25] W. E. Beardemphal put forward the argument that:

> Dress can communicate on a much more profound level than the current 'I am a male; I am a female' level. Drag can be used effectively as a cry for pity and compassion for the wrong that society inflicts. But, more importantly, it can go far beyond this expression into a wonderful world of creative art that will bring pleasure to all who will open their eyes and see. Dress can be an art form of great expression to personhood and joy of others . . . It is SOCIETY and its warped concept of 'sex-role-playing' that has robbed many homosexuals of their person-hood'[26]

The drag debate was still continuing in the 1970s, particularly as the prevalent image for gay men was a hypermasculine one, epitomised by the clone:

> The garden variety of drag is attempting personal communication and hardly ever anything else. The great majority of gay men have never cross-dressed or dragged and never had the desire to do so. For some, however, drag provides a means of self-expression in a way not ordinarily available. Halloween, New Year's Eve, Mardi Gras, and an occasional ball or pageant create the context for this expression. They may wish to be admired, or only to feel pretty. They may be tired of playing butch. They may want nothing more than to 'try it once'. For many young males

who drag, it appears to be an emphatic statement about the socially-defined femininity that they feel within themselves. Far from being an insult to women, it is the compliment of attempting to suppress their own male-ness as distinguished from person-ness.[27]

Drag, like the appropriation of an effeminate identity, was often used by young gay men as a vehicle to explore aspects of their developing sexual identity.[28]

Some men were very aware that they were playing with illusions and preconceptions of gender announced via dress. 'It's more or less a game', said Jerome:

I have honestly no desire to be a woman, so of course I feel like a man. It's more like I suppose an actor on a stage – it's a game – because when you're an actor and you're on stage you're putting yourself into someone else's place and you're convincing the audience that you are what you really are not . . . because I look conventionally like a woman, here I am sitting here eating and I'm being totally – er – accepted.[29]

Jerome is here echoing Goffman's theories of self-presentation, in which the private self is the source of the roles performed publicly, rather than 'the self' being 'fleetingly created through each performance'.[30] By the mid-1970s gay men were fully conscious of their strategies for dragging up:

I think it's mainly the idea of not necessarily wanting to be feminine – I have no desire to be a woman in any way, shape or form. But again, gay kids are characterized . . . And the gay guys are pictured as being rather nelly, you know, feminine . . . I think drag is probably something very foreign to most people in the straight realm, and its really nothing more than – than fun, than acting, as I said . . . its really sort of a camp, you know, sort of a parody, a play on things.[31]

This parodying of gender was taken to its logical extremes by the radical drag queens, by whom drag was worn as a political statement, one designed to confront or 'freak out' the straight community. Laud Humphreys says that 'radical drag differs from traditional transvestism . . . in that there is no attempt to present a consistent and deceptive performance of the opposite sex role . . . Radical drag is more than a technique, it is a new style of revolution that penetrates to the genitals of the system it calls to account.'[32] The idea behind radical drag was not to look like a real woman or a glamorous film star (like many of the drag artistes or the men attending the famous drag balls of the 1950s and 1960s), but to attract attention and cause a stir. 'We began to realise that there were ways of using drag,' recalled

Michael James. 'It's a way of giving up the power of the male role. We were holding the mirror up to man, showing that we rejected what maleness stood for.'[33] By taking the extreme stereotypes of both male and female dress, combining workmen's boots, beards and moustaches with very feminine dresses and full make-up, these gay men caused confusion through their use of conventional gender indicators, often taking its inspiration from film stars of the 1930s and 1940s[34] and from psychedelia. Interviewed for *Square Peg* magazine in 1988, John Lloyd described the clothes he and his friends wore: 'Colam would be wearing a very short white dress with boots and his beard and a badge saying "How dare you presume I'm heterosexual." I'd have my green dress on, Alice would be wearing his gold lamé and David would have a long flowing black gown and a long beard as well.'[35] Carol Warren emphasises that 'although radical drag has an element of comedy', like the professional drag artistes, it was primarily 'a proclamation of revolution against the fact that certain worlds have power over other worlds'.[36] The radical drag queen's look was one that had evolved from the street transvestites, such as Sylvia Rivera and those Martin Duberman describes as 'scare drag queens', 'boys' like Tommy Lanigan-Schmidt, Birdie Rivera, and Martin Boyce, 'who looked like girls but who you knew were boys'. These were the looks favoured by the transvestites picked out and elevated to 'superstars' by Andy Warhol, Jackie Curtis and Candy Darling.[37] This street queen look later developed into a New York 'punk' look discussed in Chapter 11. Seymour Kleinberg echoed the sentiments of genderfuck or radical drag when he wrote that 'Men in drag are not swept up in the delusion that they are women: only insane men in drag believe that. The rest are committed to ambiguity: they are neither men nor women and are only rarely androgynous; the usual aura of drag is neuter.'[38]

The spirit of the 1930s Harlem drag balls was revived in New York in the late 1980s, when groups of black gay men and transvestites bonded in 'houses' (their own version of gangs or street families, with an older drag queen as the 'mother' or leader). Instead of fighting to find the dominant group, as heterosexual street gangs would do, these houses vie with each other in 'walks' (competitions in various life-stylistic categories) at house balls. In house-ball competitions, categories are often based on imitations of realities seen not only on television or across white America but also on the streets of the black, primarily heterosexual, ghettos where the participants live. The most famous event of the house balls is the supermodel walk, in which each drag queen must sashay down the runway as his favourite superstar model and must wear a *haute couture* gown. The competitors strike poses based on those of catwalk models. This is known as 'voguing'.[39] At the drag balls of the 1930s the competitors also posed for their spectators and judges.[40] In other sections the contestants compete in gender 'realism' categories, sometimes called 'butch realism' or 'femme realism'.[41] In the 'butch-real' competition, the idea is for a drag queen to disguise himself as a heterosexual homeboy so convincingly – in backward baseball cap, baggy pants, and sweatshirt worn with a swagger – that he could walk his neighborhood streets without being found out as gay.[42] Judith Butler proposes: 'The parodic or imitative effect of gay identities works neither to copy nor to emulate heterosexuality, but rather to expose heterosexuality as an incessant and *panicked* imitation of its own naturalized idealization.'[43] In an unconscious way the 'drag queens' of the New York houses were undertaking an exposure of this very unreality of images and lifestyles. This is particularly the case where the lifestyles emulated were completely alien to and unattainable by the contestants – for instance, businessman drag, where the competitors walked and talked like surreal versions of white executives, complete with suit, wingtips, briefcase and *The Wall Street Journal*.

Drag has continued to move in and out of the fringes of gay dress. Though it had previously been present, the 1980s and 1990s saw a rise in the popularity of drag as a commercial enterprise amongst the straight population. Events such as Wigstock in New York and clubs like Kinky Gerlinky in London revived the interest in drag as a fun alternative. This was, in some respects, a reaction to the ultra macho images of gay men in the 1970s and early 1980s. One man writing in *Square Peg* magazine believed 'drag has the capacity to be a powerful rallying point, a way for gay men to get rid of inhibitions and refuse kowtowing to the rules of conventional society. If the sight alone of a man in a frock actually challenges some of the assumptions of the morality of the suburbs then it is radical.'[44] The rise in interest in the rights of and the vocal visibility of transvestites and transgendered persons, to whom clothing is just one small aspect of their declaration of identity, has furthered this debate. But drag has continued to be criticised by many gay men, who still feel that dressing up in women's clothes, whatever the motivation, does more harm than good to gay rights causes. This criticism is coupled with the belief that drag panders to an old stereotype of homosexuality: that a man wanting to wear a dress equals a man who wants to be a woman. In direct contrast to the adoption of effeminate styles of clothing or the outright donning of a dress, there is a history of gay men who intentionally (or unintentionally) wore clothes that rendered them 'invisible' as gay.

Notes

1. George Chauncey notes that the word 'pansy', along with other flower types, was commonly used to describe homosexual men in the USA in the 1920s. George Chauncey (1994), *Gay New York: Gender, Urban Culture and the Making of the Gay Male World, 1890–1940*, New York. See also Gershon Legman (1941), 'The Language of Homosexuality: An American Glossary', in George W. Henry, *Sex Variants*, New York, Vol. 2, Appendix VII, p. 1173.

2. For more details on this aspect see Carol A. B. Warren (1974), *Identity and Community in the Gay World*, New York, p. 38.

3. Charles H. Hughes (1893), 'An Organization of Colored Erotopaths', reproduced in Jonathan Ned Katz (1992), *Gay American History: Lesbians and Gay Men in the USA*, New York, pp. 42–3.

4. Chauncey, *Gay New York*, p. 291.

5. Thirty years later Donald Webster Cory highlighted the importance of drag balls to gay men: 'The gay folk do not go [to the drag balls] for the thrill and the adventure, nor are they seeking new friends. I do not believe they are primarily motivated by a need to exhibit themselves. In the main, what attracts them to the drag is the feeling that they will be among many of their own kind. Here they are known, liked, and accepted for what they are. It is a masquerade, ironically enough, where one goes to discard the mask' (Donald Webster Cory (1951), *The Homosexual in America: A Subjective Approach*, New York, pp. 132–3).

6. Dr La Forest Potter (1933), *Strange Loves: A Study in Sexual Abnormalities*, New York, p. 188.

7. Blair Niles (1991), *Strange Brother*, London, p. 211.

8. Ibid., p. 214.

9. Eric Garber (1982), ''Tain't Nobody's Business: Homosexuality in Harlem in the 1920s', *Advocate*, May.

10. Chauncey, *Gay New York*, p. 291.

11. Ibid.

12. 'On Seventh Avenue', *Afro-American*, 27 Dec. 1930, p. 9, quoted in Chauncey, *Gay New York*, p. 249.

13. 'Two Eagle-Eyed Detectives Spot "Pansies on Parade" ', *Interstate Tatler*, 10/3/32, p. 9, in Chauncey, *Gay New York*, p. 249. The declaration by these drag queens that they would have the time of their lives in the workhouse is not as unusual as it seems. The prisons of New York had developed a drag culture amongst their gay prisoners. In 1934 the *New York Herald Tribune* reported on attempts to clean up prisons. 'Men appeared for lunch, some of them heavily rouged, their eye brows painted, their lips red, hair in some instances hanging to the shoulder, and in most cases hips swinging and hands fluttering.' The article continued that the raiding party responsible for cleaning up the cells was 'greeted by cries and howls in high falsetto . . . Inside the cells were found every conceivable article of women's wearing apparel. Dozens of compacts, powder puffs, and various types of perfume were found, while silk step-ins, nightgowns and other bits of negligee were strewn about the

cells' (*New York Herald Tribune* 25 Jan. 1934 pp. 1, 9): Chauncey, *Gay New York*, p. 94.

14. Cory, *The Homosexual in America*, pp.131–2.

15. Cole interview with Daniel, 20 May 1997.

16. Cole interview with John Hardy, 12 June 1995.

17. Ibid. Stephen describes another of London's balls: 'The other thing, of course – a great mecca for the gay world – was Lady Malcolm's servants' ball at the Albert Hall [in London] every year. She was some very benevolent lady who believed in doing something for the servants; and so every year, at the Albert Hall, she organised this enormous servants' ball which I suppose several thousand people used to go to in all sorts of extraordinary garbs. I went once or twice, I think, and I saw young men dressed in a tiger skin or all sorts . . . Lady Malcolm was horrified by it; and eventually the thing was brought to an end. The other event, of course, was the Chelsea Arts Ball, which was a mixed affair, but again sort of largely patronised by the gay fraternity': Kevin Porter and Jeffrey Weeks (eds) (1991), *Between the Acts: Lives of Homosexual Men 1885–1967*, London, p. 113.

18. Brighton Ourstory Project (1992), *Daring Hearts: Lesbian and Gay Lives of 50s and 60s Brighton*, Brighton, p. 56.

19. Cole interview with John Hardy, 12 June 1995.

20. Cory, *The Homosexual in America*, p. 133.

21. Porter and Weeks, *Between the Acts*, p. 113.

22. Cole interview with Tony, 30 November 1993.

23. William J. Helmer (1963), 'New York's "Middle-class" Homosexuals', *Harpers*, vol. 226, March, pp. 85–92. Carol Warren describes similar occurrences and competitions in gay bars in the 1970s: 'The bars at Halloween are specially decorated, but the main event is the getting into drag. Many customers wear drag (just to mingle, talk and drink; in addition there is usually a drag contest at each bar. Sometimes different costumes compete; at other times the contestants rush breathlessly from bar to bar in the hope of winning more than one prize . . . winners are the most outrageous, spectacular, unusual or costly drags, not the ones that best approximate females. . . . At Midlands about one in ten of the customers were in drag ranging from evening gowns to spoofs of pregnant sluts . . . At Kenos the prizewinning costume, which won against replicas of Liza Minelli, or humorous versions of Laugh-In women, was a huge glittering butterfly. The man who wore it was young, and naked except for a small feather loin cloth and elaborate eye makeup and headdress': Warren, *Identity and Community*, pp. 60–1.

24. Helmer, 'New York's "Middle-class" Homosexuals', pp. 85–92.

25. R. W. Clark (1967), letter to 'Open Forum: The Wearing of Drag', *Vector*, April.

26. W. E. Beardemphl (1967), 'Drag – Is It Drab, Despicable, Divine?', *Vector*, May, p. 13.

27. Norman Davis (1975), 'Meditations on Drag', *Vector*, May.

28. In the 1980s one young man describes his experiences: 'It was around this time [March 1985] that I had my first cross-dressing experience. There was this old

blue dress left around and I got into tights and I was singing Marilyn records as usual. After two weeks I was thrown out of the hotel for being a wee poof, basically. It was a big struggle but I had got my allowance book and my independence. I'd thought all my troubles were over but they were really just beginning. I was doing Marilyn Monroe impressions as well as being Marilyn and I got beaten up in one hotel. I went back to the hairdresser's I was pally with and I got them to bleach my hair pure blonde. I went to school with it all lacquered and blue-eye liner and Monroe lips. I was so busy exploring my sexuality that I wasn't getting anywhere academically and I decided to leave school. . . . But it wasn't long before I started to attract men. I shaved my legs and I was walking down the street, cross-dressed and in high heels . . . I also began buying dresses and jewellery with a stolen credit card' (quoted in Bob Cant (ed.) (1993), *Footsteps and Witnesses: Lesbian and Gay Lifestories from Scotland*, Edinburgh, pp. 202–3.)

29. Warren, *Identity and Community*, p. 38. Writing in 1972 Esther Newton noted that 'The effect of the drag system is to wrench the sex roles loose from that which supposedly determines them, that is, genital sex. Gay people know that sex-typed behaviour can be achieved, contrary to what is popularly believed. They know that the possession of one type of genital equipment by no means guarantees the "naturally appropriate" behaviour': Esther Newton (1972), *Mother Camp: Female Impersonators in America*, Englewood Cliffs, NJ, p. 103.

30. Erving Goffman (1959), *The Presentation of Self in Everyday Life*, New York. Tseelon furthered this argument, saying 'this game is not an end in itself but a *means to an end* of gaining benefits. It is a game of *misrepresentation*', where the private self is sincere and the public self presents a false impression – I am not what I am: E. Tseelon (1982), 'Is the Presented Self Sincere?, Goffman, Impression Management and the Postmodern Self', *Theory, Culture and Society*, 9, p. 116.

31. Sebastian, quoted in Warren, *Identity and Community*, p. 103.

32. Quoted ibid., p. 107.

33. Quoted in Kris Kirk and Ed Heath (1984), *Men in Frocks*, London, p. 104.

34. It is useful here to compare the drag queens' dress choices with the art deco/1930s–inspired revival, characterised by shops such as Biba in London.

35. 'The Nancy Revolution', in *Square Peg* no. 20, p. 31.

36. Warren, *Identity and Community*, p. 121.

37. Jackie Curtis was 'a hip drag queen, [who] took everything to extremes. She walked around in ripped stocking and big tears in her dresses with threads hanging off . . . she had that combination of trash and glamour . . . a lot of her dresses were from the 30s and 40s, things that she'd pick up from thrift stores for 25 cents . . . she wore old-lady shoes that she sprayed silver, and her tights were always ripped . . . No one thought [she and Candy Darling] were women, no one thought they were men! No one knew what they were!': Jayne County with Rupert Smith (1995), *Man Enough To Be a Woman*, London, p. 51.

38. Seymour Kleinberg (1978), 'Where Have All the Sissies Gone?', *Christopher Street*, March, p. 8.

39. Voguing was later popularised by Madonna in her song 'Vogue', the video for which had Madonna and her backing dancers 'striking poses' like the house

competitors.

40. This is described by Blair Niles as 'a licensed masquerade party with police protection . . . a long elevated platform was set up in the center of the hall. They held back the crowd, too, while the "fairies" came on in single file, to mount the platform and slowly walk its length, pausing now and then to strike attitudes, to stiffen into statuesque poses, to drop curtsies or to execute some syncopated phrase': Niles, *Strange Brother*, pp. 213–14. In *Subculture: The Meaning of Style* Dick Hebdige identifies a series of punk dances, one in particular known as 'the pose'. In this dance one of the 'couple' (who were generally of the same sex) struck a clichéd fashion pose, while the other crouched down in an imitation of a photographer. This bears striking resemblance to the competitors at both the 1930s drag balls and the Voguing competitions of the early 1990s. Hebdige stresses how punk dances were performed in a mass of isolation, with no two people ever touching in an intimate way. This bears some resemblance to the supposed origins of the twist: 'They said it was invented by black homosexuals who wanted to dance together, which they were forbidden to do by law. By twisting, which is very erotic, they were able to dance without contact and I think it was one of the first dances in which there isn't contact': George Melly on BBC radio, 'The Story of Pop, Part 9: Twist and Shout', 10 Oct. 1973.

41. Jenny Livingston's 1990 documentary film *Paris is Burning* (1990) follows the successes and failures of a number of 'houses' as they compete against each other at the balls. Realism had been an important aspect of the drag balls from which these 'houses' evolved. The winners of the 1930s drag balls were often the men who looked most like a 'real' woman. In John Rechy's 1963 novel *City of Night* 'a Negro queen . . . a screamingly effeminate youngman in a candy-striped shirt' describes a costume he wore: 'I dressed like the Queen of Sheba, and honey, I Mean To Tell You, I looked *Real!*': John Rechy (1964), *City of Night*, New York, p. 48.

42. This mirrors the move towards 'gay lads' in England, where gay men adopt the clothing styles of heterosexuals. It also tied into an early 1990s dissatisfaction with the commercial gay scene and the images associated with it. See Toby Manning (1996), 'Gay Culture: Who Needs It?', in Mark Simpson (ed.), *Anti-Gay*, London. Also compare to passing in the 1950s: see Chapter 4.

43. Judith Butler (1991), 'Imitation and Gender Insubordination', in Diana Fuss, *Inside/Out – Lesbian Theories, Gay Theories*, London. Here Judith Butler argues that there is no original or primary gender that drag imitates, but that gender is a kind of imitation for which there is no original. Heterosexual images are just a fantasy ideal, and, in an attempt to fix the fantasy, heterosexuality is bound to fail. It therefore has to reinstate its own fantasy image, which postures as normality and reality. She is stating that if there is no *primary* reality, there can be no derogatory reference to the *secondary*, the copy.

44. 'Drag', *Square Peg*, no. 31, p. 34.

Invisible Men?

From the turn of the century right up until the 1960s, when changes in attitudes towards sexuality and men's fashions began to alter perceptions of homosexuality, the effeminate queen was the dominant public image of male homosexuals. This could mean two things. On the one hand the flamboyant stereotype diverted attention from other more guarded men and made it relatively easy to 'pass' as straight. On the other it threatened to overwhelm any other images people had of anyone they discovered to be homosexual.[1] Just as there were men who expressed their homosexuality through the adoption of an effeminate appearance in both the gay and the straight worlds, so there were men who would not or could not express their sexuality in this way. They did not identify with the feminine, and regarded themselves as homosexual but not as 'fairies'. As early as 1881 John Addington Symonds had noted that while 'a certain class of people are undoubtedly feminine, the majority do not differ from "normal" men. They are athletic, masculine in habits, frank in manner.' These 'normal' homosexuals are 'passing through society year after year without arousing a suspicion of their inner temperament.'[2]

For most homosexuals the 1930s through to the 1950s were characterised by the very real fear of exposure, blackmail and imprisonment. In both Britain and America the police were conducting a virtual witch-hunt of homosexuals.[3] In Britain this led to events such as the Montagu trials.[4] Gay men also had to contend with the threat of vigilante anti-gay violence and strove to remain invisible in public.[5] In 1948 the following 'Don'ts' were suggested as 'sane and useful advice for male inverts' in England:

> Don't commit to writing any admissions as to your inclinations; don't masquerade – on any occasion whatsoever – in women's clothes, take female parts in theatrical performances or use make-up; don't be too meticulous in the matter of your own clothes, or affect any extremes in colour or cut; don't wear conspicuous rings, watches, cuff-links, or other jewellery; don't allow your voice or intonation to display feminine inflection – cultivate a masculine tone and method of expression; don't stand with your hand on your hip, or walk mincingly; don't become identified with the group of inverts which form in every city . . .'.[6]

Dress for these gay men broadly followed conventions of fashion: they wore 'dark suits, three pieces, very quiet shirts'[7] that would not elicit comment or notice from outsiders. Dudley Cave, for example, tended to wear 'grey flannels, a sports coat and an extremely butch belt, an ex-army belt, a tie'. He 'wouldn't have dreamt of going into town in those days without wearing a tie and usually a sports jacket. Generally speaking we kept our heads down and tried to avoid being seen as what we were.'[8] John Hardy echoes the fact that everyday dress for most gay men followed conventions of fashion: 'when you were out and about in the streets and going about your ordinary day-to-day business you wouldn't think of wearing anything really outrageous. You tended to dress down and look like everyone else.'[9] In America gay men were also at pains not to express their sexual orientation through their dress. Bill Miller, owner of *Village Squire* (a shop with a large homosexual clientele in New York) said that covert or closeted homosexuals do not wish to be identified as homosexual and dress accordingly: 'they will fight fashion completely. They will want to wear a uniform, get lost in the rush. I'm willing to guess that Brooks Bros. has more homosexual customers than all the Village boutiques put together.'[10] In a novel written in 1958 a 'self-confessed fairy' decides to move away from the town he has lived in and start a new life as a 'normal' man. He changes his image from the camp effeminately dressed queen to what he perceives as 'respectable', for which we can read *not* queer.

> He thought of dying his hair black, of buying a tweed suit to fill out his figure, and of honouring his fingers with rings, big solid knots which were the emblems of athletic trophies. With square, heavy soled, box-toed shoes he would be just another Southerner in search of Manassas . . . he snipped his ringlets to the nubbin and looked almost respectable, he thought.[11]

Adhering to normative dress codes was seen as an important factor in the progression of the early gay rights movements. Frank Kameny, one of the leaders of the Mattachine Society, insisted that a strict dress code was enforced on all participants in gay demonstrations. Men were to wear suits, shirts and ties and women skirts. 'If we want to be employed by the Federal Government,' Kameny intoned, 'we have to look employable to the federal Government.' Kameny and his allies felt that it was important to look ordinary, to get bystanders to hear the message rather than be prematurely turned off by appearances.[12]

Writing in 1965 Douglas Plummer observed that in one smart members only London gay club 'it would be difficult, if not impossible, to judge any of these men as being homosexual if they were seen individually in a crowd'.[13] Stratton Ashley observed a similar clientele in New York bars, where the men were all 'young and well-groomed. On the whole they looked like a bunch of clean-cut college boys.' They were, one of them told him, 'most interested in those qualities regarded as masculine in each other. We cultivate those qualities in ourselves and look for them in others. No one is more "out" in our group than the queen who swishes.'[14] Other journalistic accounts of gay life in New York and San Francisco made reference to the smart and inconspicuous style of dress of many of the men in gay bars and clubs, where no one 'looked' homosexual.[15]

In the light of society's and the law's attitudes towards gay men, they devised a variety of tactics that allowed them to move about freely, to appropriate for themselves spaces that were not marked as gay, and to construct gay space in the midst of, yet invisible to, the dominant culture. They were aided in this effort, as always, by the disinclination of most people to believe that any 'normal'-looking man could be anything other than 'normal'. In 'The Sexed Self: Strategies of Performance, Sites of Resistance', David Bell and Gill Valentine discuss the 'managed self' in relation to lesbian identity, noting how lesbians create apparently asexual identities by avoiding reference to their personal life but bearing discreet signals that can be read by 'those in the know'. This theory can equally be applied to those gay men who remained invisible in heterosexually defined public spaces while revealing their hidden identity to those in the know through a series of sartorial or behavioural signifiers. Thus in Bell and Valentine's words they were 'putting on or taking off different "masks", sometimes maintaining multiple identities in one space at different times or in different spaces at the same time.'[16] Men who dressed conventionally in public did not necessarily continue this practice once inside their own home or in accepted gay spaces, such as pubs or clubs.[17] Grant remembered that in Brighton (which had a large and often visible gay population in the 1950s): 'The only time you saw a gay man was probably at the weekend. During the week, you would have passed him by with his bowler hat, navy suit and black shoes with a paper under his arm and a rolled umbrella.'[18]

Involvement in the gay world familiarised men with the styles of clothing and grooming, mannerisms, and conventions of speech that had become fashionable in that world, but were not stereotypically associated with effeminate homosexuals. Both gay and straight observers have noted this. Those fashions served as signs 'neither masculine nor feminine, but specifically and peculiarly homosexual', observed the writer and gay activist Donald Webster Cory in the early 1950s: 'these were difficult for [outsiders] to pinpoint', but enabled men to recognise one another even as they concealed their identities from others.[19] Whereas effeminate men used codes that were intelligible to straights as well as to gays, such as flashy dress,[20] other gay men developed codes that were intelligible only to other men familiar with the subculture:

> Most inverts are practised at spotting others, whether obvious or not, in all countries in general and their own country in particular. It is partly experience, partly intuition. I suppose I was a little quicker than the average, and fairly good at spotting the middle-class 'respectable' homosexual who tries to hide the thing, but who gives himself away by his anxiety to appear normal.[21]

Accessories, such as red ties or suede shoes, were used to allow these gay men to recognise one another without drawing the attention of the uninitiated. They were so effective that researchers repeatedly expressed their astonishment at gay men's ability to identify each other, attributing it to something akin to a sixth sense:

> Sexual perverts readily recognize each other, although they may never have met before and there exists a mysterious bond of psychological sympathy between them . . . Instances have been authenticated to me where such perverts when meeting another of the same sex, have at once recognized each other, and mutually become acquainted and have left company with each other to practice together their unnatural vices.[22]

Suede shoes are perhaps one of the better-known historical signifiers of homosexuality, especially in Britain. Observers in America in the late nineteenth century noted that 'fairies' were wearing suede shoes in New York, and Thomas Painter observed that dark brown and grey suede shoes were 'practically a homosexual monopoly'.[23] In Britain in the 1930s suede shoes were a sure sign of deviancy. Stephen 'distinctly remember[s] it was a very bad sign for people if they wore camel hair coats and suede shoes! I remember when I bought myself a camel hair coat and suede shoes I thought I was really coming out.'[24] Trevor Thomas was known as 'the man who wore suede shoes' and that 'it was known if you wore suede shoes and a Liberty [silk] tie you were [homosexual].' His 'alibis', to anyone who was not homosexual, were '(a) I was an artist, (b) I worked in a Museum and (c) I acted.'[25] By the 1950s, with a relaxing of conventions in men's leisure dress, suede shoes were not automatically a sign of homosexuality. Peter says that 'you were classed as "one of those" but it didn't really mean much. There was no seriousness in it because they didn't really know, there were a lot of normal people used to wear brown suede shoes and grey flannel trousers and cravat. But that was the fashion, particularly on the Sunday lunchtime.'[26] Dudley Cave agreed that as Teddy Boy (influenced) fashions became more popular they lost their connotations of homosexuality, but did retain a certain rebellious or anti-establishment connotation.

The colour of a man's clothing was also often an indicator that he might be homosexual. At a time when men's clothing was on the whole sombre certain colours were 'suspect'. In 1949 Mass Observation conducted a survey on sexual attitudes, and found that amongst its study group 'Pale Blue was a queer's "trade colour" – The group studied favoured pale blue for short socks, ties and pullovers.'[27] Barbara Bell noted that in Blackpool the gay men also used traditionally non-masculine-associated colours to reflect their sexuality: 'I remember vividly' she says 'one year it was pink shirts. Nobody ever had pink shirts so if you wore a pink shirt you definitely signalled that you were a gay boy.'[28] Green was also a colour that had homosexual associations. Writing in the *Urological and Cutaneous Review* in 1916 in an article entitled 'Classification of Homosexuality' James Kiernan noted that 'inverts are generally said to prefer green'.[29] In his ground-breaking book *Sexual Inversion* Havelock Ellis had written that homosexuals had a preference for the colour green, and in Paris green cravats were worn as a badge. Both these passages reflect the green carnation worn by Wilde and the rent boys of Piccadilly in London in the late nineteenth century. Peter Robins remembers the implications that the colour green had, but only because it differed from conventional heterosexual dress of the day:

> My first awareness of people actually using dress as a code was in the early fifties in Manchester. By this time I had bought a pair of bottle green trousers, cords, and I was wolf-whistled. In Heaton Park on Sunday afternoon, that's on the north side of Manchester. And I had a perfectly good Harris tweed jacket I was wearing with it and I was going out for tea, quite innocuously but some local lads certainly thought I went too far, as it were, away from the dreariness of their own clothes.[30]

Dudley Cave illustrates how despite knowing these signifiers it could often take courage to wear them:

> I had read, I think in Havelock Ellis or somewhere, gay men's favourite colour was blue or green. So when I had the opportunity, after all it was very difficult to buy clothes, I was in Simpson's and they had a rail of green sports jackets, green Harris tweed. They were so good that I took one. I bought one, but I was very embarrassed about its colour – but it showed me up, I feared. Though how everybody . . . how the straight community would know this secret colouring I have no idea.[31]

Often it was not so much the actual clothes that the men wore, but the manner in which they wore them. 'If one can only present the visible and non-identifying aspect of one's identity' Martin Hoffman noted, then 'one's physical appearance will be the central aspect that can be displayed to others.'[32] Douglas Plummer noted that 'you will observe that the men around you are well dressed. In such clubs the standard and quality of clothes is high. Most "queers" are concerned about their appearance, revealing the feminine side of their nature in a love of colour, carefully made suits, original designs, and a progressive attitude towards dress. Usually they show good taste.'[33] The emphasis here is upon how smartly dressed and well-turned out gay men were. One of the characters in Rodney Garland's 1953 *The Heart In Exile* describes the men at 'the Aldebaran', a gay bar in the West End of London. They 'looked queer, well-dressed and not tatty and no bright colours, and yet they looked queer, the way they talked and moved about . . .'.[34] In the 1950s British newspapers reflected a paranoia about the seemingly growing existence of invisible homosexuals by producing articles that offered advice on 'how to spot a homo'. They often concentrated on an over-developed sense of fashion: 'When one, two or three button jackets are in he is the first to wear them. His shirts are detergent bright, his tie has the latest knot and is always just so' and personal appearance: 'His cheeks are smooth, his hair sparkles, his nails are manicured.'[35]

Hoffman described what he observed as the typical dress of middle-class American gay men in 1968. It was:

> the same style of dress that an average college undergraduate might wear. It would consist of a sport shirt, Levi's and loafers or sneakers. In this 'typical' middle class gay bar which I am attempting to describe, extremely effeminate dress and mannerisms are not well tolerated . . . There is a tendency toward effeminacy in the overall impression one gets from observing the bar, although this may not be anything striking or flagrant . . . Also in spite of the fact that the modal bar costume is very much like that one would see on a college campus, there is a good deal of special attention paid by the bar patrons to their dress, so that they seem almost extraordinarily well groomed . . . the majority of individuals in the bar are not identifiable and would not be thought to be homosexual in another setting.[36]

Mannerisms were also vital signifiers at a time when clothing was not an obvious signal. 'The "meanings" of clothes are' John Harvey argues 'con-structions placed upon them, and are not readable in a dictionary sense as verbal meanings are. These meanings are based on the perception of specific choices (or abdications of choice) as to the material, colour, cut, newness, but there is a high degree of ambiguity as to the purposes of such choices.'[37] Consequently, he continues 'Any meaning in the clothes will, moreover, be either corroborated or qualified by posture and movement of the body inside the clothes.'[38] If Harvey's argument is correct, then signifiers such as suede shoes are only a 'possible' indication of the (homo)sexuality of the wearer: this suspicion is quantified by the mannerisms of the wearer, and so certain behaviours were an essential element of the revelation of the identity of these 'invisible queers' to one another. Many gay men who rejected crudely effeminate styles and behaviour would not have seemed 'masculine' in their interests or demeanour.[39] In the light of this argument, a mincing walk or the tilt of the head could give a man away and 'invariably you could find a queer by the way he held his cigarette'.[40] Prior to gay liberation, observers frequently commented on seeming inconsistencies of gay men's behaviour. At times they seemed fully manly, while at other times, among themselves, in the safety of the gay bar or party, they could become outrageously effeminate.[41] This was still true into the 1970s. Carol Warren's description of her friend Danny recalls how in gay company he dressed in a overly elegant style in soft colourful fabrics and behaved in a somewhat 'feminine' manner, and how his demeanour changed at a primarily straight company dance.[42]

In addressing what I have termed the invisible gay man I have concentrated on a number of signifiers and aspects of behaviour that gave an indication of homosexuality. There were always and still are many men who regard themselves as homosexual but have no desire to announce this either to other gay men or to straight society through their dress, and continue for all intents and purpose to maintain an invisible appearance. This is not necessarily through fear of exposure as gay, but may be due to their individual perceptions and the relative importance they place upon their sexuality as a defining aspect of their person.[43] In the 1950s, in attempting to pass as straight, it was possible for men to go to the opposite extreme and to become what Rodney Garland called a Male Impersonator. A male impersonator was 'obvious, because he overdoes things . . .'. One such man:

> assumed an unnecessarily deep voice and adopted gestures that were too big and too heavy for his five feet ten inches and his thirty-eight chest. Bred in London he became a caricature of a country gentleman, with his tweeds, a concealing moustache and his new vocabulary with the dropped 'g's'. It didn't need a trained psychologist to see that he was a failure . . . touchy and nasty and feminine under the disguise.[44]

It was exaggerations of masculine behaviour such as that described by Garland, coupled with an adoption of work clothes, that were to formulate a new stereotype of the homosexual in both America and Britain in the post-liberation years. By the 1970s this had developed into a new image and subsequently a new stereotype – the clone.

Notes

1. Samuel M. Steward (in his introduction to the 1982 reissue of James Barr's *Quatrefoil* (1950) recalled of this period: 'Those of us who could maintain our secret lived under an extraordinary protective umbrella: the ignorance and naiveté of the American public . . . We existed under the shadow and cover of such naiveté': James Barr (1982),*Quatrefoil*, Boston. Nonetheless, many gay men not only refused to endure the indignities suffered by the 'fairies' but resented the men who did, for they believed the flagrant behaviour of the fairies on the streets had given the public its negative impression of all homosexuals. See also Chapter 2 and George Chauncey (1994), *Gay New York: Gender, Urban Culture and the Making of the Gay Male World, 1890–1940*, Basic Books, New York, p. 103.

2. John Addington Symonds (1881), 'A Problem in Modern Ethics', quoted in Brian Reade (ed.) (1970), *Sexual Heretics*, London, pp. 251–2.

3. For Britain see Jeffrey Weeks (1990), *Coming Out: Homosexual Politics in Britain*, London and New York. For America see Eric Marcus (1992), *Making History: The Struggle for Gay and Lesbian Equal Rights, 1945–1990*, New York and John Loughery (1998), *The Other Side of Silence*, New York. The war years did see a different atmosphere and gay men felt a certain amount of freedom. For more on this period see Alan Bérubé (1990), *Coming Out Under Fire: The History of Gay Men and Women in World War Two*, New York.

4. This was one of the most famous prosecutions of homosexuals in the 1950s. Lord Montagu was accused in 1953 of indecent assault on two Boy Scouts. The chief prosecution witnesses were offered immunity in exchange for reporting on other homosexuals, which was a common practice at the time. The jury was unable to decide whether Montagu and his co-defendant Kenneth Hume were guilty. Before the retrial Michael Pitt-Rivers and Peter Wildeblood were arrested and accused of indecency and conspiracy with Montagu to commit the offences, a charge designed to prejudice Montagu's retrial. After a display of malice and prejudice from the prosecution the defendants were found guilty. This case was typical of those brought against homosexuals in the 1950s.

5. James noted the effects of this on gay men: 'I mustn't let you think that we ran around with false moustaches and beards and dark glasses, dead scared and frightened, thinking are the police going to pick me up at any minute. Some people did, some people were absolutely terrified of someone saying something out of place' (quoted in Brighton Ourstory Project (1992), *Daring Hearts: Lesbian and Gay Lives of 50s and 60s Brighton*, Brighton, p. 37).

6. Anomaly (1948), *The Invert and his Social Adjustment*, London. In 1955 James Douglas Margin offered similar advice to the readers of *One* magazine in what he called 'Margin's Theory of Masculine Deportment': James Douglas Margin (1955), 'The Margin of Masculinity', *One*, vol. III, no. 5.

7. Kevin Porter and Jeffrey Weeks (eds), (1992), *Between the Acts: Lives of Homosexual Men 1885–1967*, London, p. 62.

8. Cole interview with Dudley Cave, 21 May 1997.

9. Cole interview with John Hardy, 12 June 1995.

10. R. J. Lukey (1970) 'Homosexuality in Men's Wear', *Menswear*, February, p. 82.

11. William Talsman (1966), *The Gaudy Image*, London, p. 207.

12. Martin Duberman (1994), *Stonewall*, New York, p. 111. The influence of counter culture attitudes and associated dress codes led to a new breed of gay rights activists who countered the 1950s gay rights beliefs that to achieve gay rights it was important to follow rules and fit in, working within the system. This is dealt with in more detail in Chapter 6.

13. Douglas Plummer (1965), *Queer People: The Truth About Homosexuals in Britain*, New York, pp. 54–6.

14. Stratton Ashley (1964), 'The "Other" Homosexuals', *One*, vol. XII, no. 2, p. 5.

15. See for example William J. Helmer (1963), 'New York's "Middle-class" Homosexuals', Harpers vol. 226, pp. 85–92.

16. David Bell and Gill Valentine (1995), 'The Sexed Self: Strategies of Performance, Sites of Resistance', in Steve Pile and Nigel Thrift (eds), *Mapping the Subject: Geographies of Cultural Transformation*, London and New York. Will Finch noted that: 'All my life I had to wear a rigid mask, a stiff armour of protection, not necessarily to pretend to be what I was not – heterosexual – but not to be identified as homosexual. Not that I was ashamed of so being, but to defend against insults, humiliations and mockery': Finch diary, no date, Kinsey Institute for Research in Sex, Gender, and Reproduction Library, Indiana University, Bloomington, quoted in Chauncey, *Gay New York*, p. 273.

17. One man living in Montreal in 1916 went to work in 'tweeds; but at home among friends, at the theatre and concerts, he was delicately made up and elegantly dressed, wearing exotic jewellery and as colorful clothes as he dared. Receiving at home, he donned a bronze green robe of heavy silk: Elsa Gidlow (1980), 'Memoirs', *Feminist Studies*, no. 6, p. 122.

18. Grant in Brighton Ourstory Project, *Daring Hearts*, p. 30. Dress in other gay spaces is looked at in Chapter 3, which deals specifically with drag balls in the USA and the Arts Balls in England.

19. Donald Webster Cory (1953), 'Can Homosexuals Be Recognized?', *One*, 1, September, pp. 7–11.

20. Some gay men who were not fairies and who dressed conventionally on the whole used make-up or tweezed their eyebrows to add a slight feminine touch to their otherwise unremarkable appearance, but only in certain parts of cities, for example the West End of London. 'I did wear paint, make-up', says Daniel, 'I certainly wasn't a slut and I dressed ordinary. We had nice clothes, I mean it didn't mean to say that we had fancy clothes or feminine clothes. We looked feminine, no way about it, but you dressed *nice*': Cole interview with Daniel, 20 May 1997. Samuel Khan told of a 17-year old Italian boy who adopted 'a conventional persona in his own neighborhood, carrying himself as a fairy (by removing his hat to reveal his tweezed eyebrows) only in other parts of town': Samuel Khan (1937), *Mentality of Homosexuality*, Boston, p. 217.

21. Rodney Garland (1995), *The Heart in Exile*, London, pp. 159–60.

22. T. Griswold Comstock (1892), 'Alice Mitchell of Memphis', *New York Medical Times*, 20, p. 172.

23. Thomas Painter (1941), 'The Prostitute', Kinsey Institute Library, pp. 168–9, quoted in Chauncey, *Gay New York*, p. 52.

24. Porter and Weeks, *Between the Acts*, p. 111. In his 1930 book *Degenerate Oxford?*, Terrence Greenidge warned of 'the mass-production of the effeminate men' whose 'feet will be shod with gay suede shoes [who] speak with artificial voices of a somewhat high timbre, [and] walk with a mincing gait': Terrence Greenidge (1930), *Degenerate Oxford?*, London, p. 133.

25. Porter and Weeks, *Between the Acts*, p. 62 and 1981 television programme 'Sexual Identity' quoted in Keith Howes (1994), *Broadcasting It*, London. Dudley Cave also remembered that suede shoes were 'certainly very dubious. I did in fact buy a pair of suede shoes just before I went in to the army. They cost a guinea. A lot of money. And when I went into the army I sold them to my [a friend] . . . And people were very suspicious about him on that, but since he was very heterosexual and consequently in bed with different "Wrens" it was all right. That was distinctly suspicious, and how I came to buy them I shall never know, because I would avoid anything remotely like that, and certainly I think it was Noel Coward who said that suede shoes should only be worn by consenting adults in private. Yes, they were certainly suspicious.' (Cole interview with Dudley Cave, 21 May 1997).

26. Brighton Ourstory Project, *Daring Hearts*, p. 50. Peter Robins's father was very aware of the connotations of suede shoes – so much so that when the teenage Peter innocently suggested he buy a pair in the 1950s he angrily retorted 'Suede, do you think your father wants to look like a pansy actor?': Cole interview with Peter Robins, 4 August 1997. Roy told me (in an interview, 20 June 1994) of a circular that was sent around by the civil service, warning members of staff to be on the look out for men in suede shoes, as they were almost certain to be homosexuals and therefore a security risk.

27. Mass-Observation Sex Survey, Sexual Behaviour, Box 4, File E, Appendix 1, Abnormality. 6.7.49.

28. Quoted in Alkarim Jivani (1997), *It's Not Unusual: A History of Lesbian and Gay Britain in the Twentieth Century*, London, p. 50. George, who lived in Brighton, confirmed that in the 1950s a 'Pink shirt was definitely queer, colourful clothes were definitely queer': Brighton Ourstory Project, *Daring Hearts*, p. 52.

29. James Kiernan (1916), 'Classification of Homosexuality', *Urological and Cutaneous Review*, 20.

30. Cole interview with Peter Robins, 4 August 1997.

31. Cole interview with Dudley Cave, 21 May 1997.

32. Martin Hoffman (1968), *The Gay World: Male Homosexuality and the Social Creation of Evil*, New York, p. 59.

33. Plummer, *Queer People*, p. 56.

34. Garland, *The Heart in Exile*, p. 54.

35. Lionel Crane (1963), 'How to Spot a Possible Homo', *Daily Mirror*, 28 April 1963, p. 7.

36. Hoffman, *The Gay World*, pp. 54–5.

37. John Harvey (1995), *Men in Black*, London, p. 12.

38. Ibid.

39. The boundaries between the visible/effeminate and the invisible/masculine were permeable, partly because gay culture encouraged a style of dress and demeanour and an interest in the arts and fashion that were regarded as effeminate. Many 'invisible' gay men liked to behave in similar ways to those of the visible effeminate men when in secure private settings by adopting feminine names, using feminine pronouns and parodying gender conventions with a camp wit. While 'invisible' gay men may have derided or despised overtly effeminate men, they were also capable of seeing effeminacy as merely a style to be turned on or off at will. 'Camp' behaviour also represented some gay men's recognition of the artificiality of the social roles they regularly played in social settings in which they needed to 'pass' as straight.

40. Brighton Ourstory Project, *Daring Hearts*, p. 51. Peter Robins was living in Manchester in the mid-1950s. He remembers that at The Union pub gay men were smoking particular brands of cigarettes. Once he had noted this he used cigarette branding as an indicator of a man's homosexuality: 'I began to notice that people were all smoking either State Express 555, in a characteristic purple and egg-yolk yellow packet and this was "Like a cigarette?" . . . So, State Express 555; and another one was Passing Cloud. They were pink, I think, or something, in a pink packet, pink and pale green, and they were slightly oval as opposed to round.'

41. In the 1950s in discreet bars like The Blue Parrot in New York, 'men impeccably Brooks Brothers and as apparently Wasp as one's banker could in a flicker slide into limpness. They had available a persona that mixed ironic distance, close observation, and wit, all allies of sanity': Seymour Kleinberg (1978), 'Where Have All The Sissies Gone?', *Christopher Street*, March.

42. Carol A. B. Warren (1974), *Identity and Community in the Gay World*, New York, p. 95.

43. Discussions and arguments around this issue, have become particularly visible in the 1990s. For more details see Mark Simpson (ed.) (1996), *Anti-Gay*, London, Alan Sinfield (1998), *Gay and After*, London and Daniel Harris (1997), *The Rise and Fall of Gay Culture*, New York.

44. Garland, *The Heart in Exile*, pp. 206–7.

5

Tight Trousers: Italian Styling In The 1960s

The 'Italian invasion' in men's clothing began in Britain in the 1950s at a time when men's dress was on the whole conservative. The dark suit was the standard by which most men's dress was measured. Young men continued on the whole to dress like their fathers. But with an increase in wealth and the experiences of men who had travelled in Europe during the war and afterwards during their national service a new interest in clothes began to emerge. For those who couldn't travel these new styles could be seen in films from Italy and France and through increased exposure to other forms of communication such as magazines and television.[1] For the first time young men and women had a larger disposable income than their parents. Clothes, records and leisure activities such as attending dances were popular ways for these 'teenagers' to spend their money.[2] Young men and women were looking for new ways of asserting their independence through their dress choice. One of these new ways of dressing was the Italian look. Peter Burton remembered that 'there was a distinctly Italian look in the late Fifties. When I was about fourteen, I was kitted-out in an Italian style "bum-freezer" jacket, fairly tapered trousers and pointy-toe shoes made from woven leather.'[3] Michael confirms that this had a particular appeal to young gay men: 'Younger men – and clearly younger *gay* men – obviously didn't feel it so necessary to project such aggressively "masculine" images.'[4] Richer gay men had visited liberal-minded parts of Europe, such as Capri, on holiday throughout the 1920s and 1930s and had taken to wearing a more relaxed style of clothing seen in those countries and associated with a leisure-class lifestyle.[5] The appeal of these Italian-styled clothes to gay men was that they 'emphasised the figure. The jackets were short – that's why they were called "bum-freezers" – and the trousers tight to emphasise the bum and the crotch.'[6]

One of the first places these European-styled clothes were seen in Britain was in a shop called Vince Man's Shop (*Vince*) situated in Newburgh Street, a little-known Soho back street.[7] The owner Bill Green had begun his career as a physique photographer, and with the proceeds he made from selling a bikini-style posing brief, first to his models and then to other 'muscle-boys and butch trade', he went on holiday to France.[8] While there he noted that:

> the younger people were wearing black jeans and black shirts and I thought this hadn't been seen in Britain, everyone is so busy wearing blue jeans, which they can smuggle in from America. So I got black jeans and black shirts and similar things made in this country and they went like a bomb in those days. And I started designing stuff myself. People said the stuff was so outrageous that it would only appeal and sell to the rather sort of eccentric Chelsea set or theatrical way-out types.[9]

Green stops just short of describing a major component of his clientele – gay men.

Initially the clothes the *Vince* shop sold were based on close-fitting European casual wear, but in sombre colours; gradually Green introduced more vivid colour. Green was also innovative in his use of fabrics: 'I used materials that had never been used before – lots of velvets and silks, trousers made of bed-ticking, and I was the first with pre-faded denims – and I made everything as colourful and bold as I could.'[10] Bright colour and tight-fitting clothing had traditionally been associated with homosexuality, and this goes some way to explaining the shop's early gay clientele.[11] Just as the New Edwardians had worn snugly tailored trousers and jackets, so *Vince*'s clothing revealed the contours of the male body.[12] Peter says that 'the gay crowd took to jeans because of the close and tightness of them, showed up all the essential parts'.[13] Colin MacInnes echoes this in his seminal novel of 1950s youth culture, *Absolute Beginners*. His fashionable gay character, the Fabulous Hoplite, 'was wearing a pair of skin-tight, rubber-glove thin, almost transparent cotton slacks, white nylon-stretch and black wafer-sole casuals, and a sort of maternity jacket, I can only call it coloured blue'.[14] Bill Green said that 'everyone thought we only sold to Chelsea homosexuals but, in actual fact, we catered to a very wide public, within an age range of about twenty-five to forty . . . artists and theatricals, muscle boys, and celebrities of every kind'.[15] A closer look at the types of people Green describes underlines the gayness of his clients – 'theatricals' and 'artists' were express-ions often employed euphemistically to describe men who were or were suspected of being gay, and his list of celebrities included John Gielgud (who officially came out as gay in the 1990s, but in London circles was already known to be gay). John Hardy, who worked as an assistant at *Vince* and modelled for the mail order catalogue, confirms that a high percentage of *Vince*'s clients were gay.[16]

The association of homosexuality with Vince may not, of course, have been unquestionably good for business in those pre-liberation days. While there were many homosexuals in London who would buy his clothes, this was a limited market, and Green was keen to expand. By continuing to advertise in magazines such as *Films and Filming* Green ensured that *Vince* clothes were seen outside London, in shops such as *Bobby*'s in Bournemouth. The popularity of Vince clothes is indicated by the wholesale contracts Green established with Marshall and Snelgrove and with Macy's in New York, and by the shop's move into larger and easier-to-find premises on Foubert's Place around 1961. The formula for gay-oriented boutiques was copied by other shops such as *Dale Cavana* in Kinnerton Street, London and *Filk'n* in Brighton, which sold styles of clothing and underwear similar to *Vince*'s.[17] Brighton, which for a long time had been a mecca for homosexuals, had its own gay-oriented boutique – *Filk'n Casuals*. The owners, Phil and Ken, had both been trained in Paris, where Phil had worked for the couture house, Worth. Harry, who maintained that Phil and Ken were making these clothes before Vince started, described the clothes as 'casual shirts, jackets, trousers and under briefs, which were brief under briefs like they wear them today, which were very daring in those days'.[18]

John Stephen, who had worked as a sales assistant at Vince, initially based his menswear shop, *His Clothes*, on *Vince*, selling the same tightness, the same rainbow colours, and the same element of camp. Stephen continued to use the same fabrics and colours, which were then adopted by other men's clothing manufacturers as young men challenged conventions of acceptability and were prepared to wear more outrageous clothing. Where Stephen differed was by rapidly changing his styles and keeping costs low, even if that meant sacrificing quality of wear and finish. The success of *His Clothes* precipitated an influx of new menswear shops on Carnaby Street, such as *Donis* and *Domino Male*. Such was the success of the Carnaby Street boutique that in 1967 the chain of high-street tailors, Austin Reed, invited Colin Woodhead, the fashion editor of *Town* magazine, to launch an in store boutique named 'Cue'. Other menswear stores quickly followed suit, which resulted in similar departments in *Aquascutum*, *Harrods* (Way In) and *Moss Bros* (One Up) as the Carnaby Street look (initially developed by Vince) became available nation-wide.

The fashion historian Nik Cohn asserted that in the early 1960s, in mainstream fashion, 'it seemed less important, suddenly, to look like a he-man, to have biceps like grapefruit and hairs on your chest'.[19] However, the photographs in *Vince*'s catalogues illustrate that for a certain section of society, notably non-effeminate homosexual men, there was an appeal in adopting a more masculine look, or at least in emphasising the maleness of the body. Many of the clothes sold by Vince were designed to show off those very muscles: for example, the 'Torso Shirt', which first appeared in the catalogues in 1961 (but had been seen earlier under the name 'tailored T-shirt'). This extremely close-fitting white T-shirt was shown worn by muscular young models with the following description 'Thumbs up for this masculine modern T-shirt . . . with bicep-baring sleeves'. A later development of the original close-fitting jeans, the 'Corsair slacks' were described as 'beautifully cut Bermuda style (and that means made for a close fit everywhere)', a barely euphemistic way of emphasising the crotch-hugging nature of Vince trousers.

Vince's is generally regarded as having been the first men's 'boutique' in London. Similar shops existed in New York, San Francisco and Los Angeles, which sold tight-fitting, fashionable clothes and swimwear to gay men (and more adventurous straight men). The clothes pictured in the catalogues for *Vince*, the language used to describe them and the comments and memories of those who worked there emphasise the gay nature of its clothes and its clientele. But it is equally clear that the dress choices of gay men were influential on mainstream men's fashion: *Vince* sold clothes that once would have been worn by 'no one but queers and extremely blatant ones at that'.[20] Those heterosexual men who shopped at Vince were often rich enough or in sufficiently elevated social positions or artistic circles that they did not need to be too worried that the clothes they were wearing were typically associated with 'fairies' or 'poufs'. The lasting influence of *Vince*'s gay styling and clientele were acknowledged when George Melly joked that *Vince* was 'the only shop where they measure your inside leg each time you buy a tie!'. David Frost was still saying this ten years later when *Vince* had closed, and the joke was told later still about many other men's 'boutiques'.[21]

The flourishing of the Carnaby Street men's shop brought an essentially 'queer' look to a heterosexual market.[22] Adolescents who abandoned conventional stereotypes of masculinity and adopted 'effeminate' colours and long hair prompted a nation-wide discussion. In 1964 the *Sunday Times Magazine* reassured the public that 'there is nothing essentially queer about boys who display an overt, gossipy, fascinated interest in what to wear with what. Their other hobby is girls.'[23] Yet the association of homosexuality was still evident. A 1965 French guide to London joked that *His Clothes* should be called '*Her Clothes*, because shirts tend to be pink and the salesman only too willing to try them on for you'. The same guide brought the Jaeger shop to the attention of its readers, because it had the advantage that its staff and clientele were not 'all homosexuals, as is almost always the case in boutiques for fashionable young men'.[24] Despite, or perhaps even because of, this association fashionable young men continued pushing back the boundaries of acceptability and introducing androgyny in their clothing.

The explosion of men's boutiques in the Carnaby Street area and subsequently throughout Britain meant that these brightly coloured, tighter-fitting clothes became available to a wider consumer market. Out of this explosion was to come mod.[25] The mods were fastidious dressers, in Dick Hebdige's words ' "typical lower-class dandy" obsessed with the small details of dress . . . the angle of a shirt collar, measured as precisely as the vents in his custom-made jacket'. In her 1961 novel about London bikers and emergent gay love, *The Leather Boys*, Gillian Freeman highlights a point of crossover between the bikers and the emergent mods, where the boys involved were obsessed, in an almost feminine way, by the minutiae of their appearance:

[He] began to change. It took him a long time because he liked to look really smart . . . He always took great care of his shoes, which he had hand-made and which cost him a lot of money. Tonight he was wearing a suit but sometimes he wore a narrow-shouldered jacket with plum-coloured stripes, and sometimes a leather jacket with saddle stitching. He tied his tie carefully in front of the little looking-glass and then bent his knees so he could see to do his hair.[26]

It would be untrue to say that mod was an exclusively, or even predominantly, homosexual style. However, the clothes that the mods were wearing were those that gay men had been wearing for the previous twenty years.

The only other person we saw was a tall, well-dressed young Negro who bought a pair of the coloured denim hipster trousers. The Negro was obviously homosexual and I realized that homosexuals had been buying that stuff for years. They were the only people with the nerve to wear it, but in the early sixties the climate of opinion was changing, the Mods were wearing the more effeminate and colourful clothes of Carnaby Street.[27]

Dick Hebdige notes that in constructing a 'secret identity outside the normal social bounds of school work and family life the mods felt an affinity with black people both in Britain and via soul music from America'.[28] Their dress, he notes, was influenced by smart West Indian immigrants, and the perceived 'underworld' offered an escape to somewhere where the 'values, norms and conventions of the "straight" world were inverted'. What Hebdige fails to note, though the use of his term 'straight' world does perhaps give us an indication, is the crossover between the gay underworld and the emergent mod world. The mod quoted above noted the influence of gay men's dress, and Peter Burton makes comparisons between the mods' clubs, such as the Scene, and the homosexual coffee bars, like Le Duce of Soho, London. Both groups, he notes, were wearing the same clothes, bought at *Vince* and John Stephen's, listening to the same music, soul and Motown, and taking the same drugs, speed.[29] Jon Savage states that 'like the Edwardians, the mods assumed what had been an exclusively and outrageously homosexual style and used it as a key to cross into the "private" space of the body and of self-discovery'.[30]

It is popularly accepted that there was an element of homosexual vanity present in the mod subculture. Both Mark Feld, later to be the bisexual glam rock star, Marc Bolan and George Melly discuss this element: 'At this time clothes were all that Mod was about. The music and the dancing and scooters and pills came later. I'd say that Mod was mentally a very homosexual thing, though not in any physical sense.'[31] The first mod boys were only interested in clothes, holding themselves up to one another like mirrors. Dick, one of the 'heroes' in *The Leather Boys* (1961), echoes this view: 'One didn't only have clean shoes and a brushed suit because one wanted girls to admire one. His appearance mattered to himself. The time he spent on it was entirely for his own satisfaction. Well, perhaps not entirely. Some of it was for the other boys, in peacock competition. They were the ones who judged and criticised and appraised.'[32]

Close-fitting European-styled clothes were also popular in America. A 1959 magazine article describes the 'hip-hugging slack, loafers, below-the-navel swim trunks, the bikini-type underwear, the form fitting T-shirt along with the grey-flannel, the Italian leg, and the cowboy pocket' worn by men at Cherry Grove.

> These styles, such as the cut of Western Levi's, are taken up by the small speciality stores that have sprung up in the east side of New York and Greenwich village in the last ten years – the shops that cater to the well kept male physique and which stock 28 as a matter of course where 30 is the smallest waist size one can find ready-made anywhere else in the city . . . The new style is now called the Western look, the Italian cut, or English tailoring, according to the kind of snob appeal the particular store encourages.[33]

Four years later *Harper's* magazine reported on the same stores and the same styles of clothing: 'A number of smart men's shops in the Village and on the Upper East side feature slim cut and youthfully styled clothing designed to appeal to homosexuals. Some stores carry bikini-type underwear and swimsuits for men, and fancy silk supporters.'[34]

In a discussion on the gay influence on fashion, S. St. Clair reiterates that fashion historians have traced the influence of tighter clothing for men 'to World War II when our boys in Khaki brought European tailoring home to the US', but that during the 1950s the classic European cut was still considered too severe for most of Middle America.[35] He notes, like Michael (quoted earlier) the tighter cut of this style of clothing: 'In shirts and jackets, the European look translated into a tapered torso, snugger armholes. The pants were cut higher in the crotch, fitted to the buttocks and flared.'[36] European-styled close-fitting clothes continued to be the popular choices for gay men, especially middle-class, non-effeminate gay men, throughout the 1960s. Two observers writing in the mainstream press highlighted this dress choice. Writing in *Harper's* magazine in 1963 William Helmer informed his readers that

A premium is placed upon appearing neat, fashionably dressed, young and handsome and anyone who is slovenly or physically unattractive is severely handicapped. Fashionable dress currently means slim-cut continental or extreme Ivy League styles in suits and well-tailored, collegiate-looking casual wear. The perfect dresser is extremely up-to-date, but careful to avoid styles so radical or grooming so fastidious as to be termed 'faggoty-elegant'.[37]

This fastidiousness is comparable to that of the mods in London at around the same time. *Life* magazine's 1964 expose of gay life in America made a similar point: 'In New York City, swarms of young college age homosexuals wearing tight pants, baggy sweaters and sneakers cluster in a ragged phalanx along Greenwich Avenue in the Village . . . [In San Francisco] some bars, like the Jumpin' Frog, are "cruising" (pickup bars), filled with young men in tight khaki pants'.[38] Craig Rodwell and his teenage friends 'poured in to blue jeans or chino pants made deliberately too tight by endless soakings in hot water' to go out, 'wrecking' or taunting straights in New York.[39] The downside of this look's being associated with (young fashionable) gay men in American cities was that undercover police 'dressed to look like homosexuals [in] tight pants, sneakers, sweaters or jackets' in order to catch gay men soliciting for or having sex in public.[40]

The emphasis on body-hugging clothing for men is popularly viewed as the result of the homosexual influence in fashion. In 1970 Bill Miller, designer for and part-owner of the Village Squire shop, felt, as did many other designers and retailers, that the acceptance of tight pants, body shirts, silhouette-hugging styles, furs and brighter colours, is at least partially due to the exposure given these things by the homosexual community. However, Dr Emanuel K. Schwartz, dean and director of the Post-Graduate Training Center for Mental Health in New York, felt this assumption was far-fetched. 'Naturally,' said Schwartz,

if I'm homosexual I'm interested in a man's body, but to say that is what inspired body-emphasizing fashion is a denigration of the type of man who designs fashion. I don't think this emphasis on the male body is due to any homosexual interest in the male form; I would say that it is the result of a general phenomenon. This is the age of the body. More is being done for, about and with the body than ever before – of course this is reflected in the fashions of our time.[41]

The influence of gay men's often unconventional choice of clothing and the adoption of Italian-styled clothing were not the only influences on men's dress in the 1960s. The emergence of groups that actively challenged perceptions of social and gendered behaviour was to have an enormous impact on fashion and the lives of gay men.

Notes

1. John Hardy points out that 'If you look at those styles, the narrow jeans, say, and the skimpy shirts, that was more or less the Italian look ... if you look at some of the Italian cinema of the time, like . . . *Bitter Rice* . . . and all the men wore jeans that were very tight': Cole interview with John Hardy, 12 June 1995.

2. For more general information on men's fashion of the period see Farid Chenoune (1993), *A History of Men's Fashion*, Paris and Nik Cohn (1971), *Today There Are No Gentlemen: The Changes in Englishmen's Clothes Since the War*, London.

3. Peter Burton, (1995) 'The Way We Wore', in idem, *Amongst the Aliens: Some Aspects of Gay Life*, Brighton, p. 166. Tony was a teenager (well aware of his sexual orientation) in the early 1960s; he remembers: 'When I was in the army [the fashionable look] was the Italian look, with three buttons, that was very mod. Winklepickers, that's what I used to wear. My trousers were creased, my sleeves creased, everything: I mean I was going out like a knife and fork': Cole interview with Tony, 30 November 1993.

4. Burton, 'The Way We Wore', Brighton, p. 167.

5. Godfrey Winn recounts how, after being taken under the wing of the wealthy novelist and playwright, Somerset Maugham, in the 1920s, he was invited to stay for a month at the Villa Mauresque, Maugham's home at Cap Ferrat. 'When I presented myself in the salon, before lunch, on the day of my arrival from the train, in my orthodox English grey flannel suit, my host took one look at me and gave me my first marching orders. "No tie, no jacket, no socks. This is the South of France in August, not finals day at Wimbledon." When I returned from my room for his reappraisal, he added, "Gerald, take Godfrey into Nice this afternoon and get him some linen slacks, shirts and espadrilles at the Bon Marché, like yours"': Godfrey Winn (1967), *The Infirm Glory*, London, pp. 262–3.

6. Burton, 'The Way We Wore', Brighton, p. 167.

7. Soho had the been the centre of bohemian London for over a hundred years, with painters, musicians and poets moving among the waves of French, Swiss and Jewish immigrants. Soho's importance as a centre of gay life rested not only on its acceptance of difference but also on its proximity to the Theatre World of Leicester Square. Trafalgar Square and Piccadilly Circus on the edges of Soho had established reputations as cruising grounds for gay men and were notorious as places to meet rent boys (male prostitutes). In the 1920s gay men had begun to frequent The Golden Lion public house in Dean Street and the Black Cat café in Old Compton Street. By the 1950s Soho had established itself as a gay centre, with numerous gay clubs, bars

and cafés. For more on the development of Soho see Frank Mort (1996), *Cultures of Consumption*, London, pp. 151–7. For the development of the gay scene in Soho see James Gardiner (1992), *A Class Apart: The Private Pictures of Montague Glover*, London, 1992, pp. 17–19, Peter Burton (1985), *Parallel Lives*, London, pp. 14–45 and Derek Jarman (1992), *At Your Own Risk*, London, pp. 47–9.

8. For more detail about Green's first posing slip see Chapter 10.

9. Bill Green on 'Gear Street', part of 'South-East Special' series, broadcast 22 Aug. 1964.

10. Bill Green, quoted in Nik Cohn, *Today There Are No Gentlemen: The Changes in Englishmen's Clothes Since the War*, London, 1971. Eddie remembered: 'In the sixties, style started to change, people started to wear bright colours. If you wore a yellow sweater, it was considered very, very way out. And it was all happening in Brighton: people were wearing red socks, that was the start of red socks. And I remember about six of us all went into a shop and bought a purple tie, we were all wearing purple ties': Brighton Ourstory Project (1992), *Daring Hearts: Lesbian and Gay Lives of 50s and 60s Brighton*, Brighton, pp. 52–3.

11. At the end of the nineteenth century the Aesthetes, and later the boys of Piccadilly, were seen wearing green carnations. The colour green continued to have homosexual associations. In the 1930s gay men were to be seen wearing 'moss green cord jacket[s] with a yellow tie and matching yellow socks': Bob Cant (ed.) (1993), *Footsteps and Witnesses: Lesbian and Gay Lifestories from Scotland*, Edinburgh, p. 47.

12. Nik Cohn has referred to tightness in clothing being related very much to gay men. Cohn, *Today There Are No Gentlemen*, p. 27.

13. Brighton Ourstory Project, *Daring Hearts*, p. 56. In a pamphlet published in 1937 Eric Gill argued that the decision to force men into trousers was a threat to his virility: 'any protuberance by which his sex might be known is carefully and shamefully suppressed. It is an organ of drainage, not of sex. It is tucked away all sideways, dishonoured, neglected, ridiculed, ridiculous – no longer the virile member and man's most precious ornament, but a comic member, a thing for girls to giggle about': Eric Gill (1937), *Trousers and the Most Precious Ornament*, quoted in Colin McDowell (1992), *Dressed to Kill: Sex, Power and Clothes*, London, p. 100.

14. Colin MacInnes (1959), *Absolute Beginners*, London, p. 51. It is extremely likely that this description is based upon MacInnes's knowledge of *Vince*'s clothes. Studying *Vince*'s mail order catalogues I have noted a number of outfits that contain the elements described here by MacInnes. The clothes could have come from John Stephen's *His Clothes* shop in Carnaby Street or *Dale Cavana* in Kinnerton Street, Knightsbridge, as both of these shops sold clothes similar to those sold at *Vince*, but I have not been able to find catalogues to study. George was stopped by a policeman in Brighton and asked questions about homosexuality; he wasn't sure whether he was genuinely being investigated or picked up. 'I was in tight black drainpipe trousers which were all the rage then and brothel-creepers and a cerise-coloured suede jacket. I suppose I was quite bold. Yeah, clothes were quite bold': Brighton Ourstory Project, *Daring Hearts*, p. 54.

15. Bill Green quoted in Cohn, *Today There Are No Gentlemen*, p. 61.

16. Cole interview with John Hardy, 12 June 1995. For more information on the mail order catalogues issued by *Vince* see Shaun Cole (1997), 'Corsair Slacks and Bondi Bathers: Vince Man's Shop and the Beginnings of Carnaby Street Fashions', *Things*, no. 6, pp. 26–39.

17. Knowledge of *Dale Cavana* is based on conversations with Ray, a gay man living in London in the 1950s and shopping at *Dale Cavana*. He asserted that *Dale Cavana*'s clientele was predominantly gay: Cole interview with Ray, 19 June 1996. Nik Cohn describes *Dale Cavana* as ' a most camp establishment ... with its windows full of skin-tight trousers, lacy briefs and cards saying "For You, Monsieur"': Cohn, *Today There Are No Gentlemen*, p. 58.

18. Brighton Ourstory Project, *Daring Hearts*, pp. 52–3.

19. Cohn, *Today There Are No Gentlemen*, p. 62.

20. Ibid.

21. Ibid., p. 51.

22. Similar shops and gay men's styles in America had the same impact. Danny Zarem, men's wear merchandise manager at Bonwit Teller in New York, acknowledges that 'in the beginning of the new men's wear fashion evolution the homosexual played a very important part ... the homosexual in the creative community, that is. They were the first to snap up new ideas and give them exposure': Robert J. Lukey (1970), 'Homosexuality in Menswear', *Menswear*, February, p. 73.

23. Quoted in Farid Chenoune (1993), *A History of Men's Fashion*, Paris, p. 258.

24. Ibid.

25. For more general information on mods see especially R. Barnes (1979), *Mods!*, London, and K. Hatton (1964), 'The Mods', *Sunday Times Magazine*, 2 August. Also worth looking at for socio-economic factors are Phil Cohen (1980), 'Subcultural Conflict and Working Class Community', in Stuart Hall (ed.), *Culture, Media, Language*, London, and Michael Brake (1985), *Comparative Youth Culture*, London.

26. Gillian Freeman (1969 [1961]), *The Leather Boys*, London, p. 11. Linda Nochlin characterises the *fin-de-siècle* dandy as being obsessed by small details rather than large sartorial gestures: 'The dandy's costume, contrary to popular belief, was distinguished by its restraint – colour and textures were subdued ... restraint was exercised in richness of material and flamboyance was generally avoided, distinction provided by subtle little points of detail or refinement, noticeable mainly to other "insiders"': Linda Nochlin (1976), *Realism*, London.

27. Richard Barnes (1979), *Mods!*, London, p. 10.

28. Gay men were outsiders, they epitomised an otherness that allowed them, within certain confines, to dress differently. The black community in Britain in the 1950s and 1960s was perceived in a similar way, as alien, as other, as exotic. Thus the dress codes of such men were not as restricted by society's ideas of the acceptable, respectable and normal: to many they were perceived as outside these boundaries, in a similar way to gay men. Because they were perceived as different they were not bound by the same conventions of dress. Unusual or tight clothes were to an extent acceptable for black men, and they embraced elements of European styling. Hebdige

identifies that 'on the deviant margins of West Indian society, at least, there were significant changes in appearance. The hustlers and street-corner men, encouraged perhaps by the growth of black clubs and discotheques in the mid-60s, were sharpening up, combining hats and "shades" and Italian suits to produce a West Indian equivalent of the U.S. "soul-brother" look: tight-fitting, loose-limbed, black and yet urbane.' Dick Hebdige (1987 [1979]), *Subculture: The Meaning of Style*, London, p. 42.

29. Peter Burton (1985), *Parallel Lives*, London, pp. 30–1.

30. Jon Savage (1990), 'Tainted Love: The Influence of Male Homosexuality and Sexual Divergence on Pop Music and Culture Since the War', in Alan Tomlinson (ed.), *Consumption, Identity and Style: Marketing, Meanings and the Packaging of Pleasure*, London, p.160.

31. Mark Feld in Cohn, *Today there Are No Gentlemen*, p. 80. George Melly claimed that 'Mods remained purists and for a time re-established their pre-eminence by quite coolly turning towards overt homosexuality and going to bed with any show-biz queen who was famous and smart enough to reinforce their tottering egos': George Melly (1970), *Revolt Into Style: Pop Arts Since the 50s and 60s*, Oxford, p.169.

32. Freeman, *The Leather Boys*, p. 26.

33. Alden Kirby (1959), 'Some Folkways of the Dune People', *One*, vol. VII, no. 10.

34. William J. Helmer (1963), 'New York's "Middle-class" Homosexuals', *Harpers* vol. 226, March, pp. 85–92. Tight-fitting clothes had always had an appeal to gay men. In the 1930s 'green suits, tight-cuffed trousers, flowered bathing trunks, and half-lengthed flaring top coats' were according to Thomas Painter 'distinctively homosexual attire'.

35. S. St Clair (1976), 'Fashion's New Game: Follow the Gay Leader', *Advocate*, 24 March, pp. 18–19. Interestingly, Farid Chenoune maintains that Italian straight-cut pants were derived from the rolling gait of American GIs in the post-war period, who swaggered because of their blue jeans and tight chinos. He notes that Italian trousers underwent three alterations to imitate blue jeans: pleats were removed, horizontal cross pockets were introduced and cuffs vanished: Farid Chenoune (1993), *A History of Men's Fashion*, Paris, p. 245. Peter Burton also noted this American influence on tight trousers at *Vince*'s shop: 'because Beryl's, you remember, was the shop where you got the chino and it was the whole look that was in part to do with the American military. You know: chino being American soldiers' leisure wear': Cole interview with Peter Burton, 24 September 1997.

36. St Clair, 'Fashion's New Game', pp. 18–19.

37. Helmer, 'New York's "Middle-class" Homosexuals', pp. 85–92.

38. Paul Welch (1964), 'Homosexuality in America', *Life*, 26 June, p. 68.

39. Martin Duberman (1994), *Stonewall*, New York, p. 83.

40. Paul Welch (1964), 'Homosexuality in America', *Life*, 26 June, p. 68. The other popular way for undercover police to dress when attempting to entrap homosexuals was in rough hustler clothes: tight jeans, leather jacket.

41. Lukey, 'Homosexuality in Menswear', p. 72.

6

Counterculture and Liberation: Gay Men, Beats and Hippies

The Black civil rights movement and the anti-war movement had begun to mark changes in the way young Americans viewed society. These movements were to lead to the emergence of a countercultural movement. Many gay men and lesbians had grown up with a feeling of difference and isolation from society. For these young gay American men and women involvement in countercultural groups offered an alternative: a group that was accepting of difference, a group to belong to that was not part of the mainstream. Although these new groups were not necessarily embracing of sexual difference they did offer the chance to experiment with a new lifestyle. The beats of the 1950s and the hippies of the 1960s offered a new way of viewing and living life. An integral part of these new 'movements' was new more relaxed forms of clothing.

The place of gay men in the beat movement was recognised early by *One* magazine in 1959. An article highlights the self-acceptance of the gay men involved in the beat movement: 'There is a distinction to be made between the beat-homo and the no-beat. The beat-homo has no inhibitions. Within his own consciousness he has accepted himself and is completely integrated. He is not fighting himself, much less the rest of the world . . . Like the rest of the beat generation he simply wants to be left alone.'[1] There are comparisons that can be drawn here with the men who were involved in the early gay rights groups, such as Mattachine (initially responsible for the publication of *One* magazine) in their acceptance of their sexuality; the difference lies in their attitude to the rest of the world. The beats wanted to be left alone, while the Mattachine men wanted the world to accept them. It was the 'outsider' status, which the beats both invited and celebrated, that drew gay men (and to a lesser extent lesbians) who felt marginalised by society. Catherine R. Stimpson states that 'the beats did help to generate a reinterpretation of homosexuality . . . they created a community of naming that stripped censored material of some of their psychic burdens; brought those materials into public speech; and cheered what public speech had previously reviled – when it had been public at all'.[2]

The gay historian John D'Emilio points out that the urban Bohemias of the United States, particularly San Francisco, offered a supportive cultural environment. The bohemian and gay bar cultures overlapped in San Francisco, particularly in the North Beach area. As a result gay bars such as the Black Cat became meeting-places for the beats.[3] D'Emilio believes that after 1957, when the beats became famous, they helped, in turn, to shape the city's gay consciousness. While dress was not a consciously alternative aspect of beat culture, the clothes that they wore marked a move from the strict conventions of middle-class men's dress during this period. The choice of bohemian enclaves as gathering-points for the beats influenced their less formal dress styles. The casual, almost 'sloppy' men's clothing of the beats was seen as 'powerfully anti-establishment'. An anti-establishment style of dress mirrored the anti-establishment, freethinking attitude of the beats, which accepted homosexuality. Male beat fashion included items that were to become the staples of the clone look of the 1970s (see Chapter 7), utilitarian working men's clothes.[4] The beats, gay and straight, while having been educated to a high level (often at Ivy League schools, according to Jim Kepner) looked to the comfortable hard-wearing clothes of the working man or the military.[5]

Across America, young people began to break away from the trappings of their stultifying pasts and to imagine new ways of living. A 1966 statement from San Francisco's anarcho-radical group the Diggers summed up a sentiment that an entire generation was beginning to act on: 'Throw it all away. The system has addicted you to an artificial need. Kick the habit. Be what you are. Do what you think is right. All the way out is free.'[6] If 1967's 'summer of love' was still mostly about heterosexual love, it was of an entirely new kind. The counterculture[7] pushed at the boundaries of 1950s gender roles, breaking down monogamy and bourgeois notions of propriety. These countercultural views offered pointers to many in the gay movement. One woman remembered: 'When the hippies came it was a real liberating thing because they started wearing anything they wanted to. And that made gay people freer to do likewise.'[8] These attitudes were also carried through in dress and personal appearance; particularly, long hair for men, once a sure marker of homosexuality, became a banner of the age. Seymour Kleinberg observed that:

> With the political and social changes of the Sixties, a new androgyny seemed to be on the verge of life. . . . even straight boys looked prettier than girls. The relief at seeing male vanity out in the open, surrendered to and accepted, made it possible for homosexuals to reconsider some of their attitudes towards themselves. It was no longer extraordinary to look effeminate in a world where most sexual men looked feminine and where sexually liberated women were the antithesis of the glamorous and fragile.[9]

The first public acknowledgement of the homosexual hippie came in an article in *Esquire* in December 1969, entitled 'The New Homosexuality'. Tom Burke identified this 'new homosexual' as 'an unfettered, guiltless male child of the new morality in a Zapata moustache and an outlaw hat, who couldn't care less for establishment approval' and who 'from a polite distance [was] virtually indistinguishable from the hetero hippie'.[10] Burke compared this new liberated homosexual to the 'acceptable' face of homosexuality, the effete martini-sipping cashmere-clad 'fag' portrayed in Matt Crowley's play (and film of the play) *The Boys in the Band* (1967), and discussed this new homosexual as if he was about to take over the world. Two years later in *Trans-Action* Laud Humphreys pointed out that 'the hip, masculine image for homosexuals is not yet as universal, the transformation not so dramatic, as Burke would have us believe'.[11] What he did concede was that the image adopted by younger gay men was increasingly masculine. Earlier chapters have shown that there was always a contingent of gay men who adopted and preferred the masculine or even the overtly masculine, the male impersonator, look to the effeminate. Humphreys points out that this increasing masculinisation of the gay subculture was not based on the 'hypermasculinity of Muscle Beach and the motorcycle set', as these were parodies of heterosexuality, but on the 'youthful masculinity of bare chests and beads, long hair, mustaches and hip-hugging pants'.[12] The influence of androgyny, the so-called 'peacock revolution' that had originated in London's Carnaby Street, was leading to a blurring of lines between male and female, to what was popularly perceived as a feminisation of young men. It is interesting to compare Humphreys's association of masculinity with this look. Traditionally, certain gay men had adopted elements of female dress as a way of identifying their difference and (homo)sexual identity. Society at large was shocked by the blurring of genders, and it was the move towards the adoption of seemingly traditional gay looks by young heterosexuals that was causing concern. Female or androgynous looks were associated with homosexuality, and the older generations of heterosexuals did not want their sons looking like 'faggots'.

Gay bars were becoming increasingly indistinguishable from other straight youth hangouts. In a gay bar in Boston, Humphreys points out, 'the dress, appearance and conversations were typical of any campus quadrangle' and the men and women virtually indistinguishable from those of any other 'college-age group in the taverns of the city'.[13] By the late 1960s these new hippies were to be seen in New York gay bars. Martin Duberman noted that amongst the 'chino-and-penny-loafer crowd' that predominated at the Stonewall bar in New York could be seen 'just a sprinkling of the new kind of gay man beginning to emerge: the hippie, long-haired, bell-bottomed, laid-back, and likely to have "weird," radical views'.[14] These men could be the same as those described by Tom Burke in *Esquire*, dressed in a 'white body-shirt [which] looks beige, shaded by his resolutely tanned chest. A chain belt and tapestry-look bell-bottoms hang at his bony hips' with long hair 'secured by a Cherokee beaded headband'.[15] It was not just the young gay men involved in the counterculture that were wearing these new hippie looks. Slightly older gay men, with an eye on the latest turns of fashion, also adopted elements of this style. Burke maintains that 'homo-senior citizens' (gay men over twenty-nine) were interested in these looks because of 'the well-known homosexual compulsion to postpone old age by carefully imitating the young'.[16] This is one of the arguments levelled at gay men in both a positive and a negative light. Gay men have been accused of trying to maintain their youth long after it has passed, and it is alleged that, as they have fewer family responsibilities, they have a greater disposable income (and more leisure time) to devote to buying clothes and toiletries and experimenting with the latest fashions.

Burke was at pains to point out that the rise in gay hippies shouldn't be viewed as the psychedelic and gay subcultures aping one another, but that 'in point of fact the majority of contemporary homosexuals under forty are confirmed pot-heads and at least occasional acid trippers'. Humphreys does point out that Burke has overstated this point, and that *his* research indicated that some young gay men did smoke pot, but by no means all of them, any more than all young gay men were adopting countercultural ideas and appearances. According to an article in the *Advocate* in 1976 'the hip-hugger, the flowered print shirt and even chokers' that took hold as standard men's fashion in the late 1960s and early 1970s 'were all items the gay community had adopted at one time or another'.[17] St Clair, the author, goes on to point out that young gay people augmented the hippie look to separate themselves from the 'straight revolution', and 'this took the form of trash and glitter: studded jeans, sequinned shirts, stack heel shoes'.[18] All these are elements that were later seen in the rise of 'disco' clothing and gay punk images.

In London, after the first flowerings of the menswear revolution in Carnaby Street, the 'hip young things' moved on from Italian-influenced clothing and adopted a more flamboyant, colourful style. Hugely influenced by the American cinema and by pop stars', such as the Beatles', involvement with psychedelia, British youth began to embrace the hippie. This was evident amongst both young gay and young straight men. John Fraser was twenty when he moved to London in 1967. It was a liberating time for him,

> growing my hair long and wearing beads. That was great. Now that was liberation, you know, to have hair down to your shoulders and wear bright clothes and tight

loons and flowered shirts. That was great fun. A lot about that era is now knocked as the 'permissive society', but it wasn't: it was very open but it was very political.[19]

Heterosexual interest in clothing that had previously been worn by and associated with gay men was to lead gay men to look for new ways of dressing that would reflect their own greater visibility and growing demands for liberation and equality. Many gay rights activists had participated in countercultural, anti-war, or civil rights movements. There was, however, a lack of reciprocity amongst these countercultural revolutionaries: the issues were primarily heterosexual, and straight activists were loath to become associated with gay rights. The journalist Roger Baker wrote of his experiences in London in the 1960s: 'They were all heterosexual issues. Whether they just talked through or acted, they were interpreted in entirely heterosexual terms. Through these years of social and sexual upheaval the gay dimension was completely missing. We lacked a model for action, we lacked insight and we most lacked the confidence even if we did have them.'[20] In America there was a more active and visible history of gay civil rights demonstrations than in Britain.[21] Many of the gay men (and women) involved in countercultural protests were therefore prepared to advocate libertarian values and the destigmatisation of homosexuality.

The activists of the late 1960s did not believe in protesting quietly, dressed to look like respectable citizens, as had the previous 'Mattachine' generation. They wanted to make their dissatisfaction visible. In his instructions to participants in gay protest marches of the fifties and early sixties, Frank Kameny had insisted that 'if we want to be employed by the Federal Government, we have to look employable to the federal Government'. The dress the newer breed of activists adopted reflected their countercultural affiliations. Men like Jim Fouratt made 'a rather startling sight', dressed in black leather pants, a cowboy hat, and a brightly coloured shirt, with his long blond hair flowing loosely down his back.[22] As one man writing in *Vector* magazine in 1967 pointed out:

We are in the middle of a social revolution. One of our liberal politicians, Assemblyman Burton, has called the 'hippy' movement 'destructive'. I agree. But, 'the times they ARE a-changin' and perhaps what is being destroyed MUST be destroyed – the sex role identification of dress is ridiculous and deserves destruction. The 'hippies,' in this instance, show maturity and logic in dispensing with this inhibiting social claptrap.[23]

The Stonewall Riots of June 1969 sparked a number of meetings and discussions in New York, called by the Mattachine Action Committee.[24] It was at this point the name Gay Liberation Front (GLF) was coined, to allow for actions that were not approved by a Mattachine Society that was afraid of offending the authorities. The GLF was strongly influenced by both the international student movement and the counterculture.[25] The GLF set out to make gay men (and lesbians) visible and to achieve equal rights for both. It organised demonstrations, zaps, street theatre, and social occasions. The GLF also advocated new communal ways of living for lesbians and gay men, which drew heavily on hippie ideas. The GLF 'created a new language, a new style, a new vocabulary for being gay. It was about being contemporary, about being incredibly, outrageously, exquisitely radical and of course – and most important of all – visible; celebrating being gay rather than living an endless existence codified as "something else".'[26] The GLF advocated 'coming out' and the belief that 'gay is good', and so clothing became an important indicator of this new visible gay identity. To gay liberationists homosexuality did not necessarily mean effeminacy, pathology, or immorality. Martin Levine argues that Gay Liberation discredited camp and other evasive techniques, such as passing as straight.[27] Camp was not necessarily viewed as a self-mocking form of fun, but seen as being more about self-hatred than self-acceptance. 'I think camp' declared one liberationist 'was a way for queens to distract themselves from guilt, and today who needs it? – there used to be this syndrome of drink, guilt, camp.'[28]

Dress has traditionally been gender-specific.[29] The early gay activists had insisted on gender-appropriate clothing, much to the dismay of many gay men (and lesbians). In what was to become known as 'gender fuck', elements of both male and female dress were worn together in order to confuse the gender signals given by those pieces of clothing. As the gay hegemony moved towards a more overtly masculine look, so the effeminate or feminine was more ostracised. Gender fuck wanted to get away from the hard-edged definitions of gendered dress, and use conflicting signals to challenge and confuse heterosexual society. Clothing that would shock and confront was often the primary reason for choice. At the 1970 anti-war march in Los Angeles, Karla Jay met two of her male gender-fuck friends, Mother Boats and Jefferson Fuck Poland. She noted their lack of sartorial modesty, as Jeff was wearing a woman's bikini bottom, long hair – and nothing else.[30] Justin felt that:

> It was the more radical you could get the better, really, during GLF. So it was lots of bright colours and occasionally chaps in frocks. It wasn't drag, you'd just put a frock on and you'd go out with your boots on. It was all about making a statement and daring, really. It was military-ish, so the fashion was quite military. I remember a little black sailor top from the Army and Navy and a bit of pink braid and I was

on my way. It was mainly in your face. This is who I am. 'I'm out, I don't care' stuff.[31]

Michael Brown was also an active member of the GLF. He went for a more individual look, but kept to the essential ideas of gender-fuck:

I used to send things up – like ordinary make-up. I remember once, for example, I cut out red acetate and made lips and stuck them over mine instead of lipstick, with make-up like suntan make-up, pancake. Or I [sometimes wore] a big bow, a big velvet bow *à la* Captain Morgan, or sometimes I had a beard with ribbons in.[32]

The more conventional gay men reacted strongly to the outrageous antics and dress of many gay liberationists, echoing the reactions of 'straight' gay men of the 1950s to Quentin Crisp's presence at gay clubs.[33] Mike Brake relates how one member of a respectable homophile organization (notoriously anti-drag) puffed furiously at his pipe while complaining of being barred from a pub which had banned gay men: 'They said I was effeminately dressed. I was furious. I may be queer but at least I'm a man.'[34] The *People* newspaper noted the first dance at Kensington Town Hall: 'It's all happening at the Old Town Hall', and observed that several hundred homosexuals were present and five hundred turned away; while some of the people there actually wore dark suits, collars and ties. 'Throughout 1971 the GLF dances became freakier, the clothes more way-out, the atmosphere increasingly counter-cultural . . .'.[35]

The emergence of countercultural and hippie dress styles had a marked influence upon men's dress. It was especially liberating for gay men, whose dress choices had been pretty much limited to effeminate flamboyance if they were prepared to announce their homosexuality publicly or restrained invisibility if they were not. John Babuscio reflected that: 'The gay movement, along with such explicitly countercultural groups as the beats and the Hippies, have done much to break down the rigid boundary line separating masculinity from femininity, but the cultural definition of the heterosexual majority still exerts very considerable pressure towards conformity.'[36] Once fashion, in general, began embracing flamboyance and effeminacy, gay men could dress in a less restrained way and not necessarily be condemned as homosexuals. Even so, the fashion world was at great pains to dissociate an interest in the latest fashions from homosexuality. In 1970 the American trade magazine *Menswear* ran an eight-page article discussing the homosexual influence on fashion. The overwhelming tone of the article was that an interest in fashion was not necessarily homosexual, and that homosexuals did not set fashion trends.[37] The gay liberation movement of the 1960s and early 1970s fundamentally altered forms of gay life and subsequently styles of gay dress. As straight male fashion became increasingly effeminate or at least unisex, so the appeal of the ultra-masculine grew for gay men and led to the development of one of the most noted of gay styles, the clone.

Notes

1. Wallace de Ortega Maxey (1959), 'The Homosexual and the Beat Generation', *One*, Vol. VII, No. 7. The involvement of gay men in the beat movement was reiterated in an article in *ONE-IGLA Bulletin* from Winter 1998. Jim Kepner highlights the lack of attention that has been paid to the homosexuality of the major players of the Beat Generation, such as Allen Ginsberg and William Burroughs, and the influence that this had on both the Beat movement and gay life and culture. He draws attention to the fact that the Beat scene was 'the model for a new lifestyle' that rejected established American morality and customs and welcomed homosexuals.

2. Catherine R. Stimpson (1982), 'The Beat Generation and the Trials of Homo-sexual Liberation', *Salmagundi* 58–59, p. 390.

3. John D'Emilio (1981), 'Gay Politics, Gay Community: San Francisco's Experience', *Socialist Review*, 11, (1), pp. 77–104, especially pp. 84–5. Allen Ginsberg described the Black Cat as 'the greatest gay bar in San Francisco. It was really totally open, bohemian, San Francisco . . . and everybody went there, heterosexual and homosexual. It was lit up, there was a honky-tonk piano; it was enormous. All the gay screaming queens would come, the heterosexual gray flannel suit types, longshoremen. All the poets went there' (quoted in John D'Emilio (1983), *Sexual Politics, Sexual Communities: The Making of a Homosexual Minority in the United States, 1940–1970*, Chicago, p. 187). Gay bars were often accepting of difference in many forms, here the beats, with a reciprocated accepting of difference from the beats, who were advocating sexual and social freedom. This is comparable to London in 1977, where the proto-punks met at gay clubs such as Louise's and Chagaramas. See Chapter 11.

4. See Amy de la Haye and Cathie Dingwall (1996), *Surfers, Soulies, Skinheads and Skaters: Subcultural Style from the Forties to the Nineties*, London.

5. In adopting an anti-establishment attitude the beats often looked to black culture. The beats' musical precursor, the hipster, grew out of the same basic mythology of black culture. While the beat 'was originally some earnest middle-class college boy like Kerouac, who was stifled by the cities and the culture he had inherited and who wanted to cut out for distant and exotic places, where he could live like the "people", write, smoke and meditate', the hipster was a 'typical lower class dandy, dressed up like a pimp, affecting a very cool, cerebral tone – to distinguish him from the gross, impulsive types that surrounded him in the ghetto – and aspiring to the finer things in life, like very good "tea", the finest jazz . . .': A. Goldman (1974), *Ladies and Gentlemen, Lenny Bruce* (Panther), quoted in Dick Hebdige (1987 [1979]), *Subculture: The Meaning of Style*, London, p. 48. The hipster was appro-

priating black dress styles, language and musical forms. In a similar way, gay men in New York in the 1920s were crossing into the black ghetto, where an acceptable place had been created for 'sissy-men', and (gay) 'Negro' dress styles and language were appropriated by white gay men through their interactions: see Eric Garber (1982), ''Tain't Nobody's Business: Homosexuality in Harlem in the 1920s', *Advocate*, 13 May.

6. Quoted in George Katsiaficas (1987), *The Imagination of the New Left: A Global Analysis of 1968*, Boston, p. 146.

7. The *Oxford Concise English Dictionary* (9th Edition) defines 'counter-culture' as 'a way of life etc. opposed to that usually considered normal.' Counterculture has popularly come to signify a lifestyle, particularly prevalent amongst the middle classes in the 1960s, that advocated new communal ways of living, a return to the land and self-sufficiency, drawing inspiration from Native American and Eastern cultures and philosophy.

8. Molly McGarry and Fred Wasserman (1998), *Becoming Visible: An Illustrated History of Lesbian And Gay Life in Twentieth-Century America*, New York, p. 84.

9. Seymour Kleinberg (1978) 'Where Have All the Sissies Gone?, *Christopher Street* March, p. 9.

10. Tom Burke (1969), 'The New Homosexuality', *Esquire*, December, p. 178.

11. Laud Humphreys (1971), 'New Styles in Homosexual Manliness', *Trans-Action*, Vol. 8, nos. 5 & 6, p. 41.

12. Ibid.

13. Ibid.

14. Martin Duberman (1994), *Stonewall*, New York, p.189

15. Tom Burke (1969), 'The New Homosexuality', *Esquire*, December, p.178.

16. Ibid.

17. S. St Clair (1976), 'Fashion's New Game: Follow the Gay Leader', *Advocate*, March, pp.18–19.

18. Ibid.

19. Quoted in Hall Carpenter Archives Gay Men's Oral History Group (1989), *Walking After Midnight: Gay Men's Life Stories*, London, pp. 133–4.

20. Roger Baker (1978), 'Times They Were A-Changing', *Gay News*, no. 5, p. 22.

21. This is dealt with in many histories of gay life in America, especially John Loughery (1998), *The Other Side of Silence: Men's Lives and Gay Identities: A Twentieth Century History*, New York; and Martin Duberman (1994), *Stonewall*, New York is particularly good.

22. Duberman, *Stonewall*, p. 240.

23. W. E. Beardemphl, 'Drag – Is It Drab, Despicable, Divine?', *Vector*, May, p. 13.

24. This was a subgroup created by Dick Leitsch as a way to accommodate the young gay radicals.

25. Jeffrey Weeks testified that: 'The GLF in its early days drew its support from those who had already been touched by the New Left or the counter-culture. It had a high proportion of artists, drop-outs, social-security claimants and the young (the

typical age range was twenty-five to thirty-five) – that is, those who had least to lose by being defiantly open. But it also had a high percentage of new professional people, of students, teachers and sociologists. Some liberals dissatisfied by existing organisations were early attenders, but there was also an immediate response from the sub-culture': Jeffrey Weeks (1990), *Coming Out: Homosexual Politics in Britain from the Nineteenth Century to the Present*, London, pp. 190–1.

26. Quoted in Hugh David (1997), *On Queer Street: A Social History of British Homosexuality 1895–1995,* London, p. 228.

27. Martin P. Levine (1998), *Gay Macho: The Life and Death of the Homosexual Clone*, New York, p. 28.

28. Burke, 'The New Homosexuality', p. 306.

29. 'Why must MALES wear "men's" clothing and FEMALES wear "women's" clothing? What is the connection between what you WEAR and what you ARE? In societies, like ours, where sex identification is excessively delineated into feminine and masculine "roles," personhood and intrapersonal relations are destroyed and compensated for by exaggerated fetishes. A healthier social environment would be one in which dress was regarded as "costume" suited to the particular individual wearing it and void of its most blatant sex-identification functions. Most anthropologists and sociologists postulate that feminine–masculine role-playing is unnatural and socially imposed': Beardemphl, 'Drag', p. 13.

30. Duberman, *Stonewall*, p. 278.

31. Cole interview with Justin Stubbings, 11 July 1997. The use of drag by gay liberationists is dealt with in more detail in Chapter 3.

32. Cole interview with Michael Brown, 1 December 1993.

33. Crisp was asked on a number of occasions to leave gay clubs, as the men wanted to look as 'normal' as possible in the event of a police raid: interview with the author.

34. Quoted in Gregg Blachford (1981), 'Male Dominance and the Gay World', in Kenneth Plummer (ed.), *The Making of the Modern Homosexual*, London, p. 189.

35. Weeks, *Coming Out*, p. 194.

36. Jack Babuscio (1975), *Gay News*, August, quoted in Patrick Higgins (ed.) (1993), *A Queer Reader*, London, p. 207.

37. In Britain in 1974 the editor of *Style* magazine had the following to say: 'There has for a long time been this curious belief that an interest in fashion or an interest in wearing colour clothes was, you know, a manifestation possibly of homosexuality. For a long time there has been this nonsense. Now the younger generation has rejected that': John Taylor (1974) on 'A New Look for Him?', BBC Radio, broadcast 11 January 1974.

7

'Macho Man': Clones and the Development of a Masculine Stereotype

The counterculture movement of the 1960s and the beginnings of sexual liberation prompted men to question their roles. As straight men increasingly moved away from the rigid dress codes of their fathers and adopted a freer outlook, so gay men began to challenge public attitudes towards them and their legal and social position. The gay liberation movement had introduced questions about lifestyle and, as a part of that, acceptable clothing and behaviour. Activist groups such as the Gay Liberation Front called for an end to gender-prescribed behaviour and dressing. While most gay men found gender fuck too radical, there was a move towards a more masculine look, and they began to be attracted to the 'look of hip masculinity favoured in the counterculture'.[1] Tony Diaman summed up many gay men's disillusionment with society's view of them as effeminate: 'The straight world has told us that if we are not masculine we are homosexual, that to be homosexual means not to be masculine ... one of the things we must do is redefine ourselves as homosexuals.'[2] This attitude heralded the masculinisation of gay culture. Gay men began to regard themselves as masculine. They adopted manly attire and demeanour as a means of expressing their new sense of self, and in adopting this look they aimed to enhance their physical attractiveness and express their improved self-esteem.

There had of course been overtly masculine gay men in the past. Closeted gay men had often overcompensated for their homosexuality, becoming 'male impersonators'. There was also a tradition of men's attraction to masculine types, epitomised in the attraction (for middle- or upper-class men) to working-class men and to 'rough trade'. Male hustlers, gay and straight, were well aware of the attraction of a masculine image. John Rechy frequently refers to this type of man in his novels.[3] There were also men who frequented the leather or biker bars, projecting an image of extreme rebellious masculinity.[4] The cowboy and the biker were two archetypes that were influential in the adoption of 'butch' dress styles for men. Both had appeared as representations of masculine sexuality in physique magazines and were appearing in gay bars and on hustlers' street corners.[5] They represented a traditional but non-conforming aspect of masculinity and were 'used by the media to play up masculinity and sexuality in ways that are understood by the gay populace'.[6] Hal Fischer states that the 'Western or cowboy archetype can be seen as derivative of the natural myth . . . It would be unlikely for an American boy growing up not to have a cowboy hero' and that 'the western image is popular for three reasons. First, movies and television have made it familiar. Second, the cowboy lives a "man's life in a man's world". Third, western dress is easily translated into contemporary dress.'[7] Thus gay men were forming a 'site' for their appearance in the present comparable to an image or a point in the past, here, the cowboy in the films of their youth.

As a positive move away from effeminate stereotypes, and in search of an 'out' masculine image gay men looked towards traditional images of rugged masculinity, such as the cowboy or lumberjack, for their dress inspiration. They wore 'blue-collar garb': straight jeans (at a time when flares were all the rage), plaid shirts, hooded sweatshirts, bomber jackets and lace-up work boots; they cropped their hair short and grew moustaches. All these clothes had a clear meaning in the wider American culture: toughness, virility, aggression, strength, potency. There was a real attempt to dissociate from the ridiculed effeminate stereotyped role of other homosexuals and to become a 'real man', or at the very least to look like a real man. Assumptions about macho masculinity lay at the heart of these manly presentational strategies. The term 'macho' implied overconformity to the traditional male gender role, which was generally regarded as more masculine than the modern male gender role. Many homosexuals imitated the macho role.[8] This attempt to look like a 'real man' reflects many gay men's desire for 'rough trade' or what Quentin Crisp described as 'the great dark man'.[9] It was no longer enough for gay men to 'have men' as their sexual partners; they wanted to (appear to) be these real men. It seems clear, though, that the macho-man is a reaction against effeminacy, and this means that the masculine/feminine binary structure has not gone away, only been redistributed. John Marshall remarks on 'the extent to which definitions of male homosexuality continue to be pervaded by the tyranny of gender divisions'.[10] As this new masculinity became more poplar and more gay men adopted the look, these men became known as clones. Andrew Holleran believes that the men who began clone style were not themselves clones. They were 'people who, ironically, prided themselves (consciously or unconsciously) on separating themselves from the crowd'.[11] They were, he says 'breaking away from effeminate homosexual clichés of the Fifties'.[12]

The Queer Theorist Judith Butler views the adoption of these hegemonic images as a kind of 'subversive bodily act'.[13] However, clones were not intending to 'pass' as heterosexuals, as their predecessors had. Their appropriation opened up radical and transgressive possibilities. As Joseph Bristow has written: 'stylizing particular aspects of conventional masculine dress, [they could] adopt and subvert given identities, appearing like "real men" and yet being the last thing a "real man" would want to be mistaken for: gay . . .'.[14] Clones wore these appropriated clothes differently from heterosexual men, so there could be little doubt about whether someone was a heterosexual macho man or a gay macho man. Straight men wore this attire in an unselfconscious way, usually loosely and for comfort. Their garments might not fit or match; their facial hair might not be perfectly trimmed. In this way, straight masculinity reflected conformity to traditional male norms concerning nonchalance about appearance. Clones rejected this nonchalance and stylised these looks: 'Frank looked like a well-groomed lumberjack. Everything he wore was tailored and matched. His jeans and plaid Pendleton shirt fit perfectly. His black, wool, watchman's cap matched his black Levis and the black in his shirt. His red thermal undershirt matched the red in his shirt. The brown in his leather belt matched the brown in his hiking boots. No real lumberjack ever looked so well put together, so coordinated in color, his outfit fitting so perfectly. Frank, then, *signified* the lumberjack – appropriating the gender conformity that is traditionally associated with lumberjacks, not actually having to cut down trees to do it.'[15] Martin Humphries believes that 'for many the attraction of machismo is an acceptable way of openly celebrating the eroticism of the male body. It is a safe eroticism in that the images of desire are often those endorsed by society in general; though not endorsed as desirable by men for men. Strong, solid, clearly identifiably masculine men but with a difference – a camp difference.'[16] Clones were interested in sex and dressed both sexily and practically. The practical clothes hid well-toned bodies and 'made sense to an urban homosexual: they were impervious to the depredations of concrete and long hours of walking; they kept you warm; they worked'.[17]

Clones wore their garments in a self-consciously tight manner in order to enhance their physical attractiveness. They kept their hair short, beards and moustaches clipped, and clothing fitted and matched. The clothes worn by the clones have a quite different meaning from the clothes' original meaning – or, in Gregg Blachford's words, they 'infuse[d] the style with a new meaning of eroticism and overt sexuality – that is, they [were] used explicitly to make one appear sexy and attractive to other men'.[18] In adopting an image that was based upon a heterosexual macho image, gay men walked a tightrope between straight imitation and an interpretation that could identify them not only as real men but as real *gay* men. The macho look served a dual purpose, in that whilst attracting other gay men it also acted as a form of self-protection, explained by Ray Weller:

When you walked down the street dressed as a clone in the early days, what you wanted was straight people to be confused, and they were confused. And slightly menaced as well because it was before these looks had become clichéd. So if they saw someone with a leather jacket on, they didn't think there was a nelly [faggy] leather queen they thought there was someone who might be tough or trouble. So you were pushing the straight world away but sending out very specific signals to other gay men which was obviously sexually based. You were making yourself unattractive to the heterosexual world, or menacing, but attractive to the gay world. I remember feeling like that and talking to people about how, because of the way we appeared, nobody would ever try to mug us because people didn't understand that parody of masculinity was a gay thing.[19]

Gay men moving to major cities, such as New York or San Francisco, quickly adopted the clone look. The Castro and Christopher Street quickly became clone enclaves. Dennis Altman observed that these neighbourhoods 'seem at first sight to be populated almost entirely by men under the age of forty-five, dressed in a uniform and carefully calculated style and dedicated to a hedonistic and high consumption lifestyle'.[20] Justin Stubbings remembers:

When I went to San Francisco I just loved the way everyone looked. It was recognisable. You knew. You knew *that* was a gay man because of the jeans and the checked shirt and the moustache and the short hair, and it just seemed that was what you get into if you want to pull and that was the bottom line of it. It wasn't so much about looking good . . . it was also about being able to pull on the street. It was a fashion that suited me, it was easy. It was a move away from the perms and stripy T-shirts that were around when I came out and that was what you had to look like. And it was the first time there was a look that said its OK to be a bloke and be gay. That's what I liked about it.[21]

The clone look was, Randy Alfred argued, down to 'sexual selection. Many of these men are simply wearing the costumes that experience has taught them will attract the very men they find sexually attractive.'[22] Form-fitting Levi's and T-shirts hugged the body, revealing the contours of genitals, buttocks, and musculature. These features were often highlighted by not wearing underwear, wallets or shirts. Some men even left the top or bottom button of their Levi's undone, in part to signify sexual availability, and in part to suggest that their genitals were so large they had popped a button through sheer size.[23] The crotch of their jeans was often faded through bleaching for a similar effect. A scene from Felice Picano's 1978 novel *The Lure* illustrates these points. Buddy Vega is sent to show Noel (working undercover for the police) how to dress to be accepted in the gar bar scene of New York: 'Jeans,' Vega told Noel 'should hang low on your hips, be tight in the ass and the legs and especially full at your basket.' He selects a pair of jeans that belonged to Noel's girlfriend, which 'had been secondhand when she bought them. The pockets and cuffs were frayed . . . they felt tight, too tight too wear.' Vega tells him it is fine for the buttons to remain open, as this will emphasise the size of his genitals, and then instructs Noel on how to emphasise the bulge of his genitals by making the jeans look more worn around the crotch using a nail file.[24] Outerwear also called attention to these areas of the body. Clones wore waist-length down or leather jackets over their Levi's, which exposed and emphasised the bulge of their genitals and buttocks. These clothes could also be used to camouflage the imperfections of an imperfect body; but on the whole the men who adopted the clone looks adopted a whole lifestyle that involved using the gym and eating the right foods. Having a good body was, at least initially, as important as having the right clothes.[25]

In an article in the gay magazine *Christopher Street* Seymour Kleinberg identifies 'the uniform of the moment: cheap plaid flannel shirts and jeans, or if it is really warm, just overalls, and boots or construction worker's shoes no matter what the weather is. With the first signs of frost, a heavy leather bomber jacket is *de rigueur*.'[26] What he neglects to notice, or to mention, is that it wasn't just any jeans or plaid flannel shirt: it had to be the correct colour, style, make or brand. Ray Weller remembers this point only too well

> When that look is parodied now or people think of the Village People look they think it's almost like a pastiche – it's almost enough to put a check shirt on; but I remember at the time it was much more subtle than that, there were lots of graduations [*sic*]. You had to have the right tone of check shirt, or the right brand, or certain sorts of sportswear. And certain boots were OK and other boots weren't OK.[27]

The importance of achieving the right look or having the absolutely correct labels, rather than just the generic style, depended upon the clique to which one belonged.[28] The most important item to get right was the jeans. Justin Stubbings illustrates the importance of having Levi's: 'It was the 501 that were the prize. I remember going over to the States to get my first pair and doing the bath thing and the pumice stone just to get the bits looking right. In England it was that look with the 501s that said it – the American jeans said that this was another gay guy.' This was true in America as well as

England. Clark Henley's somewhat tongue-in-cheek guide to being a clone, *Butch Manual*, reiterated the importance of Levi's: 'Butch wears pants that show off his bulging calves, his tantalising thighs, his perfect buns, and of course, his notorious basket. There is only one pair of pants that can fill all these requirements: Levi's 501's.'[29]

As a result of increased cheap transatlantic travel the clone look was soon imported into Britain.[30] This 'stylish thug'[31] soon established himself in London and other major urban centres, and the look became essential in many gay pubs and clubs, especially in London's Earl's Court. Ray Weller tells of his first visit to the Copacabana Club in Earls Court in 1979:

> I was wearing what was [high street] fashionable for the day; French cut trousers, a heavy grey single-breasted jacket with a shirt with the collar open over the jacket. It really was all checked shirts and 501 jeans and vaguely sports tops and that kind of thing. I remember going there and really enjoying it, but really feeling that I stood out and that nobody was looking at me because I was so obviously, not just provincial, but not part of the scene or the way that everyone wanted to appear or what was considered attractive.[32]

When he returned the next week he was wearing, as was everyone else, 'Levi 501s, a red checked shirt and heavy work boots'.[33]

The gay clone look did have a precedent in Britain, just as it did in America. Some men did adopt an overtly masculine look as early as the 1950s. Michael Brown usually dressed in unremarkable clothing during the day, but at night when he was cruising for sex at Notting Hill Gate in London he wore 'a plaid workman's shirt, denim jeans and a heavy leather belt with a large buckle. This was', he asserts, 'way before the macho bit came into fashion.'[34] Vince man's shop was selling western-styled clothes, including plaid shirts, jeans and waistcoats, as early as 1952.[35]

While there was a definite basic look for the clone, it did vary from season to season and with the weather. In cold weather they wore the staples of clone wear – construction boots, straight-legged, button-fly Levi 501s, plaid flannel shirts, and hooded sweatshirts under brown leather flight jackets. During the summer, when it was warmer 'they wore green-striped, Adidas running shoes, button-fly Levi's, and either Lacoste shirts, tank tops or T-shirts'.[36] Most of the men dressed in accordance with clone fashion codes. Clones often resented intrusions by those who violated these norms:

> One afternoon, I was talking to some men at Ty's, a popular circuit bar. A group of suburban homosexuals walked in. These men wore designer jeans, LaCoste shirts with the collars flipped up, and reeked of cologne. They were obviously *not* clones . . . To the clones, these gay men were anachronisms, throwbacks to another

era of male homosexuality, of blowdried bouffant hairdos, gold pinky rings, and fey demeanour.[37]

In Britain the preppy look that had been so disparaged by New York clones found a place in clone culture. For those who didn't want to dress in the heavily macho looks or didn't feel that they were appropriate to the occasion, there was a more preppy look, which consisted of chinos and Lacoste T-shirts, but still with short hair and moustache. Ray Weller recalls:

> I was well enmeshed in the Clone look . . . and when you were a Clone and wanted to look smart it was really a kind of preppy look that was the sort of acceptable look . . . it started because the people in the Clone world . . . went to America for a couple of weeks a year . . . What they brought back was a sort of Chinos and Lacoste sort of look which was the . . . kind of the clone acceptable clothes to go to a restaurant in. That was how you could still be Clone but not look like one of the Village People if you were going to the theatre or something.[38]

As part of the clone image, gay men developed a set of codes to specify their particular sexual interests. Consequently a man could tell if a potential partner would be compatible just by the position of the keys on his belt or the colour of the handkerchief in his back pocket. In his book *Gay Semiotics* Hal Fischer defines the importance of these signifiers.

> In gay culture . . . signifiers exist for accessibility . . . The gay semiotic is far more sophisticated than straight sign language, because in gay culture roles are not as clearly defined. On the street or in a bar it's impossible most of the time to determine a gay man's sexual preference either in terms of activity or passive/aggressive nature. Gays have many more sexual possibilities than straight people and therefore need a more intricate communication system.[39]

Along with the sexually loaded codes, specific sign-vehicles were added to the basic look to project an extra butch front. They were typically associated with traditional macho icons, such as the cowboy.[40] Many of the men utilising these butch sign-vehicles did so with a sense of play inherited from gender-fuck and 'camp' sensibility, referring to their clone clothes as 'butch drag'. It was both a self-conscious, almost parodying reference to traditional stereotypical images of masculinity and a self-conscious embracing of that stereotype.[41]

By the early 1980s, Martin Levine observed 'strict butch costuming fell out of favour, as clones mixed butch elements for circuit wear and street wear. They wore either black cowboy boots or black leather Patrick sneakers, black or blue button-fly Levis, plaid flannel shirts, tank tops, or T-shirts, and black leather or down jackets. They also wore their hair longer – down to, but not over, the ears.'[42] In London there was a seasonal difference in footwear. John Campbell recalled how 'you have basically the 501s and the Timberlands, the boat shoes for summer, the hiking boots for winter. And it was originally white socks and then, because it became very "Essex", it was no socks.'[43]

Clothes that a man put on to make himself sexually attractive to other men made him, Andrew Holleran says 'entirely invisible: a non-person'. The clothes became very important; clones would only associate with and have sex with other clones. The proto-clones were quick to move on once their look became the standard dress for gay men, once it became 'clone'. The image became formulaic and tired. Holleran notes that they abandoned their plaid shirts once the majority of gay men adopted them.[44] In London too the clone look became watered down as more gay men adopted the look to be sexually attractive. Ray Weller remembered that:

> the Clone world . . . that was starting to develop was in a lot of ways was much more suburban. We often used to joke at the time about Chiswick Clones and about airline stewards about how they had this kind of look, with jeans and checked shirts, but it was all too washed and too clean and too pressed and it was essentially . . . it was much more about conforming. I mean I really wanted to conform. You knew that the way to, ehm, get a boyfriend was, kind of, to wear the right clothes in the Clone world. If you had the right shortness of hair, and the right moustache and, you know, the right vest and the right boots then that was very attractive. It didn't make you special but it [did] make you belong.[45]

The straight press had by this time identified that the macho clone was now the prevalent image of homosexuality. 'If women's [*sic*] image has changed dramatically in recent times, the image of the homosexual has changed out of all recognition. If they were once stereotyped as Julian and Sandy . . . they are now Biff and Brad . . . coming on . . . like everyone's idea of the perfect, ale-swilling Outback wallah from Australia.'[46] Like the reports of the tabloids in the 1950s and early 1960s, heterosexual society did not like the fact that it was hard to identify gay men. As long as gay men kept to their swishy, effeminate and therefore non-sexually threatening stereotypes they could be tolerated, if not actually accepted. Society could find a place for an amusing unthreatening pseudo-woman.

Perhaps ironically, the new gay macho styles began to have an influence on straight fashion. Dennis Altman notes that the 'diffusion of the macho style through advertising (for jeans for example) and entertainers like The Village People led to its being adopted by millions of straight men unaware of its origin'.[47] Rather than welcome the move, 'straight' men felt threatened by the new overtly masculine homosexual. They felt insecure in their own sexuality because the safe barrier of effeminacy had been torn down. Semiotic signals no longer meant anything. Anybody could be mistaken for a 'poofter' now that sartorial pointers had gone. Straight men began to copy homosexual styles, and leather became commonplace. John Campbell remembered when this happened in London

> And of course everything that the gay scene did within six months it was followed by the straight scene, tentatively followed. Like for instance the crew cuts without the 501s and the clones and the moustaches. The moustaches were very gay, especially the handlebars and the very full growth, but as it became straight the moustaches went. They followed, they started wearing the Lacostes and they started wearing the 501s and the white socks and all the Timberlands.[48]

Andrew Holleran believes that the death of the clones came about once the 'boys from Long Island came into town with their girlfriends on Saturday nights in bomber jackets and plaid shirts, their keys hung on the right side of their belts, like homosexuals looking for a top man'.[49]

Elements of the ideas behind the clones' adoption of masculine imagery remained even when younger gay men had begun to reject the clone image and, partially as a result of the influence of punk, look for new forms of self-expression. These were to be seen in the imagery of 'queer nation' and 'act-up' looks in America (and later Britain) and in the gay skinheads and gay rockabillies of London in the 1980s. What the clone did leave was the legacy of the masculinisation of homosexuality and an emphasis on overtly masculine images and physiques. This was to become one of the primary modes of self-presentation for gay men during the 1980s and 1990s.

Notes

1. Laud Humphreys (1971), 'New Styles in Homosexual Manliness', *Trans-action*, no. 8, pp. 38ff. See also see Tom Burke (1969), 'The New Homosexuality', *Esquire*, no. 72.

2. Tony Diaman (1970), 'The Search for the Total Man', *Come Out*, December–January, pp. 22–3.

3. Both in *City of Night* and *Numbers* Rechy describes masculine-type hustlers or trade: Johnny Rio 'is very masculine, and has been described recurrently in homosexual jargon as "a very butch number" . . . A supreme accolade in that world, "butch" means very male and usually carries overtones of roughness': John Rechy (1984), *Numbers*, New York, p. 16.

4. See Chapter 8.

5. 'Looking at Chuck and Miss Destiny – as she rushes on now about the Turbulent Times – I know the scene: Chuck the masculine cowboy and Miss Destiny the femme queen: making it from day to park to bar to day like all the others in that ratty world of downtown L.A. which I will make my own': John Rechy (1964), *City of Night*, New York, p. 97. James Leo Herlihy's 1965 novel *Midnight Cowboy* (London, 1970) also features hustlers dressed as cowboys.

6. Hal Fischer (1977), *Gay Semiotics*, San Francisco, p. 18.

7. Ibid., p. 19

8. See Esther Newton (1972), *Mother Camp: Female Impersonators in America*, Englewood Cliffs, NJ and Carol Warren (1974), *Identity and Community in the Gay World*, New York.

9. Cole interview with Quentin Crisp, 2 October 1998.

10. John Marshall (1981), 'Pansies, Perverts and Macho Men: Changing Conceptions of Male Homosexuality', in Kenneth Plummer (ed.), *The Making of the Modern Homosexual*, London, p.154.

11. Andrew Holleran (1982), 'The Petrification of Clonestyle', in *Christopher Street*, no. 69, p. 14.

12. Ibid., p. 16.

13. Judith Butler (1991), 'Imitation and Gender Insubordination', in Diana Fuss (ed.), *Inside/Out: Lesbian Theories, Gay Theories*, London, p. 19.

14. Joseph Bristow (1989), 'Being Gay: Politics, Identity, Pleasure', *New Formations*, no. 9, p. 70.

15. Martin P. Levine (1998), *Gay Macho: The Life and Death of the Homosexual Clone*. New York and London, p. 61.

16. Martin Humphreys (1985), 'Gay Machismo' in Andy Metcalf and Martin Humphreys (eds), *The Sexuality of Men*, London, p. 82.

17. Holleran, 'The Petrification of Clonestyle', p. 16.

18. Gregg Blachford (1981), 'Male Dominance and the Gay World', in Kenneth Plummer (ed.), *The Making of the Modern Homosexual*, London, p. 200. This is the process of 'stylization' that Clarke *et al.* use to describe working-class youth cultures and their 'generated' styles: 'The generation of subcultural styles involves differential selection from within the matrix of the existent. What happens is not the creation of objects and meanings from nothing, but rather a *transformation and rearrangement* of what is given (and 'borrowed') into a pattern which carries a new meaning, its *translation* to a new context, and its *adaptation*' (quoted in Gregg Blachford (1981), 'Male Dominance and the Gay World', in Kenneth Plummer *The Making of the Modern Homosexual*, New Jersey, p. 200).

19. Cole interview with Ray Weller, 26 June 1997.

20. Dennis Altman (1982), *The Homosexualization of America: The Americanization of the Homosexual*, New York, p. 13.

21. Cole interview with Justin Stubbings, 11 July 1997. James Gardiner recounted a similar experience of his visit to San Francisco in 1974: 'I think what happened to me was I first went to America in the early seventies and going to gay places on the West Coast I felt very queeny indeed and that hang over of the floral seventies and

the long hair and the bell bottoms and the floral everything, and all that jewellery, all those gold chains and all that stuff had become kind of mainstream gay fashion by 1970. It had become very very femme and I felt very very self conscious in the gay bars of San Francisco in 1974 and my friend that I was staying with took me aside and said "Darling, we really have got to buy you some real jeans" and I was taken off to one of the shops and bought several pairs of 501s and out went the platforms and on went the construction boots you know, out went the frilly shirt and on came tight T-shirt and so on and so forth and when I came back to London wearing those clothes people used to stare at me': Cole interview with James Gardiner, 24 September 1997. For a similar New York experience see Levine, *Gay Macho*, p. 47.

22. Randy Alfred (1982), 'Will the Real Clone Please Stand Out?', *Advocate*, 18 March, p. 22. See also Iain Finlayson (1990) *Denim*, Norwich, p. 113, for his theory on the two conflicting aesthetic appeals of clone style: 'high culture and low sleaze'.

23. Leaving buttons open on jeans was codified to have particular sexual meanings – usually one of availability. See also Clark Henley (1982), *Butch Manual: The Current Drag and How to Do It*, New York, p. 57.

24. Felice Picano (1996), *The Lure*, New York, pp. 55–6.

25. See Levine, *Gay Macho*, p. 87.

26. Seymour Kleinberg (1978), 'Where Have All the Sissies Gone?', *Christopher Street*, March, p. 6.

27. Cole interview with Ray Weller, 26 June 1997. Andrew Tomlin recalled how important the 'right' garment was in being accepted in the clone world: 'When I first saw a clone at Heaven [the London nightclub] I thought "I want to wear clothes like that, its easy", but my first checked shirt wasn't deemed the right one and a cute clone called Paul took me out one day to buy the right ones': Cole interview with Andrew Tomlin, 10 May 1999.

28. Compare the experiences in these two accounts. For John Campbell and his friends, the 'correct label was not the be-all and end-all. It was [important to have the right brand] to a certain extent. I mean it was more of a case of . . . the uniform was Timberlands, 501s, Lacostes and MA1s. You could have that look, but it may not be the real McCoy, provided that you almost fitted in with that, that was fine. If you took it to an extreme, if you wore a lamé Lacoste-style polo shirt, that would not have been allowed so to speak. Unless of course you decided to be a queen rather than a clone. It was quite well defined, you were either queens or clones': Cole interview with John Campbell, 31 July 1997. Ray Weller's clique was much more strict: 'I can remember going to a brunch . . . there were about 30 men there and it was a sunny summer afternoon, Saturday or Sunday and everyone was wearing a Lacoste top, everybody. There was not a single person who didn't have [one], so every pastel shade imaginable of Lacoste was present. And they had to be right because there were Lacostes that were potentially Far Eastern copies . . . And it was most important. You really felt bad if you didn't have to genuine article on': Cole interview with Ray Weller, 26 June 1997.

29. Henley, *Butch Manual*, p. 55.

30. James Gardiner maintains that it was cheap airfares offered by companies such as Freddie Laker that allowed gay men to travel easily and cheaply to New York and San Francisco, where they saw the new, out, proud and highly visible masculine clone look and brought them back to England: Cole interview with James Gardiner, 24 September 1997.

31. This is how the poet Adam Johnson described clones: quoted in Hugh David (1997), *On Queer Street: A Social History of British Homosexuality 1895–1995*, London, p. 253.

32. Cole interview with Ray Weller, 26 June 1997.

33. Ibid. 'Right after I moved to the City, I started running with a group I met at the tubs. At first, they made fun of my clothes and haircut. They really needled me! To get them off my back, I started to change. I looked at what they were wearing and listened to what they said. I started to dress the way they did and talk the way they did. All the teasing stopped after this' (quoted in Levine *Gay Macho*, p. 47).

34. Cole interview with Michael Brown, 1 December 1993. Rodney Garland describes a similar look in his 1953 novel *The Heart In Exile* 'Sartorially [Terry] was typical of at least one section of his generation all over the Western world. He had one suit, a single-breasted gabardine affair for uneasy, representative occasions. He was more at home in blue jeans, lumber-jackets, moccasins and loafers, windcheaters, cowboy shirts, in essentially masculine, revolutionary, anti-traditional, almost anti-capitalist garments. All of which emanate from the most demonstratively and aggressively capitalist state in the world': Rodney Garland (1995), *The Heart in Exile*, Brighton, p. 180.

35. James Gardiner maintains that this was a proto clone look. British gay men were taking their influence from American western films and images of men (semi) dressed as cowboys and bikers in physique magazines: Cole interview with James Gardiner, 24 September 1997.

36. Levine, *Gay Macho*, p. 61. The athletic look became especially popular after the release of Patricia Nell Warren's novel *The Front Runner*, published in 1974. The hero, Billy Sive, is a young gay athlete who favours Adidas running shoes. Ray Weller and Jonathan Jackson also remember this book's being an influence in London, though much later. 'The first year I went to Heaven on New Year's Eve, which was the first year it opened, I remember I was wearing 501s, which I was very proud of because it was really difficult to get them then, and I think a Fred Perry top and blue Adidas training shoes, and it was that look . . . it was way before the sports look': Cole interview with Ray Weller, 26 June 1997. As well as the basic, the lumberjack and the athletic looks there were a number of other clone styles that relied on specific signifying elements of clothing: Cowboy – cowboy hat, cowboy boots, denim jacket, leather chaps; Military – flight jacket, army fatigues, leather bomber jacket, combat boots, khaki army shirt, army cap; Construction Worker – construction boots, hard hat, cut down Levi's; Uniform – policeman, sailor, army captain; Leatherman – Black leather motorcycle jacket, trousers and cap, studded leather belt and wristband. The development of the leatherman will be discussed further in the next chapter.

37. Levine, *Gay Macho*, pp. 50–1.

38. Cole interview with Ray Weller, 26 June 1997. John Campbell (in interview with Cole, 31 July 1997) also underlined the importance of this 'preppy' look for clones in Britain.

39. Fischer, *Gay Semiotics*, p. 21.

40. The cowboy image was particularly prevalent, as it had figured so heavily for so long as an icon of American masculinity. Picano uses this point in his novel *The Lure*: '[Noel had] always associated homosexuality with feminine gestures and speech. But in here [The Grip - a leather bar of sorts] it was just the opposite: an extreme manliness, unruffled, almost frontiersman calm, as though all those Gary Cooper movies had come to life. Sure! That was it! The rough clothing, the swaggering walk, the drawling speech. They were acting out cowboy fantasies. How easy for him to copy!': Picano, *The Lure*, p. 64. The Village People (pop group) are a prime example of this.

41. Seymour Kleinberg, however, argues that the advent of an overtly masculine image for gay men was not liberated. By adopting a super-macho appearance gay men were following the strict binary rules of gender division, something that gender fuck and gay liberation had tried to break away from. He argues that macho looks and associated behaviour were not merely the 'new drag' but a return to the closet: 'Macho, of course, isn't a new closet; indeed, many have suspected that it's the oldest closet in the house' (Kleinberg, 'Where Have All the Sissies Gone?', p. 12).

42. Levine, *Gay Macho*, p. 61.

43. Cole interview with John Campbell, 31 July 1997. The type of footwear chosen could be used to send subtly different messages. Ray Weller recalled a friend who 'always wanted to look rough but he was frightened that people would think that he was rough trade, which he wasn't, and his compromise was he used to wear a singlet, a vest and 501 jeans, but he would never wear boots. He used to wear Bass Weegun loafers, which was a kind of an alternative but slightly smarter, but he'd wear them without socks, and he always used to say he wore them without socks 'cause that would present a rough image but people would actually see that they were actually Bass Weeguns so that they would know that he wasn't rough – that they would be going home to somewhere very nice with clean bed linen and clean kitchen and things': Cole interview with Ray Weller, 26 June 1997. Essex is a county in southern England that borders London; the term 'Essex' became a derogatory term implying that those people were suburban and behind London fashions. It was used in much the same way that New Yorkers refer to people who live outside Manhattan as 'Bridge and Tunnel'.

44. There is a link here to what Dick Hebdige calls 'the process of recuperation', which takes two forms: the commodity form, 'the conversion of subcultural signs (dress, music, etc.) into mass-produced objects and the ideological form, 'the "labelling" and re-definition of deviant behaviour by dominant groups – the police, the media, the judiciary'. He notes that one of the results of this commercialisation and popularisation of youth subcultures is the disavowal of the (commercialised/popularised) subcultures by their originators: see Dick Hebdige (1987 [1979]), *Subculture: The Meaning of Style*, London.

45. Cole interview with Ray Weller, 26 June 1997.

46. Stanley Reynolds (1983), *Punch*, April.

47. Altman, *The Homosexualization of America*, p. 33.

48. Heterosexual men's fashions had been copying gay men for many years. Refer to Chapter 5 for discussion of Vince and Carnaby Street in the late 1950s and early 1960s.

49. Holleran, 'The Petrification of Clonestyle', p. 16.

8

Hell for Leather: Bikers, S&M and Fetishisation

With the rise in popularity of overtly masculine forms of dress amongst gay men, especially the 'clones', leather became a popular dress choice. While the associations of sadomasochism (S/M) were definitely there for some men, for others it was just an extension of the strict codification of gay dress. It projected an air of dark, brooding masculinity, with associations of the rebel, of Marlon Brando in *The Wild One* (1954), of the dominator. It provided a means of furthering the image of masculine sexuality that was an integral part of the clone image. One man admits that his 'ultimate aspiration at that period would definitely have been a cross between Marlon Brando and a Tom of Finland drawing and elements of that fifties look about it'.[1] The look had been developing amongst gay men since the 1950s, and by the 1970s was a firmly established gay subculture. In his 1979 novel *The Lure* Felice Picano describes Hudson Street in New York where 'all the men seemed to be of a type . . . Some were in full leather costumes, complete with plaited chains hanging from the shoulders or wrapped around their visored hats; some even carried motorcycle helmets, though there were no bikes in sight.'[2] One of the men was 'large, broad-shouldered, with light hair that probably bleached blonder in the summer, a scraggly beard and mustache, wearing a getup from an old Hell's Angels' movie – soiled, antique black leather jacket, fat buckled garrison belt, faded skintight denims'.[3]

Participative observers of the gay leather scene, such as Larry Townsend and Geoff Mains, have noted that homosexuals regarded S/M and leather sex as archetypically masculine, mainly because it is organised around stereotypical male role performances (dominance, control, endurance) and symbols (whips, chains, leather).[4] 'To me leather sex is butch' one man noted. 'Wearing leather, doing a uniform scene, or tying someone up – that's hot. All that power and control makes me feel butch.'[5] However, it would be wrong to assume that all leathermen were into S/M and that all men into S/M wore leather. As Bryan Derbyshire pointed out 'You can be as much into S&M in a suit as you can in leathergear. It's a great mistake to believe that just because someone wears a leather jacket and chains he is auto-matically a sadist or a masochist.' Derbyshire admits that the danger of the leather scene is 'when it becomes the leather and the denim [that you're attracted to] and not the guy inside it'.[6] The growth in interest in leather led to resentment among some gay men. One bemoaned the fact that 'everyone's doing such a number that there isn't anything you can carry or wear that isn't being carried or worn by everyone in New York. Once the thing's become public, they lose their private meanings.'[7] Justin Stubbings identifies the dilemma of whether to wear leather because you like the look of it or because of its association with S/M sex: 'I liked the look, I liked the idea of it; but I didn't like the practice of it. But unfortunately those two go together. If you wear leather that's what you're into. If that's what you dress like, then play.'[8]

In America the leather look had been developing since the early 1950s, when disenchanted homosexual ex-servicemen with a penchant for rough sex and motorcycles had begun putting together a 'heavy' look.[9] In 1954 L.A.'s first gay biker club, the Satyrs, was formed. By the middle of the 1960s a whole series of clubs existed in both L.A. and San Francisco. There were no shops dealing with ready-made leather sex clothes in the 1950s; instead 'a harness was created by visiting the local saddle shop and improvising' and 'Leather pants and jackets came from Harley Davidson. Chaps came from western shops as did boots and vests.'[10] The sexual attractiveness and appeal to gay men of the biker look as a sexual look is evident in drawings and photographs in physique magazines such as *Physique Pictorial* and the films produced by Bob Mizer's Athletic Model Guild. In 1963 Kenneth Anger's film *Scorpio Rising* paid homage to the macho biker, not only addressing the decadence and ritualism involved in the subculture, but also the appeal of both these elements to gay men. The bike groups began to attract men who did not have motorbikes but were attracted to both the bikers and their style of dress. Male hustlers, who were not necessarily gay, often adopted elements of the biker look, which appealed to punters looking for 'rough trade'. John Rechy's 1963 novel *City of Night* illustrates this appeal, when the hero/narrator is dressed up by one of his punters in New York: 'There's a black leather jacket with stars like a general, eagled motorcycle cap, engineer boots with gleaming polished buckles. He left the closet door open, and I could see, hanging neatly, other similar clothes – different sizes.'[11] Gay men who were bikers would use these same elements to make themselves look like 'rough trade', to differentiate themselves from the 'flaming queens': 'Craig loved the cruising and loved the sex . . . And to make himself look older – he usually claimed to be seventeen – he wore a leather jacket and engineer boots and chain-smoked cigarettes.'[12] This 'super-masculine' type strives to:

display all the outer appearances of the ideal masculine type, [taking] an active interest, sometimes to the point of obsession, in those things that are traditionally associated with virility. He may thus strive for a muscular body, wear tattoos, take up motorcycling, hot-rodding or auto-mechanics, and maintain an appearance of a rough hewn, ribald danger loving anti-intellectual member of a gang.[13]

By 1964, San Francisco had such a well-developed leather 'scene' that it was the focus of a *Life* magazine article, 'Homosexuality in America'. The author described 'brawny young men in their leather caps, shirts, jackets and pants' alongside a photograph of similarly dressed men at the notorious San Francisco bar, The Tool Box.[14] John Rechy describes a similar club in his 1964 novel *City of Night*:

> About us in this malebar (Stirrup Club, San Francisco) are a number of men – some young, others not so young – dressed similarly: Black shiny jackets, boots. The good looking ones – and sometimes the not-so-good-looking ones – pose imperiously for the others ogling them. Just as the queens become a parody of femininity, many in this leathered group are parodies of masculinity: posing stiffly; mirror-practiced looks of disdain nevertheless soliciting those they seek to attract.[15]

Debate amongst gay men interested in leather in San Francisco in the late 1960s produced two factions, and is indicative of the way in which the leather scene was developing. There were those who were interested in leather for its S/M associations and practices and those who were part of the biking community. Mike S. identifies leather as 'a part of the "costume" that is used by fun-loving motorcyclists. It is no different than wearing shorts for tennis, special shoes for golf'.[16] He also concedes that 'even if a person has no connections with cycling at all, he may wear leather to help him associate with that group. Also to many people leather is a masculine material, and, therefore, makes the wearer appear more masculine.'[17] He sees the problem of a development of a "fetish" when 'a person gets carried away and wears complete leather outfits – leather jacket, leather pants, leather shirt, leather cap, leather boots – in addition to decorations for leather such as chains, keys, buttons etc.'.[18] This is far more the look that is associated with S/M practice and was to be seen later in the 1970s (and through into the 1980s and 1990s as a more serious fetishistic dress form, one divorced from the riding of motorcycles and leather as protective clothing.

Clubs continued to emerge that catered specifically to men interested in leather or other fetishistic forms of dress. Many clones used elements of this form of dress in their night-time clothing. In New York, clubs such as Badlands, Pipeline, the Eagle and Boots and Saddles used these dress codes to ensure that the décor and clientele matched. Martin P. Levine observed that these codes 'were typically posted near the front door, and were enforced by doormen, who generally refused entrance to anyone breaking the code. For example, the doorman at the Ramrod prohibited men wearing sandals, shorts, or dress clothes from entering the bar. Such attire violated the bar's leather image.'[19]

By the mid-1970s the gay leather scene was also well established in London. The typical uniform, which differed little from that in America, was a Muir cap, leather jacket, leather harness, leather trousers or denim jeans and leather chaps and heavy boots. It was not unusual to see men in Earls Court wearing 'boots up to here and gloves up to here and jackets out to there and they have remembered to carry their crash helmets under their arms. They come by bus.'[20] The men who dressed in leather and carried crash helmets, but had no motorbike were often mocked by those who did have bikes, or by gay men not involved in the leather scene. Justin Stubbings explained this practice as: 'It was wonderful. It was also about safety. It was about getting to and from; it's all right once you get to the venue, so its much easier going out in leather if you've got a crash helmet and you've got a line that it broke down on the Fulham Road. It's more acceptable. So it was about safety.'[21] Bryan Derbyshire identified the rise in numbers of gay (motor) bikers and motorbike clubs such as London Bikers, and Motor Sports Club (London), for which 'you actually have to have a motorbike to become a member', and points out how 'at one time everyone arrived here on the tube in their leather. Now [1976] you only have to look outside here at night and there are a hell of a lot of bikes.'[22] The leather scene, in London had been developing for a number of years before it became an established part of the gay scene, with pubs and clubs devoted to or specifically attracting leather men. Justin Stubbings remembers that 'the leather scene was around when I was about 15, 16 [in 1969], but in those days, because there weren't the clubs, everyone went back to somebody's for coffee, that was how you did it. You went to the club and you went for coffee and there were certain coffee parties that you didn't go to 'cause they were weird, and they were the leather scene.'[23] The journalist Gillian Freeman's 1961 'social problem' novel *The Leather Boys* illustrated the cross-over between the straight biker gangs and gay leather 'johnnies': 'Some men came along dressed in the whole kit, yet Reggie knew they hadn't motor-cycles, but cars parked a mile down the road. The boys laughed at them. They called then "kinky", and "the leather johnnies", but some of them went off with them.'[24] Both groups were utilising the same codes and drawing on the same iconography, particularly Marlon Brando in *The Wild One*. Freeman's description could lead to a belief that gay men were adopting the leather biker image, not as a subcultural identity in itself, but as a means of achieving sexual contact with overtly masculine (appearing) men. This argument finds a parallel in the adoption of leather jackets and engineer boots by male hustlers in America, described earlier in the chapter. By the late 1960s the Coleherne pub in London's Earl's Court was 'the bar that men in biker gear went to. There was a corner that was leather.'[25]

As in the United States before the establishment of specifically gay leather suppliers, leather clothes were available from motorbike shops. 'There have always been bikers around [so the clothes were easy to obtain], and you could always get a beat-up old leather jacket, though in the early days it wasn't about beat-up leather jackets, it was pristine leather jackets.'[26] By the 1976 Earls Court, the centre of the British gay leather scene, had its own leather shop, Hell For Leather, which supplied 'all the gear a leatherman must have', selling clothes that had been available years before in San Francisco, New York and Amsterdam.[27] The appeal of the leather look was often that it was at the opposite end of the gendered dress spectrum: it represented a huge step away from the effeminate stereotypes of the past. 'More young people are joining in the leather and denim scene now, mostly working class' Brian Derbyshire observed in 1976: 'They like its matey-ness and also because it's away from the gay stereotype.'[28]

Leather was not just about clothes. As a fabric black leather is saturated with sexual meaning. It has layers of implication: the wearing of it enhances sexual desirability through an indication of strength and power, whilst at the same time it is soft to touch and caress. Bryan Derbyshire says its appeal is:

> it's like a second skin. Also it accentuates a good body. The touch and smell of leather are enough to give me a permanent hard-on. And there's a certain butchness about it which I like. All right, I'm gay and I want to go to bed with a man. Now the way I look at it, a man is someone in a leather jacket and denims.[29]

Pat Califa believes that interest in leather is more primal, it reflects a search for something lost in twentieth-century life, it 'represents homesickness, an awareness of our human vulnerability. We miss', she argues, 'the warmth of fur, the safety of a thick hide or heavy scales, but we want to retain the sensitivity, the sensuality of our bare skins.'[30]

The gay S/M scene developed its own code of symbols to signify a desired sexual practice. Like the pinkie ring, the red tie and the suede shoes of previous decades, these signals were only for other gay men. Such codes can be likened to those of any secret or members' society; Pierre observed that:

> not unlike the Masons, West Point cadets, the brothers of Sigma Chi, the Knights of the Round Table, the Catholic priesthood, the CIA, the Hippies and the Hell's

Angel's [sic], the super-butch gay set plays at their secret rites; displaying insignia, chains on the right or left (which, like the flower worn over the ear, no one seems to remember which side means what), the jargon understandable only to the insider, the initiation ceremonies. To the new cultist these offer instant-identity: he knows who he is, because there are the jackets, belt, boots, cap and chains to prove it.[31]

However, where previous codes had signified sexuality, the new codes signified preference for particular sexual activities. 'The signs and symbols of S&M are a language all of their own. A chain, earring, belt buckle or keys worn on the left is S, on the right it means M. On the East coast it is the opposite . . . Many times keys, if worn in the middle of the back of the belt, can mean either way.'[32] In the relative safety of gay-defined spaces in the 1950s codes were developed to indicate availability:

> If you wanted to announce your sexual preference [in the leather bar world of the 1950s] you might move your belt buckle to either the right or the left of center [in an early form of the later coding of left = active, right = passive]. If you were interested in meeting a man you stood with your left side against his right side. If you saw two men standing together in a bar and you wanted to determine their relationship you would watch to see which side was either protected or exposed. If a Master stood with his left arm against the right arm of another man it meant that they were partners. If he stood with his left arm on the outside, away from the other man, it meant that he could be approached. Very formal, very subtle and not easy to figure out all the time.[33]

Bill Ruquy, owner of The Tool Box in San Francisco, explained that the bunches of keys hanging from the customers' leather belts were 'part of the sadistic business. We used to wear chains on our shoulders. Now the keys are in.'[34] Keys had been used to signify preferred roles in sexual activity since before the 1960s, dating back to the days when bikers wore their keys outside and always on the left – 'Satan's side'. By the 1970s 'people who wear their keys on the left want to be masters and the people who wear their keys on the right want to be slaves.'[35]

Coloured handkerchiefs in the back pocket became one of the most intricate and detailed systems of coding. The colours signified different sexual practices and the side of the body on which these were placed indicated the wearer's preference for active or passive roles in that activity. (See Table 8.1 for colours and signified activity.) An article on S/M in July 1975 gave an indication of what colours in handkerchiefs signified. The author points out that what he has given 'is of course, an advisory guide and subject to change as soon as the article circulates. In six months, a red handkerchief may mean you are going steady.'[36] The colours and their significance were however quickly set, as is evidenced by the number of guides issued in gay magazines and by gay shops, such as The Trading Post in San Francisco. Hal Fischer accredits the Trading Post as the first shop to promote handkerchief codes actively, in 1971. He maintains that the associations for red and blue handkerchiefs were already set, contradicting the *Village Voice*'s view that meanings were changeable.[37] In Andrew Holleran's 1970s novel of New York gay life *Dancer from the Dance*, Sutherland describes 'the various meanings of the outfits going by: the red handkerchief in the left pocket (fist-fucker), or the right pocket (fist–fuckee), the yellow handkerchief (piss)'.[38] Colour had had significance within gay dress codes long before the handkerchief codes were adopted to signify an interest in specific sexual acts. Red ties, for example, were a signifier of homosexuality early in the twentieth century. Red continued to have a very specific significance. In 1968: 'The colour red is thought of as an M colour basically because of its direct association with blood. Red, when worn with right side apparel and a thong tied tightly around the neck can lead to trouble if one is not prepared.'[39] The November 1953 edition of *One* magazine ran an appeal for information on customs in the early West from a reader who 'had heard that blue and red bandanas were worn around the wrist or neck to designate who was dancing the male and female parts at pioneer square dances when there weren't enough gals to go around'.[40]

Also associated with the S/M scene was the practice of body piercing. The work of gay body-piercers and tattooists[41] such as Doug Mallory, from the Gauntlet in Los Angeles, and Mr Sebastian in London played a large part in the formation of modern Western piercing. Before piercing and tattooing became fashionable in straight society nipples and genitals were being pierced. In *Dancer from the Dance*, Sutherland points out 'the bare chest with tiny gold rings inserted in the nipples'.[42] Just as wearing leather was viewed as a return to the 'primitive', body piercing was viewed as a form of affiliation with non-Western 'tribal' cultures. 'For me piercings are a form of tribal art', Damien put it: 'They are a conscious decision to do something with my body.'[43] Vale and Juno identify such actions as a sign of control for individuals over 'their own bodies'. Thus 'by giving visible expression to unknown desires and latent obsessions welling up from within, individuals can provoke change – however inexplicable – in the external world of the social, besides freeing up a creative part of themselves'.[44] The act of body decoration runs along the boundary between the public and private, areas that have been in a constant state of transition and sites for transgression amongst gay men for decades. For many gay men the very act of piercing made 'as strong a statement about their sexuality as coming out'.[45] Just as gay men in the 1950s hid their sexual nature behind a 'normal' facade of dress, so the pierced gay man hid his decorated body or indications of S/M interests behind a façade

Table 8.1. *The Hanky Colour Code*

Colour	Left Side (Active)	Right Side (Passive)
Red	Fist Fucker	Fist Fuckee
Dark Blue	Fucker	Fuckee
Light Blue	Wants Blow Job	Gives Blow Job
Black	Heavy S&M, top	Heavy S&M, bottom
White	Jack Me Off	I'll do us both
Yellow	Water Sports (Golden Shower), giver	Water Sports (Golden Shower), receiver
Brown	Spreads Scat/Shitter	Receives Scat/Shittee
Robin's Egg Blue	69-er	Anything but 69
Mustard	Has 8" or More	Looking for Big Dick
Green	Hustler, selling	Hustler, buying
Beige (Light Brown)	Likes to be Rimmed	Likes to Rim
Olive Drab	Military/Uniforms	Looking for same
Orange	Anything Top	Anything Bottom
Purple	Piercer/Genitotorturer	Piercee/Genitotorturee
Grey	Gives Bondage/Light S&M	Desires same
Pink	Dildo giver	Dildo receiver

of 'normality', choosing when and where to make his private body and identity visible and public. In the 1980s piercing along with tattooing and the adoption of punk styles was incorporated into new 'queer identities' that were a 'challenge against the 1980s gay gentrification of sexual identity'.[46] The increasing popularity of piercing among gay men also moved out of the exclusively sexual/personal arena into a more fashion-based arena, becoming increasingly visible on the commercialised gay scene, in discos where clothes were removed and piercings displayed as fashionable adornment. Toby Manning noted that this was indicative of 'queer' coming to suggest 'a pierced-nippled, brain-dead, club-crazy bimbo wiggling his hips to house music'.[47]

Leather has continued to play a role in gay men's dress. The advent of AIDS in the early 1980s saw condemnation of S/M sexual practices, along with the closure of gay bath houses and sex clubs.[48] Younger gay men increasingly saw the wearing of leather as something done by 'dinosaur leather clones'.[49] However, as more was discovered about the transmission of the HIV virus, S/M sex practices had a renaissance, as they involved a strict codification of sexual practice that did not rely on the exchange of bodily fluids, but went for a more polymorphous sexuality that saw the whole body as an erotic erogenous zone. The rise in interest in S/M in the heterosexual world and the gathering of people interested in S/M regardless of sexual orientation has also encouraged a new interest in associated clothing. Not only was leather a viable material for clothing, but rubber also became popular, pointing 'fetish' clothing in a new direction. Pat Califa believed that 'while leather is atavistic, pre-industrial and romantic, rubber is futuristic, technological science-fictionish . . . it represents an impossible wish to merge with the impersonal (and powerful) machine.'[50] As leather became increasingly visible outside a fetish context rubber offered a new fetishistic form of dress. James was 'always turned on by rubber. Before I heard about homosexuality, I knew I would find other people who like latex too . . . Today I have three or four rubber suits in different sizes and weights of latex'.[51]

With the advent of punk and its bricolage form of assembling outfits, elements of leathermen's wardrobe were used by younger gay men, playing with the associations held by items of clothing, what Scott Tucker described as 'the current iconoclasm – which really means a multiplication of punk, high-tech, androgynous, and indefinable icons'.[52] The clothes no longer necessarily indicated an interest in S/M sex,[53] but toyed with perceptions and preconceptions of sexual orientation, masculinity and identity.

Notes

1. Cole interview with Ray Weller, 26 June 1997.
2. Felice Picano (1996), *The Lure*, New York, p. 68.
3. Ibid., p .54.
4. Larry Townsend (1983), *The Leatherman's Handbook II*, New York and Geoff Mains (1984), *Urban Aboriginals: A Celebration of Leathersexuality*, San Francisco.
5. Martin P. Levine (1998) *Gay Macho: The Life and Death of the Homosexual Clone*, New York and London, p. 95.
6. Quoted in *Gay News*, no. 90, 1976.
7. Richard Goldstein (1975),'S&M: The Dark Side of Gay Liberation', *Village Voice*, 7 July, p. 11.
8. Cole interview with Justin Stubbings, 11 July 1997.

9. Interest in S/M and its associated clothing had been around long before the clothes were adopted by the [gay] biking fraternity. Samuel M. Steward described the clothes worn by a man he met through Dr Alfred Kinsey. When he met Mike Mikshe in 1949 he was 'lounging with legs stretched out and with his back against the trunk of an apple tree [and he] was a handsome brute with crew-cut black hair and a somewhat tough bulldog face. On his lower half were beige jodhpur trousers above brown English boots with lacings at the instep . . . for black had not yet become the imperative color for sadists. His shirt-sleeves were tightly rolled into neat bands on each arm, showing half of his remarkably well developed biceps; his belt buckle was overwhelmingly western.' 'This was', he continues, 'all long before the leather mania had codified and ritualized itself into leather-drag posturings, studied gestures, and modes of dress and behaviour': Samuel M. Steward (1991), 'Dr. Kinsey Takes a Peek at S/M: A Reminiscence', in Mark Thompson (ed.), *Leatherfolk: Radical Sex, People Politics and Practice*, Boston, MA, p. 86.

10. Thom Magister (1991), 'One Among Many: The Seduction and Training of a Leatherman', in Mark Thompson (ed.), *Leatherfolk: Radical Sex, People Politics and Practice*, Boston, MA, p. 102.

11. John Rechy (1964), *City of Night*, New York, p. 37.

12. Martin Duberman (1994), *Stonewall*, New York, p. 46.

13. Donald Webster Cory and John P. LeRoy (1963), *The Homosexual and his Society: A View from Within*, New York, p. 109.

14. Paul Welch (1964), 'Homosexuality in America' in *Life*, 26 June, p. 70.

15. Rechy, *City of Night,* p. 245.

16. Larry Carlson (1968), 'Leather: Open Forum', in *Vector*, June 1968, p. 17

17. Ibid.

18. Ibid. These very clothes are described by John Rechy. Neil is dressed 'in black mounting police pants which cling tightly below the hips revealing squat bowlegs; boots which gleam vitreously and rise at least a foot above his ankle – silver studs forming a triangular design on the tip of each boot, then swirling about the upper part like a wayward-leafed clover . . . Over a dark vinyl shirt, he wore a black leather vest, tied crisscross with a long leather strap from his chest to his stomach. On each lapel of the vest is reproduced the triangular clover-leafed pattern as on the boots (and each silver stud, again, is encircled by the beaded haloes). The vest, the shirt, the legs of the pants are so tightly molded on his stubby body that his movements are restricted': Rechy, *City of Night*, p. 245.

19. Levine, *Gay Macho*, pp. 63–4.

20. Guy Kettelhack (ed.) (1984), *The Wit and Wisdom of Quentin Crisp*, New York, p. 29.

21. Cole interview with Justin Stubbings, 11 July 1997.

22. Quoted in *Gay News*, no. 90, 1976.

23. Cole interview with Justin Stubbings, 11 July 1997. James makes a similar observation in Brighton Ourstory Project (1992), *Daring Hearts: Lesbian and Gay Lives of 50s and 60s Brighton*, Brighton, p. 107.

24. Gillian Freeman (1969 [1961]), *The Leather Boys*, London, pp. 12–13.

Figure 1. Victorian greetings card representing the aesthetic movement, 1890s. (Picture Library of Victoria and Albert Museum.)

"Yes Miss, most of the flowers 'ave done well this year, but I've 'ad a lot of trouble with the Pansies!"

Figure 2. Seaside Postcard, 1930s. (With permission, James Gardiner Collection.)

Figure 3. Fashionable young gay man and sailor friend, 1930s. (With permission, James Gardiner Collection.)

Figure 4. Two gay men in Central Park, New York, 1947. (Lesbian and Gay
Community Services Center, National Archive of Lesbian and Gay
History, Frank Thompson Collection.)

Figure 5. John Hardy and 'girlfriend', Hampstead Arts Ball, 1955. (With permission, John Hardy.)

Figure 6. Physique photograph, with model in biker-style clothing, 1950s. (Lesbian and Gay Community Services Center, National Archive of Lesbian and Gay History.)

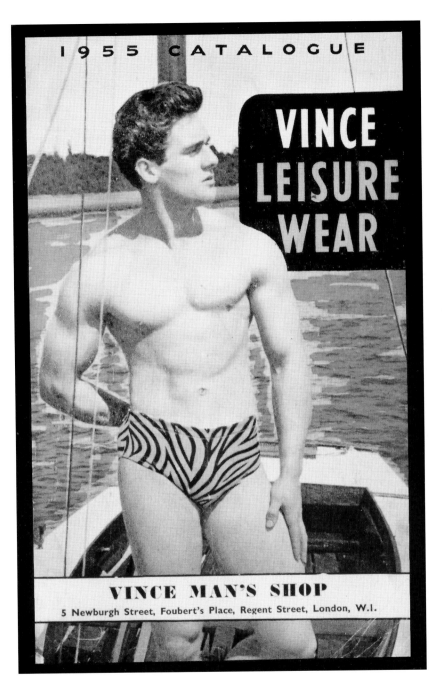

Figure 7. Cover of catalogue for Vince Man's Shop, 1954. The model is in a typical physique photo pose. (With permission, John Hardy.)

Figure 8. Group of young gay men in casual dress, mid-1950s. (With permission, John Hardy.)

Figure 9. John Hardy in Europe, late 1950s. (With permission, John Hardy.)

Figure 10. Gay youths at the beach, New York, 1960s. (Lesbian and Gay Community Services Center, National Archive of Lesbian and Gay History.)

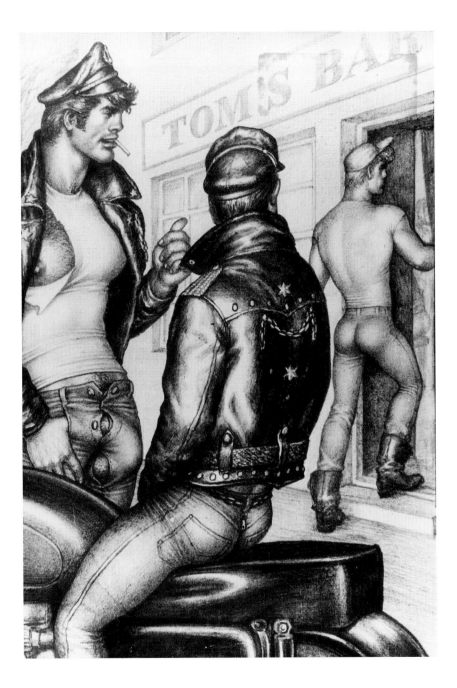

Figure 11. Tom of Finland's interpretation of a gay leather bar, 1965. (With permission of the Tom of Finland foundation.)

Figure 12. Advertisement for trousers on sale at gay-friendly boutique, The Town Squire in San Francisco, from *Vector Magazine* August 1967. (With permission of Gay and Lesbian Historical Society of Northern California.)

Figure 13. Gay fancy dress party, one man dressed in hippie clothing, 1967. (Lesbian and Gay Community Services Center, National Archive of Lesbian and Gay History, Frank Thompson Collection.)

Figure 14. Tony, on holiday in Benidorm, Spain, early 1970s, wearing canary-yellow flared trousers and flower-print pink and yellow shirt.

Figure 15. Genderfuck, Greenwich Village, New York, 1976. (Photograph by Leonard Fink. Lesbian and Gay Community Services Center, National Archive of Lesbian and Gay History.)

Figure 16. Cowboy clones, West 10th Street, New York, 1977. (Photograph by Leonard Fink. Lesbian and Gay Community Services Center, National Archive of Lesbian and Gay History.)

Figure 17. Seditionaries cowboy T-shirt, late 1970s.

Figure 18. Leathermen, Greenwich Village, New York, late 1970s. (Photograph by
Leonard Fink. Lesbian and Gay Community Services Center, National
Archive of Lesbian and Gay History.)

Figure 19. Joe Pop, gay punk, 1979. (With permission, Joe Pop.)

Figure 20. Justin Stubbings, clone, 1980s. (With permission Justin Stubbings.)

Figure 21. Jonny Slut, with decorated jacket, ripped jeans and Boy cycling shorts. (Photograph by Ted Polhemus, with permission Ted Polhemus and PYMCA.)

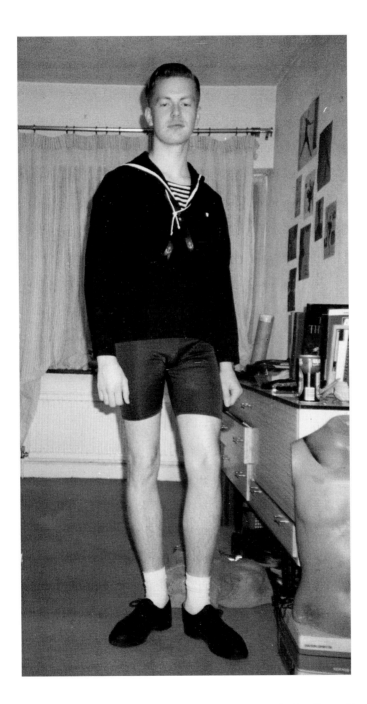

Figure 22. Cycling shorts and sailor top, 1988. (With permission Simon Rooks.)

Figure 23. Rockabilly-inspired fashion, Brighton, 1989. (With permission John Green.)

Figure 24. Gay Skinheads (Jamie and Terry), Brighton, 1990. (Photograph by John G. Byrne.)

Figure 25. Gay club fashions, London, 1990. (With permission John Green.)

25. Quoted in Murray Healy (1996), *Gay Skins: Class, Masculinity and Queer Appropriation*, London, p. 70

26. Cole interview with Justin Stubbings, 11 July 1997.

27. Jim Holmes identifies an interest in leather amongst European gay men as something copied from the Americans. He states 'in Europe the gay leather scene is perceived as something that came from the US. Some there see precedents, perhaps in the Nazis and in the European version of the Hell's Angels. But like everything else in the gay world, Americans established the leather style and Europeans simply aped it': Dennis Forbes (1984) 'Jim Holmes', *Advocate*, no. 395, 29 May, p. 34. See also Gregg Blachford (1981), 'Male Dominance and the Gay World' in Kenneth Plummer (ed.), *The Making of the Modern Homosexual*, London, p. 191. Kenneth Anger's films, notably *Scorpio Rising*, portray a flirting with Nazi fantasies and a use of fascist iconography amongst men of the gay leather scene in America in the 1950s.

28. Quoted in *Gay News*, no. 90, 1976. The establishment of the gay skinhead scene is often considered to have arisen out of or at least been nurtured within the leather scene, as it offered a very British image of working-class masculinity. See Healy, *Gay Skins* and Chapter 13.

29. Quoted in *Gay News*, no. 90, 1976.

30. Pat Califa (1984), 'Beyond Leather: Expanding the Realms of the Senses to Latex', *Advocate*, no. 395.

31. Carlson, 'Leather: Open Forum', p. 16.

32. L. Whipplasch (1968), 'Why Leather? or "What's A Nice Boy Like Me Doing Tied to a Stake Like This?"', *Vector*, June, p. 5.

33. Thom Magister (1991) 'One Among Many: The Seduction and Training of a Leatherman', in Mark Thompson (ed.), *Leatherfolk: Radical Sex, People, Politics and Practice*, Boston, MA, p. 100.

34. Paul Welch (1964), 'Homosexuality in America', *Life*, 26 June, p. 70.

35. Richard Goldstein, 'S&M: The Dark Side of Gay Liberation' in *Village Voice*, 7 July 1975. Martin Humphreys believed that 'because of the increased visibility of the macho man as an idealized sexual image it [had] become hard to understand the fine distinctions of codified dress' and that it could be 'confusing if you don't fully understand the codes and as a result imply behaviour or desire that is in contradiction to your intentions'. He says that for years he misunderstood the meaning of the key code, believing the left side indicated a desire to be the 'passive' partner, because he saw 'the left side as connected symbolically with weakness or powerlessness and therefore that wearing keys on the left fitted in with the male myth that the one who is fucked is less than male'. Belatedly he admits he realized that this was another example of gay men 'overturning straight conceptions and asserting [their] own sense of reality, i.e. camp'. Martin Humphreys (1985), 'Gay Machismo', in Andy Metcalf and Martin Humphreys (eds), *The Sexuality of Men*, London, p. 8.

36. Goldstein, 'S&M: The Dark Side of Gay Liberation', p. 11.

37. Hal Fischer (1977), *Gay Semiotics*, San Francisco, p. 20.

38. Andrew Holleran (1980 [1978]), *Dancer from the Dance*, London, p. 172.

39. Whipplasch, 'Why Leather?, p. 5.

40. *One*, vol. 1, no. 11, p. 20.

41. Tattooing is discussed in Chapter 9.

42. Holleran, *Dancer from the Dance*, p.172.

43. Derek Cohen (1992), 'Puncture Culture', *Him*, no. 60, p. 24. See also Ted Polhemus (1988), *Body Styles*, Luton; Ted Polhemus and Housk Randall (1996), *The Customized Body*, London and New York; and V. Vale and Andrea Juno (1989), *Modern Primitives: An Investigation of Contemporary Adornment and Ritual*, San Francisco.

44. Vale and Juno, *Modern Primitives*, p. 4

45. Derek Cohen (1992), 'Puncture Culture', p. 24.

46. Matias Viegener (1993), 'The Only Haircut That Makes Sense Anymore: Queer Subculture and Gay Resistance', in Martha Gever, Pratibha Parmer and John Greyson (eds), *Queer Looks*, London, p. 128. For further discussions on late 1980s, early 1990s 'queer' culture see other essays in *Queer Looks*; Paul Burston (ed.) (1995), *A Queer Romance: Lesbians, Gay Men and Popular Culture*, London; Keith Alcorn (1992), 'Queer and Now', *Gay Times*, May; Paul Burston (1992), 'The Death of Queer Politics', *Gay Times,* August; 'Queer Culture – a Celebration – and a Critique', *Village Voice*, 21 June 1994; Michael Warner (1993), *Fear of a Queer Planet: Queer Politics and Social Theory*, Minneapolis; Susan Stryker and Jim Van Buskirk (1996), *Gay by the Bay*, San Francisco, pp. 117–53.

47. Toby Manning (1996), 'Gay Culture: Who Needs It?', in Mark Simpson (ed.), *Anti-Gay*, London, p. 115.

48. See Mark Thompson (ed.), *Leatherfolk*, especially Guy Baldwin, 'A Second Coming Out', David Stein 'S/M's Copernican Revolution: From a Closed World to the Infinite Universe', and Eric E. Rofes, 'Snapshot of Desire: Surviving as a Queer Amongst Queers'.

49. As early as 1972 this was an opinion held by younger gay men. Tom Burke (1969), 'The New Homosexuality', *Esquire*, no. 72 quotes young gay men influenced by the counterculture who saw leather as something done by an older generation of gay men and associated it with the strict active/passive roles of previous generations.

50. Pat Califa (1984), 'Beyond Leather: Expanding the Realms of the Senses to Latex', *Advocate*, no. 395, 29 May.

51. Ibid. An examination of the dress codes of gay fetish clubs in the late 1980s and early 1990s indicates that rubber had become as acceptable as leather and uniforms. Rubber chaps, shorts and jackets became available from shops that had previously supplied leather to a fetish market as rubber became a popular alternative.

52. Scott Tucker (1991), 'The Hanged Man', in Mark Thompson (ed.), *Leatherfolk: Radical Sex, People, Politics and Practice*, Boston, p. 6.

53. John Preston described his experiences stopping wearing leather as an indication of his interest in S/M, and dressing '*against* the fashion' when searching for 'rough sex': John Preston (1991), 'What happened?' in Mark Thompson (ed.), *Leatherfolk: Radical Sex, People, Politics and Practice*, Boston, p. 212.

9

Body Talk

With the advent of gay liberation in the 1970s, many gay men developed an interest in projecting a more masculine self-presentation, often based on traditionally 'macho' images. As a result bodybuilding and gym culture increased in popularity, especially amongst clones, with the drawings of Tom of Finland providing 'a blueprint for the appearance of gay men in the latter part of the twentieth century'.[1] In their bid to achieve a new ultra-masculine appearance, the clones used such stereotypically macho sign-vehicles as musculature, facial hair, and short haircuts to express 'butchness'. To achieve this they developed 'gym bodies' – tight buttocks, 'washboard' stomachs, and pumped-up biceps and pectorals – which denoted the physique associated with weightlifters. Clones favoured this physique because they felt it was the most macho male build. 'Society sees musclemen as more masculine, so I work out, putting in long hours in the gym pumping iron,' one bodybuilder said. 'The results make me feel butch.'[2]

The new gay body was based on images that had been viewed by gay men for many years in physique magazines. After the Second World War, with the increased use of photography and cheaper magazine reproduction, a number of new magazines had emerged devoted to the male body. Photographers such as Bob Mizer realised that photographs of 'beefy' boys would sell to a specialist gay market. Following the restrictions set by the US post office for mailing such photographs, a 'posing strap' covered the models' genitals and they were hairless below the neck. In Britain too, influenced by the work of Americans such as Mizer, photographers began to produce physique photographs and distribute them by post. A British photographer, Bill Green, known professionally as Vince, ran a very successful business taking and selling photographs of muscle boys. As in America, genitals had to be covered, so he developed a posing pouch, which he later went on to sell.

The rise in popularity of physique magazines amongst gay men and the use of contemporary homoerotic images by artists such as George Quaintance and Tom of Finland had an immense effect upon the dress choice and self-presentation of gay men. Tom of Finland presented working-class heroes – sailors, athletes, cowboys, construction workers and bikers – in sexualised scenarios. These images flew in the face of the classic stereotype of the homo-sexual as a limp-wristed fairy. One gay man remembers finding Tom of Finland drawings amongst his friend's belongings. 'That was the first time I could see myself in a gay situation with men, because I could see myself in those pictures', he recalled.[3] The leather bars in cities such as San Francisco were also attracting men who were striving to achieve a more masculine image that owed much to the images of blue-collar working-class masculinity – bikers, hoods, cowboys – that were the staple fare of *Physique Pictorial Magazine*.[4]

Images of working-class masculinity were popular amongst gay men, and followed a tradition of the attraction of middle- and upper-class men to working-class roughs.[5] In *The Rise and Fall of Gay Culture*, Daniel Harris identifies that in the physique magazines of the 1950s the models were all working-class and heterosexual, and often 'delinquent'. In the light of this he observes that the gay body 'implicit in many physique magazines was that of a "sexless sissy" whose scrawny frame would have looked out of place' amongst the images of swaggering manhood represented in those magazines. This stereotype of the gay man had been prevalent in both Britain and America throughout the twentieth century, and proved a point of identification or alienation for gay men.[6] Discussing the changing images of gay men's sexual desire, the gay activist and writer Michael Bronski quotes an article entitled 'Boys on the Beach' by Midge Decter, in which she recalls 'the largest number of homosexuals [on Fire Island in the 1950s] had hairless bodies. Chests, backs, arms, even legs were smooth and silky. We were never able to discover why there should be so definite a connection between what is nowadays called their sexual preference and their smooth feminine skin.'[7] Bronski continued, noting that Decter saw the liberated 'out' muscular gay men in New York's West Village as a contrast to the 'sweet, harmless' queens she knew on Fire Island.[8] This highlights the way in which pre-liberation gay men were seen by sympathetic straight society as 'harmless and sexless'. This notion played a role in gay men's self-identification and was to be one of the contributing factors to the adoption of more a masculine self-image.[9]

Weightlifting and body-building became popular amongst gay men who refused to be drawn into the stereotype or who were desperate to distance themselves from the stereotype of the limp-wristed weakling. Cory and LeRoy, writing in 1963, observed 'the realisation that one is homosexual and the fear that one is therefore less than manly can and do[es] serve many as motivation to overcome and become even more masculine in physical appearance than most males' and so 'in the modern gymnasiums, homo-sexuals are seen in large numbers. They lift weights and build muscles; they ostentatiously flex their biceps in the displays that are often erotic. And at the same time they strive to enhance their own physical attractiveness.'[10] In his 1953 novel *The Heart In Exile*, Rodney Garland describes the increase in popularity of swimming pools and gyms among gay men in Britain. One man tells the narrator that the gym is 'full of queers', and the narrator then:

> remembered the occasion when Terry had taken me to a swimming pool. This was, I imagined, a new post-war trend in England. A considerable proportion of young homosexuals regularly went to gymnasia and swimming pools, not only to look at, or try to establish contact with, attractive young men, but also to improve their own physique, and thereby their chances of success.[11]

Garland's observation that gay men were improving their bodies to improve their chances of success highlights a major factor of gay men's self-identity, that of physical appearance. While this book is predominantly concerned with the way that manifested itself in clothing, body shape was important in itself, and impacted upon the choice of clothes and the way those garments looked. The body is the hanger for clothing; and for a group who were, perhaps overmuch, concerned with their physical appearance the nature of this foundation was of great importance. Jack B. stated that:

> There is little doubt that homosexuals as a group are very much pre-occupied with their bodies and all the accoutrements . . . Homosexuals have always been extremely body-conscious. The body is very important for the homosexual, more important than for any other group. You are in a competitive situation for better or for worse, so you pay attention to your physical appearance.[12]

Daniel Harris noted that many gay men were conscious of the maintenance of their bodies and that before the gym became a primary means of maintaining the body, many gay men adopted a hyper-fastidiousness over grooming 'modelled on the deportment of upper-middle-class-men'.[13] This resulted in a typically gay self-consciousness about bathing, skincare, body odours, and hairstyles. With the advent of gay liberation, and the beginnings of the rise in men's grooming products, gay publications began to devote time and space to the subject of the body's image, giving advice on beauty products.[14] The publication in 1977 of the men's grooming guide *Looking Good* highlights the importance of bodycare.[15]

The discotheques and clubs of the 1970s were filled with men who had spent hours developing their physiques in gyms. Andrew Holleran notes the importance of this in the gay world of New York: '[Malone] knew nothing of discotheques and gossip, bodybuilding and baseball caps, bleached fatigues and plaid shirts, the whole milieu of trends on which the city and the society that revolved around the Twelfth Floor thrived, even originated.'[16] If a man were going to spend time in a gym to develop a 'pumped' body, then he needed clothes to show it off. It was not only the desire to show off a muscular physique, but dancing in hot confined spaces, often after having taken drugs, that meant that gay men were looking for the sexiest clothes that would keep them cool. Certain types of sportswear offered this option. Clothes bought in gay holiday resorts, such as Benidorm in Spain and Fire Island in America, were worn on the beach during the day and then at gay clubs and night-time dancing parties.[17] The singlet (tank top, vest) was one such item of clothing that emphasised the arms and chest.[18] Ray Weller recalled how this was an extremely popular item of clothing at the London club, Heaven, in the early 1980s. In an attempt to stand apart from the crowd some men took to wearing it in a more unconventional and body-emphasising way:

there was one person who was wearing those ribbed singlets and suddenly instead of just wearing it down in the normal way you'd wear a vest or a singlet, he pulled it over his neck, but kept his arms in it so it was over the back of the neck . . . you've still got your arms in a vest, but it's sort of half off – it's pulled very tight and it pushes your chest forward. And I remember that there was somebody that used to do that, and nobody else did it . . . and suddenly a few people started doing it. I can remember when people started poking their vests into their belts, and there were just a few people who started doing it – of course they were the most muscled or the most drugged or the most out of it.[19]

The rise in images of men's bodies in photography and advertising in the mid-1980s created a new model for gay men's self-image. For Bill Wilson it was Bruce Weber's photographs of the Olympic team in *Interview* in 1984:

They were a massive inspiration to me . . . I really started to take an interest in exercise and clothes and the way I looked, really . . . I wanted to be like them, I wanted to be a sexual being like I thought they were. That came in line with the gym training and getting interested in gym. I very much wanted to be like them, really.[20]

Bill Wilson was one of the first men at his gym to wear cycling shorts, and attributes this choice of clothing to an interest in fashion as well as in how his body looked. 'At the time as well I think there was a correlation between how I physically was,' he recalled, 'because I started training at that time, and I became more aware about how my body was, really, and it encouraged me to wear tight things. There was something right about the time and how I felt and my age as well, and, you know, wearing skimpier stuff to show off my body.'[21] Just as in the clone clubs of the late 1970s and early 1980s gay men had worn clothes to show off their physiques while keeping cool, gay men in the 1980s adapted clothing to suit their needs. This was particularly visible in their appropriation of sports clothing, such as cycling shorts.[22] New fashion designers and labels, such as Jean-Paul Gaultier, Boy and BodyMap[23] quickly picked up on the interest in such clothing, and began to create their own versions. Both Bill Wilson and Nick Cook were drawn to Boy's sportswear-inspired collections, 'Boy in the Kings Road produced these long sort of white, very thin cotton lycra-y-type cycling shorts,' recalled Nick Cook,

> And of course when you're dancing and you're dancing for a long time you don't really want to be wearing a great deal more. I found that those were very appropriate; but the fact that they were showing your body off didn't particularly excite, and I just felt that they were more convenient to wear, because you weren't going to get hot and sweaty, and once you were you weren't going to soak in a T-shirt.[24]

Tattoos also served to emphasise the muscularity of a man's physique. In the West, tattooing had traditionally served as a male-bonding ritual amongst sailors, criminals and gang members. Many gay men had adopted tattoos as a symbol of this proletarian masculinity. Justin Stubbings viewed his tattoos as 'keeping that rough element . . . aggressively, coming away from being that pansy bit; I'm actually a force to be reckoned with'; and while he concedes that they did mark his feelings of difference, they were a symbol of 'moving away from being apologetically different'.[25] Studies on tattooing emphasise the transgressive nature of tattooing, along with other forms of body manipulation such as piercing, as they allow for a secret or private identity and pleasure to be carried out in public. 'It's a private thing. It's about me,' said Neil. 'I mean I don't show them off very often. I generally wear long-sleeved shirts or whatever . . . I was always fascinated by tattoos . . . I had always wanted one done. When I was 18 I had one done and sort of got carried away.'[26] For many gay men tattooing acts as a public marker: tattoos are carried out on areas of the body – the upper arm, the shoulder, the chest – that can be easily made visible, drawing attention to those areas of the body.[27] The process of being tattooed often fulfilled a 'primal need' or served as a 'rite of passage' or a 'beautification process';[28] but many gay magazines likened the selection of a tattoo to that of selecting upholstery fabric, turning what is potentially a life-enhancing or life-changing process into an act of commercialised consumption and public display: 'Pick where you want [the tattoo] to go on your body . . . Your idea should be large enough that it can be perceived and understood from a few feet away. It should be placed in a way that compliments your body, because when you move so does your tattoo.'[29]

Dennis Altman argues that gay men have a very different attitude towards displays of masculinity, in relation to body-building, than do those who are straight. Straight men repress and even deny the sexual element, while gay men are much more open, and hence much less likely to turn to aggression. He states 'body building is part of the whole assertion of sexuality that makes up much of the new gay male style [of the late 1970s], and it underlies the fact that to be gay is not, as is often thought, to be a man who would be a woman.'[30] 'Of course many bodybuilders are gay. I love the muscular aspect of myself. Yet, in effect, though different, it's similar in reversed purpose to drag. It's the opposite side, but from almost the same source. The queen protects herself by dressing in women's clothes, and the bodybuilder protects himself in muscles – so-called "men's clothes".'[31] Gay culture's advocacy of the importance of the new masculinity served to divide the gay community into a new version of the binary gender divisions: 'effeminacy' was once again derided. Gay men's body-building, which was once used as a means to 'butch' up, had become a new symbol of gay men's obsession with grooming and body image.

The advent of AIDS in the early 1980s played a role in the definitions of body type that gay men were adopting. One of the ways in which illnesses associated with AIDS manifested themselves was through drastic weight loss. For a period when AIDS was first making its devastating presence felt amongst the gay communities a fit, muscular body was associated with a healthy body. Having a 'gym-body' appeared to deny the existence of AIDS and its effects upon the gay body. Justin Stubbings offers a far more real and relevant reason for the association of gym-maintained bodies with HIV and AIDS. He recalled that:

> For a while, when, in the early days of AIDS, when people saw what it looked like, people started putting weight on, and before it all got honed into 'we all go down the gym now and we all work on our bodies', it was 'as long as you've got flesh on you you're safe' . . . but a lot of the people I know who are diagnosed make a point in joining the gym in order to have enough muscle to carry them through when they go through muscle wastage – it's not just a case of looking good, it's a case of making sure I've got something to sustain me during the times of muscle wastage.[32]

A study of images relating to AIDS and the body offers an insight into the perceptions of gay bodies in the age of AIDS. The first photographs of men with AIDS concentrated on the corpse-like appearance of the 'victims'' bodies, while later images reveal a more positive view of people living with, rather than dying from, AIDS-related illnesses. Safer sex advertising utilised images of muscular tanned bodies, continuing to reinforce the stereotype of the gym-toned gay body.[33] AIDS also had a uniting effect upon the gay communities, exemplified in the formation of the many activist and support groups formed by gay men (and lesbians) as a response to the AIDS crisis. Bill Wilson believes that this also had an effect upon the way gay men looked: 'With the onset of AIDS I think that it became necessary for people to group together to show solidarity, and there seemed to be a uniform come out of that inadvertently, which was the jeans and tight T-shirt thing.'[34]

The rise in health-inspired gym culture, partly as a result of AIDS, led to muscularity's becoming an almost certain indicator of a man's sexual orientation within urban areas with a large gay population. Daniel Harris attributes the striving to attain a uniform muscular gay body as a means of inventing 'those missing physical features that enable us to spot imperceptible compatriots, who would remain unseen and anonymous if they did not prominently display on their own bodies . . . the caste mark that constitutes the essence of gay sensibility'.[35] Gay men, he asserts, are creating the shared physical characteristic that is naturally present in other minorities. The adoption of certain dress codes had served this purpose in previous decades. The rise in uniformity of body types could also be linked to a sexual attraction as a tool to aid sexual liaisons. Just as the clones became an insular group in which many of their number would only have sex with another clone,[36] so a muscular body became almost essential (in certain groupings) for sexual attraction and liaison – culminating in the disparaging ethos of 'no pecs, no sex'.

By the late 1980s the gym-pumped body had become a common sight in gay areas of cities. With the increase in drug use throughout the 1970s and 1980s and the rise of large commercial discotheques gay men were dressing to show off their bodies as a matter of course. Images that were on offer in gay magazines and especially in gay pornography offered a well-developed musculature that was almost entirely hairless. This image runs counter to many of the 1970s images of gay muscularity, which emphasised the secondary sexual characteristics, such as hairiness, as a symbol of masculinity.[37]

In direct contrast to the hairless muscleboys another subculture developed known as 'bears'. Reviling the artificiality of the body type developed by the 'buffed baby boys',[38] some gay men gloried in what they perceived as 'real' masculinity – hairiness, big bulky bodies, muscle developed by manual labour rather than in the gym, often a belly (in direct response to the washboard stomach). The Bears' costume drew on the staples of the clones – jeans, plaid shirts, work boots – reflecting (and continuing) the desire to appear to be 'real' men. Bear culture operated almost in direct opposition to the cult of youth that permeated gay culture, and in adopting this image men were accepting and glorying in their ageing bodies. For many the appeal of the bear lay in its perceived masculinity. The overdeveloped bodies of the 'gym queens' were viewed as (almost) effeminate. One man claimed: 'I don't find the muscle mary attractive, because it's almost camp, but I like the bear because often it's a butch version of the muscle queen – it's not all toned. It's big muscles on a working man – he's not gone to the gym, he's been building his muscles on a construction site.'[39] While the fantasy of a working man ran through the iconography of the bear (just as it did with the clones), it was often just a fantasy. Many of these men didn't develop their bodies through manual labour, but were natural big-built. However, the reality of the bear culture was an embracing of the diversity of body type, a move away from the homogenisation of the gay body into what is described as the 'circuit queen' or 'muscle mary.'[40]

In his 1984 observation of gay life in London, *Queens*, the author Pickles described the men he saw in the pubs and clubs of London. One of the 'types' he identifies is the YMCA queen:

> The guy with the wet tousled hair and pink day-pack slung over his pink Lacoste T-shirt is wildly in love with his body... He has just come from the YMCA, where he has just seen enough well-toned bodies to feed his imagination ... Physical jerks stimulate his sex-drive, and his nipples harden at the slightest sense of strain ... He stands, legs apart, shifting his weight self-consciously because he likes to accentuate their shape. So he wears tighter jeans than many YMCA queens, and always tennis shorts in summer ... It is hard to tell whether he looks better on or off the glossy *GQ* page.[41]

This image was to become a new stereotype of gay men by the 1990s, and was criticised as homogenising gay life, which, critics argued, should be based upon a celebration of difference.[42] Toby Manning notes the uniformity of appearance and points out that a 1990s gay 'sensibility' could be said 'to encompass dance music, female comediennes, muscular bodies, designer clothes, Calvin Klein underwear, cappuccino, bottled beers and Ikea furniture'.[43] These are the trappings that the media disseminates as 'official' gay culture in articles noting the importance of the pink pound. An image that had first been appropriated and developed as a positive move away from negative stereotypes, has developed into a new stereotype, a new clone.

Notes

1. *Daddy and the Muscle Academy*, written and directed by Ilppo Pohjola, Filmitakomo Oy, 1991.

2. Martin P. Levine (1998), *Gay Macho: The Life and Death of the Homosexual Clone*, New York, p. 59.

3. Interviewed in *Daddy and the Muscle Academy*, written and directed by Ilppo Pohjola, Filmitakomo Oy, 1991.

4. See Chapter 8.

5. See Chapter 1. In the late nineteenth century the culture of the athlete and its associated muscularity became central to a dominant ideal of manhood. With the rise in popularity of athleticism came publications such as *Physical Culture*, aimed at body-builders and containing photographs of almost naked men in classic Greek poses. In the 1920s these magazines began to feature articles and advertisements, encouraging men to develop their physiques, based on the images in the magazines. Perhaps one of the best-known is Charles Atlas, whose advertisements showed how through his diet and exercise regime a man could transform himself from a 'ninety-pound weakling' into the man of steel in his photographs. For a brief introduction to muscle magazines in the nineteenth and the first half of the twentieth centuries see F. Valentine Hooven, III (1995), *Beefcake: The Muscle Magazines of America 1950–1970*, Cologne, Chapter 1.

6. See Chapter 2.

7. Michael Bronski (1991), 'A Dream is a Wish Your Heart Makes: Notes on the Materialization of Sexual Fantasy', in Mark Thompson (ed.), *Leatherfolk: Radical Sex, People, Politics and Practice*, Boston, MA, p. 60. An examination of the collection of 'beach' photographs held by the National Archive of Lesbian and Gay History in New York reveals a collection of similarly hairless bodies.

8. Martin P. Levine quotes one older man who said 'Just look at these clones, dear. With their pumped-up bodies and thick mustaches, they all look so "butch". But I remember them when everyone was "nelly". What a joke! . . . Over the last few years, I have watched many of these girls change as the times changed. A couple of years ago, they had puny bodies, lisping voices, and elegant clothes. At parties or Tea Dances, they came in dresses, swooning over Garbo and Davis. Now they've 'butched up,' giving up limp wrists and mincing gaits for bulging muscles and manly handshakes, giving up fancy clothes and posh pubs for faded jeans and raunchy discos': Levine, *Gay Macho*, p. 55.

9. For further thoughts on the contradictory ways in which gay men have been viewed as harmless sissies on the one hand and a threat to society on the other see Frank Pearce (1973), 'How to be Immoral and Ill, Pathetic and Dangerous, All at the Same Time: Mass Media and the Homosexual', in Stanley Cohen and Jock Young (eds), *The Manufacture of News: Social Problems, Deviance and the Mass Media*, London.

10. Donald Webster Cory and John P. LeRoy (1963), *The Homosexual and His Society: A View from Within*, New York, p. 83. Drawing on Judith Butler's arguments about gender performativity, Eve Kosofsky Sedgwick has considered the role of shame and shaming in the naming of 'queer': 'for certain ("queer") people, shame is simply the first, and remains a permanent, structuring fact of identity'. While Sedgwick is using 'queer', in its most recent context it applies equally well to those men who perceived themselves as 'queer', i.e. homosexual, in the 1950s. Thus her arguments can be brought into play when viewing the adoption of body-building by gay men

to counteract any association with former stereotypes: Eve Kosofsky Sedgwick (1993), 'Queer Performativity: Henry James's *The Art of the Novel*', in *GLQ*, 1, p. 14.

11. Rodney Garland (1995), *The Heart In Exile*, Brighton, pp. 135–6.

12. Robert J. Lukey (1970), 'Homosexuality in Menswear', *Menswear*, February 1970, p. 72.

13. Daniel Harris (1997), *The Rise and Fall of Gay Culture*, New York, p. 91.

14. The 1980s saw a new rise in grooming products for men, particularly straight men. Advertising and discussion centred around how to market these products to non-gay men and how to dissociate the use of such products from homosexuality. This is now popularly linked to the New Man: see Frank Mort (1996), *Cultures of Consumption: Masculinities and Social Space in Late Twentieth-Century Britain*, London.

15. Charles Hix (1979), *Looking Good: A Guide for Men*, London. 'I remember walking into a bookstore and seeing this book full of colour photos of guys, often really butch muscular guys, clones,' said Andrew Tomlin, 'and sneaking a copy home. I was fourteen. It's what I wanted to look like': Cole interview with Andrew Tomlin, 10 May 1999.

16. Andrew Holleran (1980 [1978]), *Dancer from the Dance*, London, p.113.

17. By the 1970s certain items of swimwear began to be worn off the beach and in the clubs at gay holiday resorts. Tony was given a pair of black-and-white swimming trunks that he had worn on a modelling job. 'I'd wear these [swimming trunks] with this [black lace] shirt', Tony recalled. 'I mean in those days one would go on the beach at ten o'clock [in the morning] and . . . [in the evening] it was straight off to the disco . . . When I went back to London I wore them there as well': Cole interview with Tony, 30 November 1993. Swimwear and underwear are dealt with in more detail in Chapter 10.

18. Keith Howes noted how the singlet became a part of gay erotic iconography through its appearance in such films as *Querelle* and Derek Jarman's *Edward II*. Keith Howes (1994), *Broadcasting It*, London, p. 747. This has continued to be a staple item of gay clothing, as an examination of photographs of venues in the gay press will illustrate.

19. Cole interview with Ray Weller, 26 June 1997. 'As the summer months approach, Butch packs away his T-shirts in mothballs and gets out the tank tops. These are either worn tightly to broadcast stomach definition, or worn loosely, which allows the nipples to play "Hide 'n' seek"': Clark Henley (1982), *The Butch Manual: The Current Drag and How to Do It*, New York, p. 58.

20. Cole interview with Bill Wilson, 10 August 1999. Bruce Weber was the photographer responsible for the images in Charles Hix, *Looking Good*.

21. Cole interview with Bill Wilson, 10 August 1999.

22. James Laver has noted that the increase in leisure time and sporting activity and the adoption of its associated clothing into a non-sporting context has been one of the primary motivators for changes in men's fashion since the eighteenth century: James Laver (1977), *A Concise History of Costume*, London, p. 257.

23. David Holah, one half of BodyMap, was a young trendy gay man who drew some of the inspiration for his designs from the clothes he saw being worn in the gay clubs he frequented.

24. Cole interview with Nick Cook, 27 August 1997.

25. Cole interview with Justin Stubbings, 11 July 1997.

26. Quoted in Frank Mort (1996), *Cultures of Consumption: Masculinities and Social Space in Late Twentieth-Century Britain*, London, p.195.

27. For more details on the transgressive nature of tattooing see David Bell and Gill Valentine (1995), 'The Sexed Self: Strategies of Performance, Sites of Resistance', in Steve Pile and Nigel Thrift (eds), *Mapping the Subject: Geographies of Cultural Transformation*, London and New York and David Curry (1993), 'Decorating the Body Politic', *New Formations*, 19, pp. 69–82. For a history of gay men and tattooing up to 1970 see Phil Sparrow (1970), 'Tattooing and Sex: How Much Do You Reveal About Yourself?', *Vector*, August.

28. Cole interview with Joe Pop, 19 May 1997. For further details on the history and motivation behind tattooing see V. Vale and Andrea Juno (1989), *Modern Primitives: An Investigation of Contemporary Adornment and Ritual*, San Francisco.

29. *Drummer*, no 141, August 1990, p.19.

30. Dennis Altman (1982), *The Homosexualization of America, The Americanization of the Homosexual*, New York, p. 13.

31. John Rechy (1978), *Gay Sunshine*, quoted in Patrick Higgins (1993), *A Queer Reader*, London. Jack Fritscher's 1990 novel *Some Dance to Remember* is the story of gay body-builders living in San Francisco between 1970 and 1982, in what Fritscher calls 'The Golden Age'. The novel concentrates on the interaction between the world of gay clones and that of professional body-builders, emphasising the sexual desirability of men with heavily developed muscular physiques.

32. Cole interview with Justin Stubbings, 11 July 1997.

33. See Carolyn Watts (1995), 'AIDS and the Body', *Rouge*, no. 21, pp.16–19 and Ted Gott (ed.) (1995), *Don't Leave Me This Way: Art in the Age of AIDS*, London.

34. Cole interview with Bill Wilson, 10 August 1999. See Chapter 13 for a description of what Michelangelo Signorile termed 'the new clone' and 'queer' political gay dress of the late eighties and early nineties: Michelangelo Signorile (1990), *Outweek*, 28 November.

35. Harris, *The Rise and Fall of Gay Culture*, p. 35

36. 'If you had the right shortness of hair, and the right moustache and, you know, the right vest and the right boots then that was very attractive . . . I can remember [a friend] meeting somebody and having a date with them and in between the time he'd met them and the date they'd shaved off their moustache and he couldn't go through with the date with them because they'd shaved off their moustache. And that's kind of how narrow it was': Cole interview with Ray Weller, 26 June 1997.

37. In the late 1980s and early 1990s there was a call for images of hairy and big men to be portrayed in pornography, and magazines such as *Drummer* and *Bear* attempted to fulfil this desire.

38. *Drummer*, no. 119 quoted in Harris, *The Rise and Fall of Gay Culture*, p. 105.

39. Cole interview with Andrew Tomlin, 10 May 1999.

40. In London another reaction to the stereotyped hairless, muscular 'disco bunny' has been the emergence of clubs aimed at fatter men, such as Bulk: see Megan Radcliffe (1994), 'The Incredible Bulk', *Independent*, 4 August 1994, p. 16.

41. Pickles (1984), *Queens*, London, pp. 23–4.

42. In 1963 Cory and LeRoy wrote: 'It would be ironic, indeed, if supermasculinity, the cult of the body-builders, the muscle-men and the sports fans, should grow side by side with effeminacy, symbolized by the screaming hairdresser, as the two new stereotypes of the homosexual.' How ironic indeed! (Cory and LeRoy, *The Homosexual and his Society*, p. 91).

43. Toby Manning (1996), 'Gay Culture: Who Needs It?', in Mark Simpson (ed.), *Anti-Gay*, London and New York, p. 106.

10

Down to Basics: Swimwear and Underwear

Whilst this book has prioritised the visible aspects of gay men's clothing, this chapter explores gay men's self-presentation in public spaces and in spaces that, because they had been appropriated by gay men, *became* safe, semi-private spaces. It analyses items of clothing not generally noted as being affected by the sexual orientation of the wearer – underwear. However, in a 'community' or a series of burgeoning communities that were, at the least, conscious of, or, at the most extreme, obsessed by, the male form, both beach wear and underwear play important roles in dress choice.

Studies have shown that the development of men's swimwear (and to some extent men's underwear) has entailed a struggle between nudity and modesty, just as the history of gay dress has entailed a struggle between masculinity and femininity. Because stylistically swimwear is a form of underclothing worn in public, it has epitomised the problematic attitudes to the body that have emerged in Western culture. The sight and site of the body as revealed or alluded to by clothing, has prompted waves of public outrage and hysteria over issues surrounding perceptions of modesty and immodesty.[1] Gay men were challenging ideas and thoughts about the body and about the gender-appropriate disguise or revelation of the body.

One of the locations traditionally associated with gay men displaying their gym bodies is the beach. Cory and LeRoy observed that standard attire for 'the narcissistic and exhibitionistic amongst the homosexuals [was] bikini bathing suits for men, so thin that they are nearly transparent when wet.'[2] These 'outrageous' forms of swimwear were sold in shops that had a gay clientele, well aware of the sensation they could cause in such attire. William Helmer noted the existence of 'A number of smart men's shops in the Village and on the Upper East Side [which] carry bikini type underwear and swimsuits for men, and fancy silk supporters. Swimsuits of this sort cannot be worn on public beaches, but certain parts of Fire Island (and sometimes other beaches) have become the more or less exclusive domain of the gay crowd, and there they have more freedom to dress and behave as they please, and generally "camp it up", i.e. act homosexually without inhibition.'[3]

In *The Face of Fashion*, Jennifer Craik says that 'Trends in swimwear have run parallel to fashions in underwear as well as with other sportswear such as bike pants. The development of men's swimwear featured a concern with modesty that interfered with practical techniques of swimming and, in so doing, sexualised a previously unremarkable garment by drawing attention to the sexual attributes of the body.'[4] Gay men have run counter to this concern with modesty, choosing swimwear (and underwear) that reveals or appears to reveal as much as possible. John Rechy reflected exhibitionism amongst certain gay men in Los Angeles in the early 1960s, who wore bathing suits that were 'made of a flesh-colored material which, when wet, was almost transparent'. One particular 'fairy' in a show of exhibitionism would go into the sea for very brief periods, just long enough to wet his bathing suit, and then stand apparently naked at the water's edge.[5] This type of exhibitionism amongst gay men was also evident in Britain. In a Mass-Observation study on sexual behaviour a group of gay men were observed on a day trip to Brighton. One of them 'Arthur [aged 25, a young musician] first bathed and was then snapped (after Arthur had very carefully draped his body on the towel on the beach) in a pair of excessively brief "briefs" – very small, tight and almost transparent – bought by Arthur in Paris the previous year.'[6] Denis Shorrock recalled the bathing suits he bought in Cannes, which was a popular gay holiday resort in the late 1950s and early 1960s:

I bought up a wardrobe of bikinis because there was a shop there, just off the Croisette, that tailor-made bikinis to fit you and they did literally *fit* you, in terms of the garment fitting and showing all that you had. But the two old blokes there, or one particular one, he liked to actually make sure that he hand-fitted everything. And I suppose I bought about 20 of them, and you couldn't buy anything in England like that, and it was great fun to come back with those. But even for Cannes, the stuff from that sort of place . . . it was exceeding . . . it wasn't out-rageous, it was making a very definite fashion statement about me, that I'm confident . . . that I'm quite confident wearing these and flashing my 'lunch'.[7]

In his history of gay life in New York, George Chauncey noted that, in the 1930s, gay men claimed a certain section of Coney Island beach for them-selves. These gay men did not necessarily have body-builder bodies, and behaviour in the gay section of the beach was notably camp.[8] Gay men were also attracted to the muscle beach section, where they'd view the bodies on show and look for possible sexual partners. John Rechy observed a similar distribution at 'Crystal Beach' in Los Angeles:

the queens in extravagant bathing suits, often candy-striped, molded to the thin bodies – tongued sandals somehow worn like slippers; the masculine-acting, -looking homosexuals with tapered bodies and brown skins exhibiting themselves lying on the sand, trunks rolled down as far as possible – or going near the ocean as if undecided whether to dive in, posing there bikini-ed, flexing their bodies, walking along the long stretch of beach, aware of the eyes which may be focused on them: the older men who sit self-consciously covered as much as the beach-weather allows, hoping perhaps for that evasive union, more difficult to find now – ironically now, when the hunger is more powerful, the shrieking loneliness more demanding; the male-hustlers, usually not in trunks, usually shirtless, barefooted, levis-ed, the rest of their clothes wrapped beside them, awaiting whatever Opportunity may come at any moment, clothes, therefore easily accessible for moving quickly for whatever reason.[9]

The British photographer Bill Green, known professionally as 'Vince', ran a very successful business taking and selling photographs of muscle boys. As in America, genitals had to be covered, and so he developed a posing pouch, which he later went on to sell. This was the beginning of his new business venture, a clothes shop selling underwear, swimwear and form-fitting clothes to, amongst others, more daring straight men and gay men. Green tells his own story:

I used to be in the RAF and when I was in the western desert, we were persuaded by some of the boys on the squadron to start a weight-lifting club, which I did in order to keep fit, and I carried it on after the war when I got demobbed. When I got demobbed I opened a studio, primarily to photograph children and actors and actresses, stage photography in a rather dramatic style, which I like. I used to carry on weight-lifting in a Gymnasium, and one day I was asked to photograph one of the boys at the club, which I did. The result, the dramatic style which I used, was quite popular: magazines started to use the pictures and asked me to photograph other weight-lifters, which I did. Now, these boys used to turn up in rather unsuitable gear to be photographed, so I got a girl friend to make some swimwear which I thought right to photograph these boys in, and I kept them in the studio. They were actually made from women's roll-ons from a well-known chain store. They were cut down and made very comfortable, very slick, very brief, swim shorts, so that the boys could be photographed and would appear well. The result is they all wanted to buy these swim trunks. I had to get these made wholesale, and we sold them. Within six months after that I had to close down the studio, because the business on the swimwear on the mail-order side and people coming in to buy had overwhelmed the whole thing. I was then in business originally selling rather brief, and considered by some people outrageous, swimwear.[10]

Fashions in swimwear for gay men were closely mirrored by choices of underwear. Often the same items were worn both as bathing costumes and underwear. Jennifer Craik argues that the history of men's underwear was almost unseen, as if 'keeping men's underclothes plain and functional could secure male bodies as a bulwark against unrestrained sexuality'.[11] Until the advent of Y-fronts in 1939, men's underwear consisted of loose shirts, singlets, long johns and drawers that revealed little of the body's form. Y-fronts were revolutionary in that, owing to the way the fly was angled for modesty when urinating in public, the seams drew attention to the male genitals. This held an obvious appeal for gay men, who had less qualms about drawing attention to their genitals than straight men. Dennis remembered the appeal of Y-fronts when he first saw them:

> During the war you didn't wear underclothes because you couldn't get them. I didn't wear any underclothes until I was about eighteen, when I got my first pair of Y-fronts, which I thought were ever so outrageous. I'd seen them advertised in American magazines, because they came over from America. Apart from that all you had was horrible flannel things that were nasty, anyway, and revolting. And when I finally got these Y-fronts, I thought they were fabulous.[12]

Shops whose target audience was gay men were selling underwear that was even more revealing than Y-fronts. Bill Green was selling his posing brief, developed for physique models as underwear; and in Brighton:

> Phil and Ken sold casual shirts, jackets, trousers and underbriefs, which were brief underbriefs like they wear them today, which were very daring in those days. They used to make them out of odd materials. They had a whole range of them done in cotton gingham, those red gingham squares and blue gingham squares, and they used to be all tailored, and the pouch was shaped at the front with a seam down it ... It was very daring to wear their sort of clothes, you didn't find it anywhere else. The nearest thing to their underwear were Y-fronts which were quite big, but these were proper briefs with sides. They used to make them in several sizes, they used to make dozens of them.[13]

Kevin remembered another shop in Carnaby Street that produced skimpy underwear bought predominantly by gay men:

> There was a men's boutique in the Carnaby Street area called Carnaby Male. They brought out a line of men's underwear, briefs in various colours. Today they are everywhere, but until then men had worn bulky and unattractive underwear, forever white or off-white. The boutique manager knew his market, gays flocked to buy them, so much so that a leaflet was inserted in the packaging inviting the purchaser to join the Carnaby Male Club. For a small subscription one would receive a

newsletter with contact ads . . . Eventually Carnaby Male decided it wanted to distance itself from the organization – perhaps there had been complaints from straight men into fancy underwear – and from then on it was known as CMC.[14]

American shops and underwear manufacturers, too, were selling a wide range of revealing underwear and swimwear to a specifically gay market. The first advertisement to appear in a gay magazine was for a diaphanous satin nightshirt and see-through nylon harem pants available from 'WINMOR of California', which appeared in *One* in October 1954. In 1965 Regency Square of Hollywood offered over twenty different styles of underwear, from the 'male pouch. This next to nothing – but complete cover up – offers the maximum support with a minimum of brief' to 'contour shorts, cut low and contoured to fit – the only fit that shows you at your best', all of which were shown on drawn or photographed models heavily influenced by Tom of Finland's work and physique magazine photography. Other companies, including The Town Squire, Ah Men and Parr of Arizona, sold garments specifically designed to appeal to a gay consumer market, offering one of the earliest visual representations of a distinctly gay subculture.[15] The increasing fashionability of tight trousers during this period (discussed in Chapter 5) led to an increased demand for brief underwear that did not wrinkle under the trousers, allowing them to follow the contours of the wearer's body unimpeded. In April 1969 the fashion page of *Vector* recorded that the 'run on such underwear is so strong that The Town Squire has had a difficult time keeping one of their briefest, Immenence, a French Import, in stock'.[16] In the catalogues for Vince Man's Shop the names that were given to the clothes in the catalogues indicated knowledge of gay language and holiday resorts. Green must have had his gay clients in mind when naming his swimwear ranges, as many of the styles were named after gay holiday destinations – 'Tangier', 'Mallorca', 'Capri' (in 1963), and 'Bondi Beach' (1964) and 'Bondi Bathers' (1965). The 1967 catalogue illustrated the 'Ibiza' and 'Fire Island' shirts, again named after well-known gay resorts.[17]

The sexual appeal of underwear was important to gay men, and not just to those who were building their physiques into a Charles Atlas perfect man. Daniel, who was by his own admission effeminate and of slight build, knew his own sexual appeal, and played on this when he was working as a nurse by carefully selecting his underwear. 'Of course the underwear one wore was nylon, see-through, you know, we never went in for butch jockey shorts or anything like that, but those were nice', he recalled. 'The guys used to go to pieces 'cause they used to run their hands over my buttocks and all that and feel the nylon silk, you know. I was, very very naughty. I used to tease them a lot about it – that was my undoing, of course.'[18]

With the fashion revolution of the late 1960s men's underwear underwent a process of heterosexualisation. Fancy underwear was no longer targeted at gay men, and it was now acceptable for men to wear underwear other than conventional white jockey shorts or Y-fronts or boxer shorts. Skimpier brightly coloured briefs began to be produced by the major underwear companies and were overtly promoted for their erotic connotations, as what Valerie Steele calls 'a prelude to sexual intimacy, the attraction of concealment, and the libido for looking (and touching)'.[19] Magazine advertisements of the 1970s market underwear as a means of sexualising the body to attract members of the opposite sex.[20] With the hypermasculine posturing of the clones it became *de rigueur* not to wear underwear but to allow the genitals to be displayed through the tight-fitting worn denim of jeans. Clark Henley's *Butch Manual* confirms that 'Butch knows a con game when he sees one, and he is certainly not being fooled by the underwear industry. *Underwear is completely unnecessary*, and only gets in the way.'[21] Underwear did however continue to hold its sexual attraction for gay men, and its increasing eroticisation led to the instigation of events such as underwear parties at gay clubs, which continued to grow in popularity throughout the 1980s. Armistead Maupin's fictionalised account of life in San Francisco in the 1970s recounts such an occasion – the jockey shorts dance contest at the End Up night-club: 'Five contestants had already vied for the hundred-dollar prize. Another was competing now, thrashing across the plastic dance floor in nylon leopard-skin briefs . . . Michael chided himself silently for selecting the standard white jockey briefs. This mob obviously went in for flash . . . [but] An hour later he got the news. He had won.'[22]

The adoption of 'flashy' underwear by heterosexual men precipitated a move for gay men back towards plain white underwear. Such garments were the least likely to detract from what they were trying to reveal while keeping it concealed. In 1982 Calvin Klein erected an enormous billboard in New York's Times Square advertising his men's white briefs. It was an overtly sexual image of a perfectly formed muscular man wearing nothing but white underwear. The nods towards homoerotic imagery were overt.[23] Klein's billboard has been credited with a heralding a new era in the imagery of men in advertising, and with precipitating a new fashion in men's underwear. This campaign ran just a few years before the revolution in men's magazine production and advertising, which resexualised the male form as a hairless muscular object of sexual desire. Pictures by photographers such as Bruce Weber and Herb Ritts enhanced their homoerotic appeal.[24] By the beginning of the 1990s Calvin Klein white cotton briefs were the most popular item of underwear for gay men, enhanced by the use of increasingly sexual images such as the 1992 campaign featuring the rap star Marky Mark. The image of the muscular tanned gay body clad in white (or black or grey, varying from season to season) Calvin Klein (or one of the other seasonably fashionable brands, such as 2xist or Armani) has become one of the overriding images of gay men in the final decade of the twentieth century.

Notes

1. See Jennifer Craik (1994), *The Face of Fashion: Cultural Studies in Fashion*, London, p. 136.

2. Donald Webster Cory and John P. LeRoy (1963), *The Homosexual and His Society: A View from Within*, New York, p. 135.

3. William J. Helmer (1963), 'New York's "Middle-class" Homosexuals', *Harpers*, vol. 226, March, pp. 85–92.

4. Craik, *The Face of Fashion*, p.141.

5. John Rechy (1964), *City of Night*, New York, p. 229. In 1968 Bill Green was the first to make wet-look swim trunks. He got the idea from a pair of gloves he saw a woman wearing made from a wet-look fabric, and 1965 saw the introduction of 'Black Leather Briefs for sunbathing only. Bikini style in soft leather', possibly a recognition of the growing interest in leather as a fabric for clothing other than jackets, but also an indication of awareness of the use of leather for fetish clothing for gay men, especially in America.

6. Mass-Observation, Sex Survey Article 1 Sexual Behaviour, Box 4, File E, Appendix 1, Abnormality. 6.7.49.

7. Cole interview with Denis Shorrock, 11 August 1997.

8. George Chauncey draws attention to the fact that gay men sometimes put on a 'show' (that outpaced the shows at clubs in Greenwich Village and Harlem) for other beachgoers, turning their towels into dresses and fancy hats, swishing down the beach, kicking up their heels. Chauncey quotes from a report of a male beauty contest held at Coney Island's Washington Baths in the summer of 1929 in *Variety* magazine: '[One] pretty guy pranced before the camera and threw kisses to the audience,' the reporter, who was also a judge, wrote. 'One man came in dressed as a woman.' Chauncey remarks on the confidence with which gay men moved in these claimed spaces, enough to wear make-up and act camp; he also highlights the humorous way in which the event is reported. George Chauncey (1994), *Gay New York: Gender, Urban Culture and the Making of the Gay Male World, 1890–1940*, New York, pp. 183–4.

9. Rechy, *City of Night*, p. 212. The men's beach in Brighton, on the south coast of England, attracted large numbers of gay men. See Brighton Ourstory Project (1992), *Daring Hearts: Lesbian and Gay Lives of 50s and 60s Brighton*, Brighton.

10. Bill 'Vince' Green on 'Gear Street', part of the 'South-East Special' series, broadcast 22 August 1964.

11. Craik, *The Face of Fashion*, pp. 121–2.

12. Brighton Ourstory Project, *Daring Hearts*, p. 52.

13. Ibid., p. 53.

14. Quoted in National Lesbian and Gay Survey (1993), *Proust, Cole Porter, Michelangelo, Marc Almond and Me: Writings by Gay Men on their Lives and Lifestyles*, London, p. 57.

15. These magazines also served another purpose, that of soft-core pornography. In the absence of other images of naked men they were avidly consumed, especially by men living outside major metropolitan centres: see Daniel Harris (1997), *The Rise and Fall of Gay Culture*, Boston, p. 162. Peter Burton reflected that Vince catalogues 'could *almost* be classified as an early gay magazine': Peter Burton (1985), *Parallel Lives*, London, p. 30.

16. Gale Whittington (1969), 'Fashion . . . The Male's Emergence', *Vector* (April), p. 16.

17. The catalogues also showed a familiarity with *polari* (the underground gay language) that to the unsuspecting would have seemed perfectly innocent. Swimtrunks called '*Butch*' and '*Trade* Wind' and a jacket called 'Sun *Cruiser*' all illustrate this familiarity. *Polari* (Parlare) was a British underground slang associated with the gay community. It was probably derived from the language of eighteenth- and nineteenth-century theatre and showpeople, as well as from a version of Romany known as 'parlyaree'. The version known to gay men appears to have been passed on through the merchant navy. It drew words not only from theatre slang and romance languages but also from cockney rhyming slang, back slang and Yiddish. In the 1960s *polari* was popularised by Julian and Sandy and the radio programme, *Round the Horne*. In *polari Butch* meant Masculine, *Cruising*, looking for sex and *Trade* referred to men who were sexually available, though not necessarily homosexual.

18. Cole interview with Daniel, 20 May 1997.

19. Valerie Steele (1989), 'Clothing and Sexuality', in C. Kidwell and Valerie Steele (eds), *Men and Women: Dressing the Part*, Washington DC, p. 56.

20. See especially those adverts for Fruit of the Loom underwear. The presence of women in the catalogues for Ah Men's underwear also highlights this process of heterosexualisation. One token, not particularly sexually portrayed, woman shown indulging in a 'camp' scenario with a group of (gay) men was replaced by the late 1970s by a buxom beach 'babe', who was the focus of attention of the men in the shot. This also served to heterosexualise the gaze of the viewer by drawing attention away from the (homoerotic portrayals) of the male models.

21. Clark Henley (1982), *The Butch Manual: The Current Drag and How to Do It*, New York, p. 66.

22. Armistead Maupin (1988), *Tales of the City*, London, pp. 166–7.

23. On being questioned about the homoerotic appeal of their advertising , a spokesperson for Calvin Klein stated, 'We did not *try* to appeal to gays. We try to appeal, period. If there's an awareness in that community of health and grooming, then they'll respond to the ads': Karen Stabiner (1982), 'Tapping the Homosexual Market', *The New York Times Magazine*, 2 May, p. 34.

24. These images and advertising campaigns also served to create a new image of heterosexual man and increase his role as a consumer of fashion and grooming products. Manufacturers, advertisers and commentators strove to disassociate these forms of consumption from homosexuality. This phenomenon has been described as the rise of the New Man. See amongst others Frank Mort (1996), *Cultures of Consumption: Masculinities and Social Space in Late Twentieth Century Britain*, London; and Sean Nixon (1992), 'Have You Got the Look? Masculinities and Shopping Spectacle', in R. Shields, *Lifestyle Shopping: The Subject of Consumption*, London, pp. 149–69.

11

Trash, Glamour, Punk

In 1976 punk appeared on the streets of London and New York as an opposition subculture that expressed the estrangement from society experienced by youth in the 1970s. The early punk subculture in both America and Britain had developed as 'a reaction against the massive commercialization of both music and fashion for the young',[1] and was characterised by anti-commercialism and anti-romanticism. Whereas British punk was a working-class response to economic depression and authoritarian ideology, in America it was more a middle-class expression of alienation from and disgust with mainstream values. Punk had similar origins in both London and New York, arising out of an alternative, disaffected scene of young people who embraced and encouraged difference and individuality. It was this that attracted gay men (and women) to, and made them important players in, the formulation of punk.

In New York the scene that had developed around Andy Warhol's Factory, with its transvestites, transsexuals and rent boys, gave rise to a whole new music and fashion scene, based at the bar, Max's Kansas City, and later at the Mercer Arts Centre and the CBGBs night-club. This art-based music scene gave rise to what became known as the glitter scene, and evolved into punk. Legs McNeil noted that:

> Glitter rock was about decadence: platform shoes and boys in eye makeup, David Bowie and androgyny. Rich rock stars living their lives from Christopher Isherwood's *Berlin Stories*, you know, Sally Bowles hanging out with drag queens, drinking champagne for breakfast . . . Decadence seemed so lame, because decay suggests that there's still some time, and there wasn't any more time . . . Compared to what was going on in the real world, decadence seemed kind of quaint. So punk wasn't about decay, punk was about the apocalypse. Punk was about annihilation.[2]

A magazine that discussed music and other issues important to this group of young people was started. The magazine was named *Punk*, a popular term of abuse that summed up the attitudes of the writers and the target audience. In issue three of *Punk* Peter Crowley pointed out to readers the origins of the term. Punk was prison slang for 'the boys who gave up their ass to the "wolves"'.[3]

It was soon 'cool' for rock stars 'to paint up and wear glitter and outrageous clothes'. As homo- or bi-sexuality was a part of the whole glitter or glam world, it quickly became 'hip' in the music world. Jayne County points out 'that being gay and bisexual had always been taboo in rock, but it got pushed through from the underground scene, into the rock world'.[4] David Bowie, influenced by this New York underground scene, announced his bisexuality, and others followed suit. Alice Cooper, who was straight, allowed people to think he was gay because it was fashionable to 'act queer'. In her auto-biography, Jayne County recalls Alice Cooper's gig at Max's Kansas City, where Cooper wore 'false eyelashes, garish make-up, a woman's yellow and pink flowered dress and leather trousers. Someone in the audience yelled "Queer!" at Alice, and he just looked at them and went, 'Hmmmm . . . you'd better believe it, honey . . . [5] Leee Black Childers pointed out that 'gay people make up much of the audience'.[6] In an article on 'gay rock' in the *Advocate* in 1982 Adam Block confirms the popularity of glitter or glam rock and the sexual experimentation that was associated with it:

I was back in the States by '73, primed to watch glitter-rock sweep the continent. Lou Reed scored with 'Take a Walk on the Wild Side', and suddenly there were addicts, transvestites and hustlers lounging in the Top 20. Ziggy Stardust toured, while critics raved about the outrageousness androgyny of The New York Dolls. Fourteen-year-old boys were filching their mommie's mascara as Bowie sang Rebel, rebel, how could they know? Hot tramp, I love you so.[7]

The groups who were leading the punk movement in America, such as Wayne County and the Electric Chairs (who were 'taking sexuality to the extreme'), were often gay or ambivalent about their sexual preferences, dressed in 'genderfuck'-style drag, and sometimes sang about gay sex. The New York Dolls, one of the earliest bands to develop out of the CBGBs club scene, were dressing in a form of drag that they described as 'Puerto Rican sluts', and promoting 'polymorphous pan-sexuality'. This look owed much to the transvestites and transsexuals of Andy Warhol's Factory. When Leee Black Childers interviewed The New York Dolls for *Melody Maker* in 1970 'they were all in women's clothes and make-up. Women's clothes were especially cool then . . . I thought they were all gay. I was wrong, of course. But they were . . . very funny, which is more important to me than a woman's blouse, or hetero, or homosexual, which I thought they were, because they talked very gay. They were playing gay.'[8] The New York Dolls' style of dress at this point was heavily influenced by the 'two most famous downtown drag queens' and cohorts of Andy Warhol, Jackie Curtis and Candy Darling. Jayne County describes Jackie Curtis as

> a hip drag queen, [who] took everything to extremes. She walked around in ripped stocking and big tears in her dresses with threads hanging off . . . she had that combination of trash and glamour . . . a lot of her dresses were from the 30s and 40s, things that she'd pick up from thrift stores for 25 cents . . . she wore old-lady shoes that she sprayed silver, and her tights were always ripped . . . No one thought [she and Candy Darling] were women, no one thought they were men! No one knew what they were![9]

It was this mixture of trash and glamour that the New York Dolls adopted and adapted as their gimmick. It was this 'wonderful transvestite-type group' that so impressed Malcolm McLaren when he went to New York in the early 1970s. As the self-proclaimed founder of English punk, McLaren took his experiences of managing the New York Dolls and the things he saw on this American Punk scene and incorporated them into his ideas for the shop, called Sex, which he ran with his wife Vivienne Westwood, and into his ideas for forming and managing a new band, the Sex Pistols.

While the New York Dolls and Jayne County were following styles, if they could be called styles, set by transvestites and drag queens, other punks were looking to a more masculine deviant image. The Ramones wore the ripped jeans and skimpy T-shirts worn by cheap hustlers who worked the corner of 53rd Street and Third Avenue in New York. Their acknowledgement of the influence of hustling was evident when they sang a song called '53rd and 3rd', which was based on Dee Dee Ramone's experience of working as a male prostitute.[10]

In London the clubs where the proto-punks met were gay and lesbian clubs in Soho, the most famous being Louise's on Greek Street. Into what was described in the popular press of the time as the 'seedy twilight world of the homosexual' stepped the disillusioned kids from the suburbs. This was a mixed group in which 'no one was criticized for their sexual preferences' and 'the only thing that was looked down upon was suburbia . . . it was small and narrow-minded'.[11] Louise's club was discovered by Siouxsie (later to become the singer with punk band Siouxsie and the Banshees), who introduced it to her friends because they were accepted there – no one cared once they had paid their entrance fee. Debbie Wilson, one of London's earliest Punks, says 'People think that the early days of Punk were all banging along at Sex Pistols gigs, but for me it was camping it up and down Park Lane with a gang of trannies . . . it was the most outrageous place in the world. All these queens going around in Punk gear and black leather going "Ooooooh!".'[12]

Punk was a time of freedom for many, especially young gay people. Not only was it liberating to be able to dress up: groups such as the anarcho-punks were encouraging thinking about sexual politics, and the first punk groups or cliques were made up of 'lesbians, gay men, transvestites, prostitutes, midgets. It was like a carnival, like a bizarre carnival of people, bizarre people, every combination you can imagine, subterranean people, every combination you can imagine, the sleaziest people, drug dealers, everything.'[13] Jordan, an early Punk and shop assistant at *Sex*, believed that punks 'are not as bigoted as their peers. They are more awake and are going to accept ideas which are generally accepted as anti-social.'[14]

Jon Savage identifies that in 1976 London's gay scene was still in the 'wedge' era, just before the rigid separatism of the clone look. Amongst teenagers, he points out, the softer wedge hairstyles (as opposed to the clones' crop that was to develop into an important part of gay men's images for the next two decades) and outrageous camping proclaimed their difference and their liberation from the world of work. George O'Dowd (later to become pop star Boy George) described the gay hairdressers at Vidal Sassoon as 'spindly queens with wedge haircuts and jumpers [sweaters] tied around their shoulders'.[15] Berlin, one of the now infamous Bromley crowd, describes the (gay) clubs he and his group frequented: 'We'd go to Chageramas, a dingy dive where the worst transvestites went and all these businessmen. There was the Masquerade in Earls Court . . . There was the Sombrero. I can't tell you the parallels between those days and *Goodbye to Berlin*. We were living it out, the whole bit.'[16] The first gay club George O'Dowd went to was Bangs, a Monday night gay club on Charing Cross Road. After being turned away from a soul night at the Lyceum Ballroom, off the Strand, 'a swishy boy in rubber trousers threw us a lifeline "Why don't you come to Bangs. You can wear what you like there."' There, amongst the 'shirtless queens in white shorts, jiving, high-kicking, and flicking their wedges. Older men with Zapata 'staches [swinging] their sweat drenched T-shirts above their heads' were other punks, including the 'punk legend' Sue Catwoman.[17] While the clubs that the first punks were frequenting were gay clubs, Simon Barker observed that 'Punk wasn't necessarily a sexual thing: it was something that enticed people . . .'.[18] Jonathan Jackson reiterates this sentiment: 'I mean I always knew I was gay, that wasn't really relevant for dressing like a punk. That wasn't the attraction of it at all: it was wanting to look different from everyone else but the same as the people I thought were where it was at.'[19] Joe Pop states that it was 'the curse of David Bowie' that encouraged experimentation with dress and to some extent sexual identity:

> Basically we were blighted, and for me, the way I looked . . . I didn't really equate anything to do with sexuality. I didn't see anything in the way I looked, I didn't

realise that it wasn't sexy until quite a long time afterwards; but then I wasn't trying to be sexy. I saw it as being exotic and decorative . . . felt exotic and glamorous, but not sexy.[20]

Before punk established itself fully, there was a distinct look worn by gay teenagers, who did not want to become part of what was on offer on the gay scene, and the 'weirder straight teenagers' who were later to become punks. This, like the New York punk look, drew on rent boys' style, borrowing their 'Rent Boy Red' hair colour for their exaggerated wedge hairstyles. Joe Pop was one such teenager, who had 'what was called a beret cut, which was very short on one side, dyed bright orange . . . it was this big wedged hairdo and when it was done properly it looked like a sort of spaceship on my head'. The clothes that made up this pre-punk look he described as:

the most uncomfortable clothes in fashion ever. Mohair jumpers, which I'm allergic to. I had one in pastel pink and then I used to wear Osh Kosh jeans, blue and white pinstripe ones that had little pockets on the side and then the most ridiculous thing for the feet imaginable. Lurex socks, which are like wearing a cheese grater, 'cause they've got little strips of metal rubbing your feet, and plastic sandals.[21]

This was also the look favoured by soul boys. Isaac Julien's black (gay) soul boys in his film *Young Soul Rebels* (1991) wear similar clothes. George O'Dowd describes the 'soul look' favoured at the Black Prince in Bexleyheath as 'Smith's American jeans, bright-coloured combed-out mohair jumpers, wraparound shades, and winklepickers'. He goes on to describe how the 'more full-on types were starting to wear plastic bags and trousers, feather earrings, safety pins on their clothes and in their ears'.[22] The new punk look was an obvious move from the earlier look, allowing the participants a free rein in what they wore.

A look that was adopted by the gay proto-punks not interested in the soul boy look was influenced by the interest in the 1950s. Westwood and McLaren's shop *Let it Rock* (as *Sex* was previously named) had sold teddy boy clothes and other 1950s paraphernalia. Jonathan Jackson recalls it was:

the first time I really remember identifying with something . . . I went to work in Kensington High Street, and it was right at the beginning of when punk had first started, and Johnsons had just opened in Kensington Market, and it used to be a second-hand clothing place then, and everybody used to kind of wear old retro jeans, fifties, it was a kind of fifties-inspired look. And I can remember the first thing that I remember buying where I looked really different to everybody where I lived. It was when people were still wearing flares, and I'd gone off to a shop in Lewisham that was called Paraphernalia, and they sold fifties pegs, and I'd seen some boys up in Kensington Market wearing fifties pegs and a short-sleeved kind of fifties shirt and those plastic sandals that are now called jellies, and I can remember I must have been fifteen going to an evening at school and I wore these jellies and these zoot suit trousers and this short-sleeved shirt that I thought was the absolute business and everyone thought I was the most outrageous thing, because they had flared trousers, platform shoes, you know. No one wore trousers that went in and were narrow.[23]

David Bowie exerted a huge influence upon the youth of the 1970s. This was especially true of boys who were just beginning to address feelings of homosexuality. In his biography *A Bone in my Flute* Holly Johnson (who was later to achieve fame as the openly gay lead singer of the pop group Frankie Goes to Hollywood) explains the importance of David Bowie:

It was not enough to play 'Ziggy Stardust and the Spiders from Mars' full blast on the teak radiogram. Honey Heath and I had to embrace the lifestyle of the then 'openly bisexual' pop star . . . The record had a huge effect on kids of my generation, not just the homosexual ones. Bisexuality became a fashionable pose, along with the idea of androgyny in fashion. Small pockets of girls and boys (especially of the apprentice hairdresser variety) all over the country started to experiment with their appearance as a direct result of the current fashions in Pop music. Bowie, Roxy Music, Alice Cooper *et al.*[24]

A Teddy Boy interviewed at the time punks were first seen on the streets said that to him punks 'look effeminate, they look like some third sex. They look like invaders from another planet or something.'[25] Joe Pop echoes the teddy boy's 'alien' description: 'Basically [gay men] all suffer the curse of Bowie. Mine was being an alien, a transsexual alien. That's all we wanted to be, really, a transsexual space alien.'[26] David Bowie influenced many (gay) teenagers, such as George O'Dowd and Jonathan Jackson, who became punks, and their pre-punk looks were influenced by Bowie's ever-evolving personas.

Gay punks were drawing upon the androgyny and gender play made visible by Bowie, Marc Bolan and Roxy Music to express their formulating of their identities. Like the radical drag queens of the early 1970s the young gay punks wanted to challenge society, to make people stare in confusion and shock. Thornton and Evans emphasise the adoption of traditional trappings of masculinity by female punks, who were seeking to look 'tough, menacing and threatening', their manipulation of 'the illicit iconography of sexual fetishism'[27] and use of dress to attack traditional concepts of acceptable and mainstream female dress. Within this context it is interesting to note the influence of the key female punk figures such as Siouxsie, as opposed to the male role models such as the Sex Pistols, on the dress choices and style of gay punks. Seeing David Bowie kindled an interest in Jonathan Jackson's appearance that had hitherto been unawakened: 'I can remember being very young and wanting to look like David Bowie in his Ziggy Stardust days and I can remember that you know a few of us . . . had reddish hair all standing up on the top and long down the back.'[28] David Bowie was also an early inspiration for George O'Dowd. When Bowie returned from his self-imposed exile in Berlin in 1976 George was there with hundreds of other fans to welcome back his hero. 'Bowie had abandoned the drag of Ziggy Stardust for the Thin White Duke: slicked back hair, white shirt, and pegged trousers. I copied the look, wore one of my Dad's white shirts, and greased down my hair.'[29] The New York Warhol crowd (perhaps via David Bowie, who had worked with Warhol and written a song included on his 1973 album Aladdin Sane) also had an influence on the teenagers who were to become London's first punks. Berlin describes how 'we'd go round [Steve Severin's] house and listen to Velvet Underground. In a way, Siouxsie mirrored herself on all those pop stars, Nico and Patti Smith, and Severin modelled himself on John Cale, Lou Reed, which is where he got the name Severin from: "Venus in Furs".'[30]

Gay punks developed their own style. There was a less macho edge than in the popular perception of punk clothing, which developed once the Sex Pistols began to achieve fame and other Punk bands sprang up. Jon Savage identifies this point, that the Sex Pistols':

> link with the subterranean sexual world would be conveniently forgotten once the music they played became part of the music industry and once the people that actively supported them and contributed to the package became mere 'fans'. Once defined, the Sex Pistols became a Rock band and Rock bands are not usually tolerant of homosexuality, either in their music or in the way they are treated by the media. Just as in New York, ambiguity would turn to disavowal and then under the wrong conditions, prejudice.[31]

Joe Pop records that early on punk had a less harsh, macho edge – the looks were based more on androgyny: 'Punk very early was all about poofs and women basically, that Bowie-inspired sort of thing, and basically if you look at it as being a polarization of butch and femme, if you like, or Bowie and not Bowie. Basically were you for the Banshees or the Clash, do you know what I mean?'[32] Punk women had for the most part rejected conventional notions of feminine beauty, mocking sexist stereotypes through exaggeration, inversion and parody. As Daniel Wojcik identifies 'themes of sexual ambiguity and gender confusion were explored by members of both sexes through their body adornment'.[33] This embracing of an asexual nature upset conventional ideas about displays of masculinity and femininity in much the same way that gay liberationists (male and female) had challenged boundaries and conventions by their combining of male and female clothing.

The gay punk look could be viewed as a continuation of glam rock: the over-the-top clothes and make-up and the insistence on bisexuality. The hero(ine)s and sartorial inspiration were David Bowie, Marc Bolan and Siouxsie Sioux. Punk, for many young gay men, was about dressing up, wearing make-up and having 'big hair'. 'Boys were all wearing make-up; I had this big hair and only a few girls had hair like this', recalled Joe Pop: 'I dressed up like mad and wore loads of make-up.'[34] Jonathan Jackson recalled the clothes that were popular amongst the gay punks:

> One of my favourite things, and I remember it took me absolutely ages to get it, was the dreaded mohair jumper. I mean, it was just the thing at the time; it didn't much else matter what else you wore, as long as you had a mohair jumper, you know, preferably in a huge bright colour. Most of the time then it was kind of a very narrow-legged black jeans, skin-tight, pointed, like, suede or leather winkle-picking boots and then a mohair jumper on the top, with hair that was . . . very long but all standing up and out at right angles; loads of black make-up round your eyes kind of look, and a deathly white face . . . When David Bowie did that Earls Court tour when he had those pleated trousers with about eight pleats at the top and went really narrow at the bottom . . . I remember that I had them on with a pair of those punk suede boots with the seam up the front, very pointed. It was probably with a great big mohair jumper on top of that, looking utterly out of place for Bangs.[35]

Vivienne Westwood and Malcolm McLaren, the self-proclaimed inventors of punk, appropriated gay pornographic imagery to adorn the clothing that they sold in their shop, Sex. Clothes worn by gay men, and particularly those worn by leathermen, were also adapted for sale at their shop. Vivienne Westwood later commented that Malcolm McLaren 'thought the best way to confront the English Society was to be as overtly obscene and pornographic as possible'.[36] In the early seventies the radical drag queens and other members of the GLF had staged demonstrations and street theatre events that often verged on the pornographic, and were designed to challenge British sensibilities. McLaren had been in New York at the beginning of the seventies, and had associated himself with the New York punk scene that was growing out of Andy Warhol's Factory. Hebdige identified two principal signifiers of punk: nihilism, or blankness, and, more importantly to this study, sexual deviance or kinkiness.[37] Daniel Wojcik comments that 'forbidden and deviant connotations were especially evoked by the punk use of the entire repertoire of bondage wear and sexual fetishism'. The flaunting of sadomasochistic accessories and sexual imagery served primarily to 'shock, threaten or expose culturally constructed ideas about "deviancy" rather than to entice'.[38] Vivienne Westwood and Malcolm McLaren borrowed designs from the gay S/M scene – a shirt was made with straps resembling those of a leather body harness – and printed images of gay sex on their T-shirts.

> In 1973 we renamed the shop 'Too Fast to Live, Too Young to Die'. We were thinking of images like *Rebel Without a Cause*. Also about Kenneth Anger's *Scorpio Rising*. This added homosexual and pornographic undercurrents to biker imagery. We also became interested in rubber and fetish clothing. The research we did for this led us into an underground fetish and sadomasochistic world. In those days not many people knew about that sort of thing. Malcolm found some under the counter catalogues with examples of weird fetish-wear items and we started to crossbreed the biker look with fetish wear.[39]

Joe Pop describes the T-shirt he used to wear: 'I had a Vivienne Westwood porno T-shirt, I used to troll to school at 15 with a fistfucking sailors T-shirt.'[40]

In the early days of punk the gay scene had accepted the new punk crowd who were dressing unconventionally. As the punk movement became more established, punks were less accepted on the gay scene: 'Gays were as straight as the straights. We were bad-news queers, refusing to abide by their unspoken code of discretion.'[41] The punks were seen as an intrusive, noisy, brash crowd interested in dressing up and causing outrage rather than the sex, drugs and disco music that were a particularly important part of the gay and especially the Clone world. Clones' gay fashion consciousness, according to Boy George 'amounted to check shirts, white vests, and jeans. Predatory fashions to show off the balls and biceps.'[42] New York's gay scene was dominated by the same fashions. Legs McNeil noted that by 1977:

> Gay Liberation had really exploded. Homosexual culture had really taken over – Donna Summer, disco, it was so boring. Suddenly in New York, it was cool to be gay, but it just seemed to be about suburbanites who sucked cock and went to discos ... So we said, 'No, being gay doesn't make you cool. Being cool makes you cool, whether you're gay or straight.' People didn't like that too much. So they called us homophobic ... But as far as us being homophobic that was ludicrous, because everyone we hung out with was gay.[43]

This attitude also had to do with music as well as fashion. In 1978 Andrew Kopkind reported that: 'No one hates punk worse than a gay disco purist and no one has more venom for disco than a gay punk.'[44] Adam Block, however, held an opposing view. Punk, he said did appeal to gay men, and the experiences of young gay men in London reinforce his view. Block noted that 'Homos who had grown up in the 60s flocked to both [the disco and the punk] scenes. But if disco was upwardly mobile and coolly hedonistic, punk was downwardly mobile and aggressively nihilistic. Though both developed in alternative "fringe" music scenes, they came to view each other as the enemy.'[45] As disco became the music of the gay scene and the clone became the dominant way to dress, gay punks were left feeling in limbo. Gay punks were 'rejecting both the mainstream rock and the mainstream gay scenes. They were creating an arena that welcomed sexual ambiguity, revolt. They were also a declaration against mainstream gay stereotypes.'[46] Joe Pop's experience reiterates this experience of gay clubs: 'We were a bit too weird, we weren't that loud but we weren't well behaved, and often it was more a case of we'd make half a lager last all night, so we were either asked to leave or we just didn't feel right in them.'[47] As punk became more popular and more developed, it lost its tolerant attitudes. The dilemma for young gay punks like Pop was whether to go to the straight punk clubs where people dressed similarly and listened to the same music but disapproved of his sexuality, or to go to commercial gay clubs aimed at clones, where gay punks were now not welcome. Phillip Salon was physically thrown out of gay clubs for not conforming to the approved gay images.[48] In an article on Punk in *Gay News* in 1978 Faebhean Kwest expressed his sadness at the gay scene's indifference to Punk, considering that:

> the thing itself developed in the gay clubs. Punk, its music, its fashions and its attitudes [had] much to offer gays who [didn't] fit into the gay scene in any shape or form . . . many of the gay punks [who were 15 or 16 in 1978 were] not afraid of telling people that they are gay any more. The gay scene in Liverpool and London had nothing for me. There's a lot of gay kids, gay punks that are as rough and as common as muck and they're all on the dole or working in factories. They're just not into 'polare' or drag or this 1930s fucking talk; they can't relate to all that. It's 1978. It's the New Wave.[49]

Holly Johnson noted that what had been exclusively gay looks began to be seen on the straight boys in the punkier clubs: 'It was strange going to a straight club and seeing straight boys starting to dress up. They may have been liberal enough to wear unusual clothes and a bit of eyeliner, but they were still a bit uncomfortable about real live Queers.'[50] Faebhean Kwest echoes Johnson's observations, stating:

> One of the first places that the Sex Pistols played was a [gay] club called Louise's. And now you see all these people wearing the leather and the plastic and the rubber at punk concerts . . . well, you'll see exactly the same thing in the gay pubs like the

Coleherne. All these tough-looking, strange-looking people who, when you talk to them, you realise are mostly really very nice and friendly.[51]

Holly Johnson maintained that dressing exclusively from Seditionaries or Acme Attractions, also on the King's Road in Chelsea, was 'unoriginal', and that he was not 'a punk, I often repeated "I am an original"', echoing Philip Salon's desire not to be labelled.[52] Johnson does concede that he may have been jealous of Rutherford and that Seditionaries clothes were an important part of the look. In his film *Young Soul Rebels,* Isaac Julien portrays his memories of gay punks in Billy Boy, who dresses exclusively in clothes from Seditionaries. In the film Billy Boy is derided for being a St Martin's art-college parody of punk.[53] The desire for individuality that had inspired many of the early punks led to the beginnings of a new movement, where the emphasis was on style. The invitation to Steve Strange and Rusty Egan's Billy's Club at Gossips read 'Bowie Night. A Club for Heroes'. It had, Boy George maintains, 'more to do with decadent pre-war Berlin than reflecting life on a South London council estate'.[54] The influences that had inspired many young gay men to become involved in punk, David Bowie, Christopher Isherwood's 1930s Berlin, Andy Warhol's Factory were again important in setting the tone for this new 'movement', which came to be known as the New Romantics.

Notes

1. Elizabeth Rouse (1989), *Understanding Fashion*, Oxford, p. 297. The development of punk is dealt with in more detail in the many books on the subject, including Dick Hebdige (1987 [1979]), *Subculture: The Meaning of Style*, London, Tricia Henry (1989), *Break All Rules: Punk Rock and the Making of a Style*, Ann Arbor, MI and London, and Neil Nehring (1993), *Flowers in the Dustbin: Culture, Anarchy and Postwar England*, Ann Arbor, MI. For a contextual background of (British) society in the 1970s see Bart Moore-Gilbert (ed.) (1994), *The Arts in the Seventies: Cultural Closure*, London.

2. Legs McNeil and Gillian McCain (eds) (1996), *Please Kill Me: The Uncensored Oral History of Punk*, London, p. 318.

3. Jon Savage (1991), *England's Dreaming: Punk Rock and the Sex Pistols*, London, p.139. Earlier the term had been used to describe homosexual prostitutes – rent boys. See Richter Norton (1992), *Mother Clap's Molly House: The Gay Subculture in England 1700–1830*, London, p. 47.

4. Jayne County with Rupert Smith (1995), *Man Enough to be a Woman*, London, p. 51.

5. Ibid., p. 90.

6. Savage, *England's Dreaming*, p.139.

7. Adam Block (1982), 'The Confessions of a Gay Rocker', *The Advocate*, 15 April, p. 43.

8. Quoted in McNeil and McCain, *Please Kill Me*, pp. 117–18.

9. County, *Man Enough to be a Woman*, p. 51.

10. Savage, *England's Dreaming*, p.139.

11. Siouxsie Sioux quoted in Savage, *England's Dreaming*, p. 183. Some of the clubs that New York's punks were frequenting were also gay: 'Since the (transvestite) Club 82 had this outcast image for so long, the punks and the early glitter kids were treated very openly by the management. They didn't think they were weird and didn't try to cash in on 'em – they'd been dealing with weirdos for forty years!': Bob Gruen quoted in Clinton Heylin (1993), *From the Velvets to the Voidoids*, London, p. 188. Andy Warhol's Factory and associated scene had encouraged transvestites, transsexuals, rent boys, gay men, lesbians to get along together and celebrate their differences and individuality as something positive and creative – anyone could be a 'superstar'. British punk's ethos of 'anyone can form a band' echoed this sentiment.

12. Savage, *England's Dreaming*, p.183.

13. Bertie Marshall, 'Berlin', quoted on 'Punk and the Pistols', BBC television arts programme 'Arena', 1995.

14. Quoted in Keith Howes and Alan Wall (1978), 'Punk, Wot's in it for Us?', *Gay News*, no. 136, p. 22.

15. Boy George with Spencer Bright (1995), *Take it Like a Man*, New York, p. 52.

16. Savage, *England's Dreaming*, p. 184.

17. Boy George, *Take it Like a Man*, p. 74. Simon Barker also emphasised the point about acceptance of the proto-punks at gay clubs regardless of their sexual orientation: 'purely because of the way we looked we were a distraction, a threat. The straight clubs either didn't want you in there or they wanted to cause a fight. We used to go to Bang sometimes: there were two thousand people there, and none of them would hassle you': Savage, *England's Dreaming*, p. 186.

18. Savage, *England's Dreaming*, p. 187.

19. Cole interview with Jonathan Jackson, 26 August 1997.

20. Cole interview with Joe Pop, 19 May 1997.

21. Cole interview with Joe Pop, 3 December 1993.

22. Boy George, *Take it Like a Man*, p. 59.

23. Cole interview with Jonathan Jackson, 26 August 1997. The fifties-inspired look was also popular on the burgeoning (gay) punk scene in Liverpool: Holly Johnson describes the apprentices from a trendy Liverpool hairdressing salon 'A Cut Above the Rest' arriving at the gay pub 'decked out in various styles, some with a thrift shop Fifties look, all with dyed hair and too much make-up ... In the pre-punk early Seventies it was all very new' (Holly Johnson (1994), *A Bone in My Flute*, London, p. 47).

24. Johnson, *A Bone in My Flute*, p. 34. Some contemporary commentators were appalled at the games of make-believe that Bowie's fans were engaging in and were

worried about the oppositional content of youth culture. Taylor and Wall were concerned particularly about Bowie's alleged 'emasculation' of the 'Underground' condition: 'Bowie has in effect colluded in consumer capitalism's attempt to re-create a dependent adolescent class, involved as passive teenage consumers in the purchase of leisure prior to the assumption of "adulthood" rather than being a youth culture of persons who question (from whatever class or cultural perspective) the value and meaning of adolescence and the transition to the adult world of work': Ian Taylor and Dave Wall (1976), 'Beyond the Skinheads', in Geoff Mungham and Geoff Pearson (eds), *Working Class Youth Culture*, London, p. 123. The views of some of Bowie's teenage followers shows that Bowie *did* have a profound effect and did encourage an oppositional element in teenage youth culture, i.e. a questioning of sexuality and gender roles. What seems apparent is that these contemporary commentators were not willing to acknowledge a questioning of heterosexual norms as a valid form of youthful opposition. Hebdige also acknowledges this point, noting that Bowie's teenage followers '*did* "question the value and meaning of adolescence and the transition to the adult world of work" . . . and were challenging at a symbolic level the "inevitability", the "naturalness" of class and gender stereotypes': Dick Hebdige (1987 [1979]), *Subculture: The Meaning of Style*, London, pp. 62, 89. This is not dissimilar to the 'games' played by those gay men adopting radical drag and genderfuck styles. Michael Brown attributes much of glam rock's flaunting of bisexuality and androgynous images to the influence of the GLF's radical dress ideas: Cole interview with Michael Brown, 1 December 1993.

25. Quoted on 'Punk and the Pistols', BBC television arts programme 'Arena', 1995.

26. Cole interview with Joe Pop, 19 May 1997. Evans and Thornton, drawing on Dick Hebdige's two principal signifiers of punk, point out that 'the nihilistic anti-sexuality of punk was partly a way in which it differentiated itself from previous subcultures, particularly from the (ageing) hippie values of authenticity and love. It contributed to the intimidating alienness of punk, a feature shared by both men and women', and that 'the device of gender confusion inherited from glam rock and David Bowie was used for its power to make it strange, to render alien': Caroline Evans and Minna Thornton (1989), *Women and Fashion: A New Look*, London, pp. 118–19. The hippie spirit of love had contributed to the ethos of early gay liberation movements such as the Gay Liberation Front.

27. Evans and Thornton, *Women and Fashion*, p. 19.

28. Cole interview with Jonathan Jackson, 26 August 1997.

29. Boy George, *Take it Like a Man*, p. 49. David Bowie had developed his Ziggy Stardust and Aladdin Sane images partly on the basis of what he had seen of the New York Factory scene. David Bowie was obviously aware of the influence of Warhol's Factory crowd. Jayne County met David Bowie when she was in London for Andy Warhol's *Pork*. The *Pork* crowd went to see Bowie play at a club called Country Cousins, where they sat in the audience 'with our black fingernails and dyed hair . . . Leee Childers had gotten a Magic Marker and coloured his hair all different bright colours'. County was disappointed by her first sighting of Bowie:

'we'd heard that this David Bowie was supposed to be androgynous and everything, but then he came out with long hair, folky clothes'. They met afterwards and Bowie spent some time with the New York *Pork* crowd, and as a result of this 'David started getting dressed up. I'd gotten the shaved eyebrows thing from Jackie Curtis, and David started shaving his eyebrows, painting his nails, even wearing painted nails out at nightclubs, like we were doing. He changed his whole image and started getting more and more freaky': Jayne County, quoted in McNeil and McCain, *Please Kill Me*, pp. 117–18. By the same token, emergent American punk stars were looking to England's glam music performers. Iggy Pop, for example moved to London to work with Bowie.

30. Savage, *England's Dreaming*, p. 184.

31. Ibid., p. 190.

32. Cole interview with Joe Pop, 3 December 1993.

33. Daniel Wojcik (1995), *Punk and Neo Tribal Body Art*, Jackson, MS, p. 10.

34. Cole interview with Joe Pop, 19 May 1997.

35. Cole interview with Jonathan Jackson, 26 August 1997. Both Boy George and Holly Johnson describe wearing similar clothes in their biographies. See Boy George, *Take it Like a Man*, p. 91 and Johnson, *A Bone in My Flute*, pp. 67–9. Mohair jumpers had been extremely popular amongst effeminate gay men in the 1950s and 1960s. Michael Brown recalled in the late 1950s that 'mohair pullovers were still in fashion in pastel colours, and chiffon scarves' and for Tony 'Mohair sweaters were fabulous, you used to wear them in powder blue. They were so popular, you'd go anywhere to get a mohair sweater'; interviews with author.

36. Quoted on 'Punk and the Pistols', BBC television arts programme *'Arena'*, 1995.

37. In *Subculture: The Meaning of Style* Dick Hebdige looks at punk and other post-war subcultures in terms of class and race, but not gender, or sexuality. Gender was addressed by Evans and Thornton in *Women and Fashion*; issues of sexual orientation have been pretty much neglected or avoided. Michael Brake noted that 'subcultural studies of youth never mention homosexuals, and this is hardly surprising given the masculinist emphasis of practically all youth subcultures': Michael Brake (1985), *Comparative Youth Culture*, London, p. 11. It is conceivable that the invisibility of homosexuality in 'subcultural studies' has at least as much to do with the authors' concerns not to damage their 'street cred' with their informants and with their own aspirations as with the alleged 'masculinist emphasis' of the subcultures themselves. Murray Healy's *Gay Skins: Class, Masculinity and Queer Appropriation* is one of the few books to address this issue in any detail. Channel 4's gay magazine programme *Out on Tuesday* did tackle the issue of punks and gay men and lesbians.

38. Wojcik, *Punk and Neo Tribal Body Art*, p. 19.

39. Fred Vermorel (1997), 'The Godparents of Punk' in *NE Trains* magazine, written in Vivienne Westwood's voice to coincide with the publication of his book *Fashion and Perversity: A Life of Vivienne Westwood and the Sixties Laid Bare*. It was McLaren and Westwood who emphasised the sexual deviance in the clothes they designed and the imagery they appropriated for T-shirts. A number of the images

on T-shirts drew upon gay pornography, showing naked young men and in one instance a Tom of Finland-style drawing of two trouserless cowboys with their penises almost touching (see Figure 16). This was one of the shirts for which McLaren and Westwood were successfully prosecuted: 'With them [the pornographic T-shirts] you could find out where people's sore spots are and how free you really are. Sex is the thing that bugs English people more than anything else, so that's where I attack': Vivienne Westwood (1980), quoted in ZG, no. 2.

40. Cole interview with Joe Pop, 3 December 1993.

41. Boy George, *Take it Like a Man*, p. 81.

42. Ibid., p. 81.

43. McNeil and McCain, *Please Kill Me*, pp. 342–3.

44. Quoted in Adam Block (1982), 'The Confessions of a Gay Rocker', *The Advocate*, 15 April, p. 46

45. Ibid., p. 46.

46. Ibid., p. 46.

47. Cole interview with Joe Pop, 3 December 1993.

48. See Boy George, *Take it Like A Man*, p. 78.

49. Quoted in Howes and Wall, 'Punk, Wot's in it for Us?', p. 25

50. Johnson, *A Bone in My Flute*, p. 79.

51. Quoted in Howes and Wall, 'Punk, Wot's in it for Us?', p. 23.

52. Johnson, *A Bone in My Flute*, p. 80. Philip Salon never called himself a punk, although he was friendly with the Bromley contingent (and years later advised the V&A on punk clothes for its Streetstyle exhibition, selling them one of his early 'punk' outfits). He dismissed the term, saying 'labels, dear, labels: I want attention. It's those that are petrified of attention that are abnormal.' This was a sentiment echoed by other gay punks. Pete Shelley, the lead singer with the punk band The Buzzcocks, had similar hopes for punk, believing that 'it's a climate where people are accepting that everybody's different and everyone wants to express themselves in the way that suits them best. That's why a lot of people are forming bands, others are writing fanzines about the music, others are just making their own clothes or badges. And they are questioning things like the family and love . . .' (quoted in Howes and Wall, 'Punk, Wot's in it for Us?', p. 23).

53. Holly Johnson notes how Paul Rutherford adopted the Seditionaries look as he came to terms with his (homo)sexuality. 'His hair had become very spiky in a carbon copy of Johnny Rotten. He even managed to get his mum to buy him a genuine bondage suit from Seditionaries, Vivienne Westwood and Malcolm McLaren's new King's Road shop': Johnson, *A Bone in My Flute*, p. 80.

54. Boy George, *Take it Like A Man*, p. 118.

12

Express Yourself: Clubbing at the Blitz, the Batcave, and Beyond

By the late 1970s the aesthetics of punk had become commercialised and given birth to a whole series of new subcultural groups. The look of punk itself had become increasing masculinised, and a uniform had appeared that was represented in the popular press and on television as a green-haired, safety-pin-pierced, black-clad yob (hooligan) of either gender. The commercialisation and masculinisation of punk alienated many of those who were at first attracted to its embracing of difference and individuality. Boy George described how, by the middle of 1978:

> Punk had become a parody of itself, an anti-Establishment uniform, attracting hordes of dickheads who wanted to gob, punch, and stamp on flowers . . . It was sad because I loved the energy and music of punk. In the beginning it was screaming at us to reject conformity but it had become a joke, right down to the £80 Anarchy T-shirts on sale at Seditionaries.[1]

These people began to look for new ways of dressing to express their character. Holly Johnson described outfits that he wore in a post-punk phase in Liverpool: 'I remember one night painting my face white and wearing a black ski jumper with a multicoloured yoke, below which I wore a pair of red ballet tights and ballet slippers.'[2]

In London, Steve Strange and Rusty Egan[3] tapped into this need for a new alternative to punk, opening a series of one-night clubs, often on quiet nights at gay clubs. The best-known of these was on Tuesday nights at the Blitz,[4] a wine bar in Great Queen Street in Covent Garden. Drawing influence from David Bowie, glam rock and the new electronic music of bands such as Kraftwerk, these clubs encouraged a dressed-up escapist fantasy. Robert Elms echoed Siouxsie Sioux's sentiments about punk's escape from suburbia when he described this new club scene as a 'refusal that life had to be grotty . . . we just said we've had enough of this we're going to go and party.'[5] Steve Strange confirmed that 'It was like a competition. Your outfit actually outshone everyone else, so that you would actually compete, the way that you were dressed you would be on show for that night. And the style was that anyone who got through the doors could be themselves, be as creative as they liked and dress up – even if it was escapism, they could dress up and be themselves.'[6] This escapism appealed to many young gay men, especially those who were not attracted to the hypermasculine commercial gay scene, but were more drawn towards to the rebelliousness of punk. 'Most of the boys who did that were gay,' Jonathan Jackson recalled. 'There weren't like hundreds and hundreds, it was a very mixed-up kind of crowd, you know, there were straight men that weren't the kind of laddishy, macho, they were a bit arty and a bit sensitive and whatever. Most of the boys were gay and the girls were kind of like, you know, it didn't matter to them . . .'.[7]

This new club scene quickly attracted the attention of the press, which gave it names like Blitz Kids, Peacock Punk, New Romantics;[8] but for the people who were attending the club and dressing up labelling was un-important. What was important was the costume, the appearance, the pose. Jonathan Jackson concedes that it was about attracting attention: 'I think the Blitz lot, we wanted attention, you know, from people. Going to the Blitz you wanted people to gasp as you walked down the streets . . . gasp with horror usually, but when you got there you wanted the admiration of your uniqueness and your daringness from your peers, you know.' A number of the people who went to Billy's and the Blitz and their successors Le Kilt, Hell and Club for Heroes, had been either soul boys[9] or punks who had been driven off the punk scene by being 'called poser because [they] wore makeup and frills'.[10] Wearing make-up and frills became one of the primary images of the New Romantics,[11] although a number of particular 'looks' were seen – the pierrot, the squire, the eighteenth-century dandy, the toy soldier[12] – as the New Romantics plundered, in a magpie fashion, not only post-war fashion but the whole of modern history. Noting this prevalence for 'make-up and frills', Caroline Evans and Minna Thornton emphasise the importance of transvestism and cross-dressing amongst the male New Romantics.[13] Although there were a number of men who did cross-dress – Marilyn, attired in re-creations of the screen legend, was the most notable – many men took elements of dress that were traditionally feminine-associated, such as make-up, silk, satin, lace and frills, and incorporated them into their 'costumes' rather than actually dressing to imitate women. For young gay men this was a revelatory move:

I remember getting caught up in the Blitz crowd. And we just dressed like . . . well, it was just for outrage really. And plus the fact you belonged to this kind of, you know, gender-crossing set, when people weren't really sure whether you were a boy or a girl. You were just this thing with tons of make-up on and hair that stuck up all over the place . . . it was to be not what was to be considered the general kind of trend of the country, but to be something that was a little bit elite.[14]

The straight world emphasised the requirement of masculinity (many of the post-punk subcultures were masculine in their appearance, a tradition of many youth subcultures); and even the established gay scene favoured masculine dress choices, frowning on the effeminate. Martin Levine has alluded to the stigmatisation of gender-role nonconformity. He observed that 'Like all boys, homosexual and heterosexual "sissies" learn the male gender role stereotyping during childhood . . . To ward off sanctions, "sissies" actualize this training in late childhood or early adolescence. They "de-feminize", replacing feminine activities with manly behaviour, becoming appropriately masculine.'[15] What New Romantic clubs and dress styles offered was not only a validation of nonconformist gender-inappropriate behaviour, but also a celebration of 'effeminate' or at least effete imagery. For young gay men they offered acceptance of their naturally non-manly demeanours.

What was notable about the Blitz was its initial lack of emphasis on sexual orientation, which manifested itself, like glam, in declarations of homosexuality or bisexuality. Once again it had become fashionable/trendy to be gay, even as pretence.[16] While acknowledging this trend, Jonathan Jackson doesn't believe that the Blitz looks were necessarily associated in the minds of the public with a gay look:

I don't know that people really associated it with a gay look, you know – it was something different. I don't even know that that was part of the drive, really: sexuality it wasn't, it was almost like a bit of a love affair with yourself, do you know what I mean? . . . When you were getting ready in the evening you didn't think, or I didn't think, 'If I put this on I'm going to be like desperately attractive to so-and-so.' It wasn't like that for me. Having said that, when I met a boyfriend looking like that (he was a jeans and checked shirt merchant) he thought he was getting on to something a bit exciting and a bit different.[17]

In cities outside London similar club scenes grew out of punk culture, often at the more liberal and accepting gay clubs. In Liverpool a group of gay former punks were wearing increasingly outrageous clothes:

a wonderful pair of tartan trousers . . . The tartan was a white background with red and yellow printed plaid . . . With these I wore a pair of steel-toed brogues dyed pillar-box red. I somehow acquired a pair of red-and-white satin basketball shorts that I wore over the top of my tartan trousers. I also wore a collarless motorbike jacket I'd bought off Paul, often with no shirt underneath.[18]

Boy George described the clothes he and his friends wore in Birmingham, where a similar scene had grown up: Martin Degville 'wasn't like all the other punks, he was wearing stiletto heels and had a massive bleached quiff and huge padded shoulders'.[19]

Exclusivity was a primary factor in attendance at the clubs. Melissa Caplan recalled the division between the initial innovators and the later crowds who imitated and emulated, saying 'there was a right and a wrong place to stand depending on whether you were an innovator or a copyist. And if you were an innovator you must never be seen with people who copied you.'[20] In London stereotyped New Romantic images began to be seen. Elements of the image were adopted almost wholesale by people influenced by the culture, but not daring or imaginative enough to be truly original:

That whole Spandau Ballet thing and the New Romantic and the frilly big white shirts and all of that kind of thing came along. I mean, I don't think they specifically influenced me then, because I think I'd moved on a bit; but I remember seeing loads of people in clubs with that look. . . . That Spandau Ballet thing appealed to the same sort of gay boys, but the more . . . perhaps the more suburban. The ones who weren't looking for the sexy look, they were looking for a way of perhaps expressing they were different. Because it was always . . . if you were in a club and a group of boys came from outside London, you could guarantee that that's what they were going to look like – Spandau Ballet clones, with big baggy trousers and little T-shirts and the bandanna around their head.[21]

The extensive press coverage accorded to these new clubs and the groups that evolved from the Blitz club scene, notably Visage, Spandau Ballet, Duran Duran and Culture Club, took these new outrageous images far afield. For many young men living outside London who were beginning to question their sexuality, this experimentation offered a way of expressing their burgeoning self-awareness. Richard explained the first time that he felt influenced by fashions:

I remember when I first saw Spandau Ballet and Visage, I thought they looked great – the clothes, the hair, the make-up. I wanted to dress like that, to be like them. All the boys at school said they were poofs. I thought: so what, they look fabulous. Looking back, I'm sure it was partly that association that drew me to them – it allowed a freedom, and expression of my difference.[22]

John didn't necessarily associate the New Romantics with being gay, because as he noted there was a lot of denial; but it was about playing with gender, and this appealed to him:

There was this idea behind that, that you didn't have to behave in a particular way, or look a particular way to still be a man. When you feel that you're different . . . because I never felt I could live up to this, like, hard sort of masculine sort of image – that never felt right for me, 'cos I mean all through growing up I was what other people would call soft, because I didn't sort of like football or any kind of sport. I just didn't identify with – at that point – with that very sort of constricting image of what a man or boy should look like or behave like. And I think that was why the New Romantics appealed, because it was challenging that – it was challenging gender stereotypes. There was an androgyny, and that men and women could look the same. Men could dress flamboyantly and wear make-up.[23]

For Bill Wilson the New Romantic images offered a form of escapist dress, and an incentive to experiment with clothes. Influenced by Spandau Ballet, he created an outfit for his school Ball:

It was made out of some sort of tweedy fabric, it was double-breasted, and it had short sleeves and it had leather thong drawstrings around the waist somehow, so it was like a tunic. It was inspired by Spandau Ballet, I must admit. And it came with a matching accessory of a little leather headband . . . It was a really good way of expressing myself I suppose, especially since I made it.[24]

Wilson also affirms that the New Romantics club scene influenced a whole generation of club-goers, and appealed especially to gay men. 'The look wasn't so overtly masculine,' reflected Andrew Tomlin. 'I'd done punk, but it'd become very straight, so this was a safer, more flamboyant image. But I mostly did it because I knew that's how you'd get contact with other gay teenagers.'[25]

New Romantics opened up a whole host of new images for men's dress. Many young designers had been a part of that early clubbing scene. For some a new, smarter, more masculine image was attractive, with a move away from the (now stereotyped) frills and make-up. Johnny Melton recollected coming to London in the post-New Romantic phase and going to clubs such as Le Beat Route, where Latin-influenced music had become the latest thing and zoot suits were the staple of men's dress. Jonathan Jackson moved on from the New Romantic looks once they became more mainstream and almost clichéd. He was influenced by the new style magazines, in particular one entitled *Boulevard*:

I can remember very clearly reading in a magazine, because Antony Price then had a shop in the King's Road . . . And I remember there were these drawings in this magazine and he brought out these trousers that were absolutely leg-huggingly tight. Straight, you know: not particularly drainpipes, a bit looser on the ankles; but they were cut so they accentuated your bum and made them [sic] look really round and like absolutely desirable; and I can remember going, and these trousers cost £18, which was like tons of money then; and I remember going and buying about three pairs of them and being absolutely delighted, and wearing them with the tightest T-shirts you could ever imagine.[26]

It was at this time that his motivation for choosing clothes changed from seeking to be outrageous and individual to being more sexual:

Before that . . . which was like really strange, because like before that it . . . you didn't want to show your body off, you wanted to show your clothes off. And we all used to starve ourselves so that we'd be stick thin and look wonderful in clothes; and all of a sudden there was this look that you were showing your body off and you had to start paying attention to whether you really had muscles.[27]

Others, influenced by New Romantics and punk, continued to experiment with make-up and clothes, but to move away from the now cosy, Queen Mum look of Boy George, the frilly shirts and knickerbockers of Lady Di and teenage girls, or the Latin gangster looks of Spandau Ballet and Blue Rondo *à la* Turk. For Jonny Melton a new club, the Batcave, offered an escapist form of dress:

I read about [the Batcave] . . . I used to come down to clubs like The Beat Route, just post New Romantic, Blue Rondo *à la* Turk, really crap. There were people like me there, really out of place, just went there for no better reason than . . . I dunno! . . . [The Batcave] was a light bulb for all the freaks and people like myself who were from the sticks and wanted a bit more from life. Freaks, weirdos, sexual deviants . . . .[28]

Joe Pop had been a punk, but was disillusioned by the increasing machismo of punk and was attracted to the Batcave when it opened:

The Batcave was really odd because you could drag up like that. The Batcave was great because there was [sic] a lot of us around looking for something and there was a lot of us proto-Goths . . . What happened was you'd go to a gig and the sort of Punk that I was interested in was that artier end of punk – the Banshees and Adam and the Ants and Bauhaus . . . You could go to the Batcave and look pretty nancy . . . Anyway Jonny Slut, I thought he looked amazing. He was mincing around wearing a thong and a bit of fishnet; and I remember the time I wore quite . . . I wore . . . I used to wear leather trousers, plain black shirts and things, and I had big, big black hair. I prided myself on having some of the biggest hair for a boy going.[29]

While the Batcave was not a gay club, it did have a free enough atmosphere to attract gay men. The Batcave was essentially about music; but like the Blitz and the other New Romantic clubs, it encouraged individuality and outrageousness. 'I think it attracted all sorts', recalled Jonny Slut. 'A lot of people who didn't realise they were gay or care if they were gay. It attracted a lot of the Skin Two crowd: there was a lot of rubber, leather and chains around, and it was great for that, it was a really healthy cross-section of diverse people.'[30] Jonny was one of the more outrageous, wearing outfits created by a friend:

the best thing she made me was kind of like . . . I wanna look like a cat, and she made me this elephantine, four-foot-long rubber tail, and it was about the width of a small tree trunk and it would come from the base of my spine, over my shoulder and around my neck. It was like a rubber tail with about a thousand studs on it. And it was like held on to my body by a harness and chains. Most outfits did start off with a very body-conscious fishnet sort of thing and then built on to them.[31]

Other regional cities also had a burgeoning scene, which had evolved from punk and the New Romantics. Storm Constantine described this:

Birmingham in the eighties: we were doing the Rum Runner and Holy City Zoo. [Martin] Degville and [Boy] George posing in the Ladies powder room and we just screamed at the delight of it. Screamed and screamed, my dear. We were listening to Tubeway Army and Human League (yes, Human League), and the colours were pink and purple, dayglo leopardskin coming in on the heels of punk. Then it grew teeth and claws . . . hanging out with the sweet transvestites, who dragged the Gothic in from the bones of New Romanticism by the nose . . . Everything went black . . . the dangerously exciting melding of the gay and alternative scenes, the outrageous trannies who taught us where to buy our clothes: sex shops mainly. The fashion was everything . . . Makeup and plastic, fishnet, any kind of netting. But it had to be black![32]

Richard, too, recalled the merging of the gay and alternative scenes:

When I first came out my great dilemma was whether to go to the alternative club or the gay club. On the one hand I wanted to get dressed up in my most outrageous shocking clothes and dance to the music of Siouxsie and the Banshees and the Virgin Prunes and on the other hand I wanted to be in a club where I could meet a boyfriend, or, once I had a boyfriend, to be able to kiss him and hold hands.

Luckily I wasn't the only one like this: there were a number of gay men who were, what I suppose would now be described as Goths, who really wanted the best of both of these two worlds. The funny thing was that the one gay pub in town did attract a lot of the Goths: it was somewhere that they could go and not be thrown out for the way they looked. There had been a gay club that attracted the 'alternative' gay crowd, but this shut down quite soon after I discovered it; but I do remember on the few occasions that I went that it was heavily populated by punky poofs and dykes.[33]

Steve Parker noted that 'the first thing that strikes the newcomer about Cardiff's gay population is its outrageous originality. Punks abound . . . giving a refreshing bohemianism to the Cardiff Scene and noticeably distancing itself from the ubiquitous gay scenes of plaid shirts and Levi 501s'.[34]

The theme of outrage and individuality remained central within London's radical club scene, notably at Taboo, which opened in January 1985. 'Taboo was certainly the most important club around' Jonny Slut recalled:

It wasn't about music, it was about Leigh Bowery and Michael Clark, people like that. The whole kind of transgender thing seemed a lot more interesting. There were a few characters like Lana Pellay and stuff around that seemed to be movers and shakers at the time . . . all the clubs we are talking about aren't sex clubs, and it hasn't really ever been an issue. If you've got something flamboyant going on, yeah, obviously you are going to get gay men, because the two of them go arm in arm really. It was pretty much anything goes, and it was hot and it was happening.[35]

Leigh Bowery had been invited to host Taboo, because of his outrageous and original approach to dressing. He set the ethos of the club – 'dress as though your life depends on it, or don't bother'.[36] As with New Romantic clubs and the Batcave, sexuality was not a primary motivator for attendance at Taboo, although P. P. Hartnett, who frequently photographed the clubbers at Taboo, felt that there were a large number of gay men at the club.[37] 'Taboo was the last time that people really were self-indulgent about getting dressed up and going out,' reflected Bill Wilson. 'There seemed to be a more sombre attitude in the air after that . . . was genuinely good fun and there wasn't so much of a sexual atmosphere in there, although it was very sexy.'[38]

From 1985 to 1989 a whole host of new club nights sprang up in London catering to a gay or mixed gay and straight crowd. 'It was very much the post-New Romantic, it was still the same ethos,' Bill Wilson recalled. 'It was being glamorous, dressing up, looking fantastic, not wanting to look like anyone else . . . it didn't particularly matter what sexuality you were . . . it was less blatant somehow, but there were a lot of gay people there just expressing themselves.'[39] The focus was on dressing up, often incorporating elements of dress that were not traditionally masculine, jewellery and (for one or two seasons, thanks to fashion designer Jean-Paul Gaultier) skirts:

> The first time I was aware of seeing two gay men was when I came to London and went to [Steve Strange's club at the Lyceum Ballroom] The Playground. There were two men who I thought were dressed so stylishly. They were wearing white shirts, black shawl-collared tuxedo jackets with huge diamante brooches pinned on them, white socks, black Dr Marten lace-up shoes and black ankle-length skirts. They both had amazing bleached blond quiffed hair. I remember thinking they looked fantastic and wishing that I had the nerve to dress like that at home.[40]

Frank Mort states that 'pre-punk, the overriding concern of all youth subcultures was to offer coherent images to young men in opposition to the symbols coming from the dominant culture' and that 'what's now cool is not the assertion of a fixed masculine identity but a self conscious assemblage of styles.'[41] Although Mort's main focus is on young straight men's changing self-identity and approach to clothing, he notes that younger gay men were also critiquing established role models, such as the clone, and that the newer styles of gay dress were being adopted by straight men frequenting 'mixed' nights. Bill Short described one season's look, popular in the clubs: 'This summer he has been wearing gypsey-style [sic] headscarves or Pearly King hats; his shirts are loud and ride above the navel and any jacket he wears has to be customised with badges, condoms and photographs of his heroes or himself. He may wear lycra cycling shorts or a baggier variety reminiscent of a 1950s Norman Wisdom film.'[42]

For many gay men in the 1980s, the arrival of an organised club scene provided a new opportunity to express themselves. Individuality was as, or even more, important to teenagers than belonging to a labelled youth subculture. Androgyny was the buzzword in many fashionable circles in the 1980s, and made popular by pop stars such as Boy George, Marilyn and Annie Lennox. As in genderfuck of the early 1970s, traditional signifiers of masculinity and femininity were combined, in a gender-distorted bid for self-expression. Having grown up in a post-gay-liberation age, many young gay men did not feel the need to express their sexuality through blatant declarations of masculinity; but for others the appropriation of new masculine images and the emulation of working-class icons and subcultures proved an equally important means of expressing sexual orientation.

Notes

1. Boy George with Spencer Bright (1995), *Take it Like a Man*, New York, p. 118. Westwood and McLaren's Kings Road shop Sex was renamed 'Seditionaries' in 1977.

2. Holly Johnson (1994), *A Bone in My Flute*, London, p. 84.

3. Steve Strange was a former punk who had moved to London from Wales, becoming the singer with the pop group Visage. Rusty Egan was an ex-punk who had been the drummer for the band, The Rich Kids.

4. I will refer to Blitz throughout this chapter, as it was the best-known of the 'New Romantic' clubs; however, I do include other clubs, such as Billys, Le Kilt, Hell, St. Moritz and Le Beat Route.

5. Quoted on 'Peter York's Eighties', BBC television, 1996.

6. Ibid.

7. Cole interview with Jonathan Jackson, 26 August 1997.

8. 'New Romantics' is now the name most popularly used to describe this subcultural group, and the one I shall use: see Amy de la Haye and Cathie Dingwall (1996), *Surfers, Soulies, Skinheads and Skaters: Subcultural Style From the Forties to the Nineties*, London and Ted Polhemus (1994), *Streetstyle*, London.

9. See Chapter 11.

10. Boy George with Spencer Bright (1995), *Take it Like a Man*, New York, p. 118.

11. Ian Birch (ed.) (1981), *The Book With No Name*, London offers a good range of photographs of the members of this club-based subculture.

12. Jonathan Jackson recalled how 'one of the things I can remember that was, like, a most essential item was one of those army raincoats, you know, belted at the waist and one of those little – I don't even know what they're called – those little army hats, you know, the ones that just go like that [makes a gesture indicating a hat to one side of the head tilted to one eye], fold flat. You had to have one of them, and if you weren't wearing it, it had to be tucked flat under the epaulette of the coat': Cole interview with Jonathan Jackson, 26 August 1997.

13. Caroline Evans and Minna Thornton (1989), *Women and Fashion: A New Look*, London, Chapter 3.

14. Cole interview with Jonathan Jackson, 26 August 1997.

15. Martin P. Levine (1998), *Gay Macho: The Life and Death of the Homosexual Clone*, New York and London, p.16.

16. A study of London's club culture would reveal a shifting trend in the fashionability of gay clubs. At various points gay clubs have been the most trendy and favoured clubs in the city, for example Heaven around 1983 and Trade in 1991. The same could be argued of any major city in Britain or USA. This shifting trend could be attributed to the fashions that are worn at the various clubs, or to the music played at them, as people like to see what is new and 'in' amongst different groups, particularly gay men, who have traditionally had a reputation for being at the cutting edge of fashions. There is scope for a more in-depth study on the appeal of gay club culture to non-gay participants.

17. Cole interview with Jonathan Jackson, 26 August 1997.

18. Holly Johnson (1994), *A Bone in My Flute*, London, p. 96.

19. Boy George, *Take it Like a Man*, p. 103.

20. Quoted in Sally Brompton (1984), *Chameleon: The Boy George Story*, London, p. 69.

21. Cole interview with Jonathan Jackson, 26 August 1997. 'I remember meeting two American boys over to see the alternative scene and get involved in it. They were desperate to meet a group of us at Heaven because we were all dressed up in frills and long shirts': Cole interview with Andrew Tomlin, 10 May 1999.

22. Cole interview with Richard, 19 August 1998.

23. Cole interview with John, 7 June 1997. The transgressive image portrayed by Boy George, Marilyn and other post New Romantic 'gender benders' offered a similar point of identification to that which David Bowie had offered to pre-punk gay teenagers in the early 1970s. See Chapter 11 and Richard Smith (1999), 'Oh No Love You're Not Alone', *Gay Times*, no. 250, July, pp. 32–6 for David Bowie's influence on Boy George and others; see Shabbaz Chauhdry's discussion of the influence of Marilyn in Bob Cant (ed.) (1993), *Footsteps and Witnesses: Lesbian and Gay Lifestories from Scotland*, Edinburgh.

24. Cole interview with Bill Wilson, 10 August 1999.

25. Cole interview with Andrew Tomlin, 10 May 1999.

26. Cole interview with Joe Pop, 19 May 1997.

27. Ibid.

28. Jonny Melton quoted in Mick Mercer (1991), *Gothic Rock*, Birmingham, p.102. Jonny's reminiscences of the crowd of people attracted to the Batcave echoes Berlin's reminiscences of the early punk crowd who went to Louise's and Chageramas.

29. Cole interview with Jonathan Jackson, 26 August 1997.

30. Cole interview with Johnny Slut, 11 August 1998.

31. Ibid.

32. Storm Constantine, quoted in Mick Mercer (1991), *Gothic Rock*, Birmingham.

33. Cole interview with Richard, 19 August 1998.

34. Steve Parker (1984), 'Cardiff and South Wales', *Him*, 65, p. 41.

35. Cole interview with Johnny Slut, 11 August 1998. The Pyramid in New York was a similar bar attracting 'gay, straight, artists, famous models, actors and on weekends, transy cruisers galore': Rupaul (1995), *Lettin It All Hang Out: An Autobiography*, London, p. 76.

36. Hilton Als (1998), 'Cruel Story of Youth', in Robert Violette (ed.) (1998), *Leigh Bowery*, London, p. 16. And he dressed accordingly, wearing a different outfit each week. One of his most popular was 'a short pleated skirt with a glittery, denim, Chanel-style jacket teamed with scab make-up and a cheap, plastic, souvenir policeman's hat': Sue Tilley (1997), *Leigh Bowery: The Life and Times of an Icon*, p. 57.

37. Conversation between Cole and P. P. Hartnett, 15 September 1994.

38. Cole interview with Bill Wilson, 10 August 1999.

39. Ibid.

40. Cole interview with Richard, 19 August 1998. 'At one point the diamante was everything. I remember whole days spent buying up the stores and making diamante medals. God knows what we looked like with these pinned on flapover tartan shirts': Cole interview with Andrew Tomlin, 10 May 1999.

41. Frank Mort (1988), 'Boys' Own? Masculinity, Style and Popular Culture', in Rowena Chapman and Jonathan Rutherford (eds), *Male Order: Unwrapping Masculinity*, London, p. 204.

42. Bill Short (1987), 'Social Trends at Heaven's Pyramid', *Gay Times*, September, p. 53. Adorning jackets and hats with badges and found items was a popular trend, noted by magazines such as the *Face* and *i-D*, and was an extension of the Buffalo styles of the mid 1980s dealt with in more detail in the next chapter. Richard Dyer observed that the adoption of knee-length baggy shorts was attributable to gay men – that it followed in a long tradition of gay men wearing clothes that were socially unacceptable or unfashionable and 'reworking' them to give them a new credence and hence 'behold the ripple of queerness as one or another gay style spreads back out into society': Richard Dyer (1994), 'Fashioning Change: Gay Men's Style', in Emma Healey and Angela Mason (eds), *Stonewall 25: The Making of the Lesbian and Gay Community in Britain*, London, p. 188.

13

Hard Boys: Masculine Appropriations in the 1980s

While gay liberation had questioned the constrictions of gendered behaviour and its effects on gay people, the rise of the new masculine images for gay men had, many commentators criticised, merely pandered to the stereotypes of male and female behaviour.[1] However, the clone had encouraged a rethinking of gay men's self-image. Although the clone was still prominent in the mid-1980s,[2] it was perceived by many younger gay men as an outmoded form of dress and behaviour, belonging to the generation who had come out and been active in a pre-AIDS gay society. These younger men looked for alternative ways of dressing that allowed them to express their sexuality. Some looked to images that were not 'butch' and chose their clothes 'for the same reasons that an earlier generation might have chosen to be camp (i.e. the desire to be noticed, a desire to escape, a reaction against a straight world, a ghetto mentality and so on). He strives to find a new image that will fit a new set of values.'[3] For others, the realisation that to be gay did not equate to effeminacy had a marked impact on their dress choice. To adopt the clone image, however, would have been to adopt the clothes of an outdated generation, and so they looked to other subcultural images as a way of asserting their masculinity. In particular, two subcultural styles were being worn by gay men in the wake of the clones and punk, both of which made a nostalgic nod towards a historical masculinity, via a post-punk reappropriation: 'When the real is no longer what it used to be, nostalgia assumes its full meaning. There is a proliferation of myths of origin and signs in reality; of second hand truth, objectivity and authenticity.'[4] The rockabilly and the skinhead, while seen as ostensibly heterosexual subcultures, made a marked impression upon the map of gay dress styles.

The British rockabilly revival evolved from an interest in 1950s American rock and roll and associated clothing, but disliked the stereotype of the British Teddy Boy (which also saw a revival in the 1970s). It coincided with a post-punk interest in earlier subcultures. By the early 1980s it had become established on the London club scene, and plundered a whole range of 1950s teen clothing styles, from dressy pegged pants and box jackets to jeans and bowling shirts.[5] The interest was nostalgic, drawing on a romantic fiction-alised notion of 1950s America portrayed in the spate of high school/coming of age films such as *Grease* (1978) and *American Graffiti* (1973). In the same way that the second wave of Teds in 1970s Britain could, as Dick Hebdige commented, float on a 'wave of nostalgia situated somewhere between the Fonz of television's *Happy Days* and a recycled Ovaltine ad,'[6] because they were free from time and context the rockabillies existed somewhere between a fictional remembrance of 1950s American high schools and the gritty reality of unemployment in 1980s Thatcherite Britain. The revival recalled a time that seemed surprisingly remote and, by comparison, secure.

The rockabilly image was picked up by gay men disillusioned with the now-dated clone image who were searching for an alternative look. 'I started to go to the Bell in King's Cross [a pub in North London that attracted a non-clone, young, 'alternative' gay clientele], and the most common gay look there was a sort of Rockabilly' recalled Richard, 'and I remember finding it immensely amusing, because one of the things that people there were immensely proud of was the fact that they weren't part of the clone scene, even though they were all in the same way dressed within a very few signature items, and you had to have them . . . and to be attractive you had to have them. It was when . . . really, I suppose when Clone has two meanings: it means that specific way of dressing, but it also means conforming, and there has always been that and there still is.'[7] One of the rockabilly styles comprised denim and checked shirts, clothes that were also worn by clones. The very overt masculinity of such apparel, which had appealed to the clones, appealed in a similar way to what *Gay Times* called 'clone-a-billies'. Joe Pop observed that the similarity between the gay rockabillies and the clones lay in the 'sexiness' of the look: 'I remember I used to go on Sundays to the Time tunnel night [at the Bell]. I remember there being a look that a lot of people did that was the gay rockabilly look and the flat top and the 501s, the sort of James Dean-y kind of thing . . . It was butch and it was cute . . . It was unisex; boys and girls did it. It was deceptively casual, but obviously involved quite high maintenance, and I think it was . . . for some years you could say it was the younger version of the moustached clones, and so it was sexy and sort of roughty tufty.'[8]

For gay rockabillies the romantic fantasy of 1950s Americana mirrored a sexual fantasy based on an American vision of masculinity. It was not so much a copy of the original and straight rockabillies as an interpretation of an ideal of what that original was. There were of course gay men who were involved in what was known as the 'rocking scene', whose sexuality was often secondary to their involvement in the lifestyle – wearing authentic clothes, listening to the music and collecting 1950s furnishings. For many of the 'clone-a-billies' combining elements to create a sexy and stylish image was more important than authenticity.[9] Jonathan Jackson believes that the appeal of the rockabilly look was that it was 'a very masculine look or boyish look that was kind of quite glamorous to do and was quite different, markedly different, from what you saw everyone in the street wearing'.[10] The emergence on the gay scene of rockabillies coincided with a general interest in the 1950s. Interest in James Dean and Marlon Brando as icons grew, and advertising nodded a nostalgic head towards the fifties, with adverts such as the 'Launderette' and 'Bath' advertisements for Levi's jeans.[11]

In his biting fictionalised account of the London gay scene, the author Pickles described the gay rockabilly in somewhat derogatory terms, emphasising what he saw as a despondent pose. They saw themselves, he wrote, as 'avant-garde skinheads' who 'might wear a slick suit, or look like a tastefully arranged mess: bits of black paramilitary gear draped about with careless flair, perhaps a donkey-jacket and duffel bag, topped with an ice-cream mop and tapering away to huge black boots or dainty canvas slip-ons and thin hairy ankles'.[12] This studied dishevelledness was a key factor in the image. Just as the clones had worn their utilitarian masculine clothes in a self-consciously sexily styled manner, so these young rockabillies were donning a seemingly careless combination of clothes that signified a sexual attractiveness rooted in the icons of fifties Americana.

If the rockabilly styles had originated in a wave of imagined nostalgia for 1950s America then the eighties skinhead (revival) originated in a myth of the working-class authenticity of the original 1960s subculture. The original skinheads had developed as a reaction to the perceived feminisation of mods. Their values were, in the words of George Marshall, 'masculinity, male dominance and male solidarity',[13] and their dress reflected these values. The boots, braces and cropped hair that the skinheads adopted were considered appropriate and hence meaningful because they communicated the desired qualities of 'hardness, masculinity and working-classness'. In *Resistance Through Rituals* Stuart Hall proposed that appropriated objects reassembled in the distinctive subcultural ensembles were 'made to reflect, express and resonate . . . aspects of group life'. He cited the skinheads as exemplifying this principle, claiming 'The symbolic objects – dress, appearance, language, ritual occasions, styles of interaction, music – were made to form a *unity* with the group's relations, situations, experience.'[14] The working-class masculinity that the skinheads were reflecting and representing was outwardly heterosexual.

There were however gay men involved in the first waves of the skinhead subculture. In his 1996 publication *Gay Skins: Class, Masculinity and Queer*

Appropriation, Murray Healy gives accounts of a number of gay young men who became skinheads. Much of the appeal was because it was ostensibly working-class. It also reflected a masculinity that was at odds with many of the perceived and available images of homosexuality, which were still predominantly grounded in a post-Wildean leisure-class form.[15] Peter Robins was at pains to point out that 'you shouldn't run away with the idea that we were all like [Quentin Crisp], that . . . even if we wanted to be, because there is . . . again its anthropological, if you want to attract your east London lad you try to look like your east London lad. I mean I knew a guy in the early days of gay liberation in the seventies who had his bovver boots and his red braces and his short haircut and his gorblimey accent, and it wasn't until I got him into bed that he confessed he'd been to a public school and wanted actually to be with an east end bovver-booted boy.'[16] Robins's experience highlights the 'erotic fascination' that drew gay men to skinheads. For middle-class gay men the attraction was in the tradition of the working-class rough, as Nick was aware: 'The image of working-class masculinity . . . I think it's quite an old-fashioned thing now, but I should imagine, years ago, middle-class men would have a bit of rough on the side; manual workers, soldiers, obviously masculine.'[17]

Magazines aimed at gay readers did not overlook the existence and appeal of the skinhead. As an alternative to the American forms of physique magazines available, *Young Londoners* featured photographs of skinheads, at first using straight models but later gay skinheads. The images were of a British, rather than an American fantasy ideal. *Jeremy*, one of the first British glossy gay magazines, observed the existence of a growing gay skinhead subculture in 1970: 'All those skinheads aren't quite what they seem, and certainly at this particular tavern [the Union Tavern] there's very little to worry from in the way of aggro.'[18]

With the post-punk skinhead revival came a renewed interest in the subculture and the image amongst gay men. Again this was initially grounded in a working-class appeal. Nick recalled that 'it was definitely a class thing, we were working-class guys'. Ian Walker, writing in *New Society* in 1980, believed that 'the accent, like the clothing, is constructed from the cartoon worker, the navvie. Skinhead style takes the bourgeois caricature of its own class (dumb and violent) and makes it yet more extreme.'[19] Aspects of the skinhead revival focused on the overtly aggressive side of the skinhead ideology rather than its roots in Jamaican music and rude boy dress (something that was to become a huge debate in both the gay and straight skinhead worlds, as racist violence and accusations of racism were embraced and denied by various factions). The association of aggression was often an attraction to gay men. 'The implication of violence cannot be ruled out of the attraction', wrote gay skinhead Mike Dow, 'The fetishism centred on the boots is merely part of the inevitable fact that the connection between sex and violence is part of the human psyche.'[20] This perceived relationship was responsible for the appearance of gay skinheads in bars that attracted an S/M clientele: for example, the Coleherne had been one of the few venues in Britain to attract a crowd interested in S/M, and as such had become the centre of London's gay leather scene.[21] 'Gay Skins are associated with rough sex and I am interested in power games', said Bobby, interviewed in *Square Peg*.[22] Many of Healy's respondents also made the association between the leather and S/M scene and the skinhead scene, from the 1970s through to the 1990s. Commenting on the rise in British macho identity, Jamie Gough observed 'more specialist images: the leatherman/biker, the construction worker, the squaddy, the skinhead, the biker',[23] tying the skinhead to these other aggressively masculine images.

Like the clones, the gay skinheads were drawing on items of clothing that had a working-class association. Closer analysis reveals that these were essentially the same items of clothing – work boots and jeans. The journalist Richard Smith believes that the skinhead presented the same working-class icon to British gay men that the lumberjack or construction worker offered to Americans, and as such had become 'a new clone'.[24] The comparison with the clones becomes evident on examination of the fetishisation of clothing by skinheads: 'The tight jeans, it's obvious, show off your boots, show off your bum, show off your, er, equipment. And your braces – either you have them under your bum to show of your bum, or you have them up to pull the whole lot up around your stuff ... The bomber jacket ... it exaggerates your shoulders and the broadness of your back.'[25]

In the 1980s gay men adopted and embraced the skinhead culture and style on a number of levels. An article in *Square Peg*, the gay arts magazine, concluded that gay skinheads were 'gay men who have adopted the fashion as a sexual image'.[26] While this was, and still is, in many cases true, it does not adequately encompass all the motives that gay men may have for becoming a skinhead. For some it was fashion-based. 'I see it as a fashion style for the gay scene,' said Tony, 'it's more individualistic than other styles.'[27] For others, like Mitch, 'It's my way of life. Teddy boys and mods have come and gone, but they all still look as though they're wearing a fashion. Being a real skinhead has nothing to do with a fashion. It's shouting, "I'm a skinhead."'[28] For Peter: 'its an image I choose for myself as a gay man and a sign of rebellion against the person I was before: a nice middle-class boy at university. By being a skinhead, I can't be called "not a man", and by being a gay skin, then I can take that image and use it.'[29] 'I'm a skinhead first, gay second' became quite a common declaration amongst gay skinheads as a reaction to those they saw as 'plastic' fashion skinheads, attracted to the look because of the prospect of rough sex or the association of masculinity. George Marshall, the straight author of the skinhead bible *Spirit of '69*, believed that 'anyone can claim to be a skinhead and as long as he looks the part who's to say he's not?'[30] Some gay men saw the appropriation of the skinhead image as a transgressive tool, challenging society's perceptions – 'Being a skin raises questions constantly for myself. If straight men are scared of me, I'm always totally surprised, as I don't see myself like that. It can be very useful, as I feel confident and very safe. I act polite and quite normal, and to see the relief in people's faces and the power of giving that is really good.'[31] One black gay skinhead was attracted to the image because he was not supposed to look at skinheads because of their supposed homophobia and racism. The issue of skinheads' racism did cause concern within sections of the gay 'community'. Some gay skinheads were open about their affiliation with right-wing (racist) skinheads groups, while others emphasised their anti-racist affiliations.[32]

While the association of working-class identity was still a factor in some men's decision to become skinheads in the eighties, this was not always true for all men, and to the dismay of those who considered themselves real skinheads many adopted the look and the stance for its sexual appeal or its fashionability. Jamie Crofts believed that 'the look is so obviously a queer one, a thing that gay men got into, because everything about the look originally was sexy'.[33] The attraction of the sexy look led many men to adopt the look because it was a way of meeting other skinheads – like attracts like. 'I'd always fancied skinheads', Richard recalled, 'I think there was something about them being the forbidden, frightening other; but they had never looked at me. I realised that if I wore jeans and boots and braces and shaved my head then I started getting attention from skinheads. I also quickly realised that there were a lot of others who were dressing this way because it was sexy and you got to have sex.'[34] Writing in the gay paper *Out* Mike Dow emphasised the non-class-specific nature of gay skinheads, stating that 'generally speaking, gay skins come from a far broader background than straight skins. Many are found in highly respectable and skilled jobs . . . He has usually decided to become a skinhead after consideration and preparation for some sacrifice, not simply because he comes from a tower block in Canning Town and his mates are doing it.'[35]

The interest in skinhead-styled images coincided with a trend in the London clubs towards a less flamboyant image that had been a staple of the New Romantic styles. This became known as the 'Hard Times' look (after an article in the *Face* in 1985). The look was also a reflection of the general mood in Britain, marked by the economic depression and social turbulence of the first few years of Tory Government. Sue Tilley observed the move away from glamour and how it became 'chic to be on the dole and flaunt your new-found poverty. Ripped jeans and faded T-shirts were *de rigueur* but it was perfectly all right to go out in your pyjamas . . . It was the height of fashion to slash the neck off your T-shirt or cut off the sleeves . . . studded belts and wristbands made a comeback and no one was properly dressed without at least one belt slung around their hips. Mesh was everywhere and girls and boys styled tops out of dyed dishcloths.'[36] While Tilley's description described the dressier end of the hard times spectrum, the masculine looks associated with the skinheads and rockabillies fed into this move. Mike recalled the Bell was 'where the skinhead look crossed with the fashion look. Guys who were wearing short hair and DM boots and jeans.'[37] The signifiers of the skinhead (which were coincidentally almost identical to those of the clone and the rockabilly, but worn in subtly different ways) – Doctor Martens (work boots), Levi's 501s, bomber jacket, cropped hair – became a new urban gay uniform signifying less the macho queen than 'gay man/homosexual/ queer'. The presentation of these styles of dress by out gay pop stars such as Jimmy Somerville served to present these images to a wider audience and in becoming role models to a generation of younger gay men widened the appeal of the image.[38]

The political dress of many radical left groups in the 1980s was informed by the hard times urban image. Items of clothing were drawn from pur-portedly fashion-resistant items, such as Doctor Marten boots, Levi's jeans, workwear and shaved heads.[39] These elements of dress, which were the basis of rockabilly, skinhead and clone dress styles, formed a new androgynous image that was markedly adopted by politically motivated gay men and lesbians. Most androgyny in the eighties had been grounded in an adoption of effeminacy by males. This new masculinsed androgyny drew on a history of lesbian cross-dressing and feminist arguments about the gendered nature of clothing, and produced a shaven-headed, booted activist, proclaiming her/ his alliance to AIDS or anti-homophobic protests on T-shirts and badges – the new image of a 'Queer Nation'. In *Outweek* magazine Michelangelo Signorile, emphasizing the 'heavy sexual innuendo' in the choice of clothes, named this the 'new clone'.[40]

The Hard Times feature in the *Face* was one of the many to be styled by Ray Petri. Petri (who died in 1989) has been credited with changing the face of both men's fashion and men's fashion magazines. Petri plundered a whole series of fashion styles to create new images of masculinity, which became known as Buffalo, and were, Jamie Morgan recalled, 'strong and sensitive – they showed you didn't have to drink beer and beat people up to be tough. He gave men a sense of pride in the way they dress which has been hugely influential.'[41] For Bill Wilson, Petri's influence was in the way he used clothes in unconventional ways, which invited the viewer to question how he could assemble his own style: 'I think what he did was make you start thinking about clothes really, and looking, which is something . . . it sounds really obvious, but people don't often do that. I mean he did take trousers and make them into cardigans or whatever, and he used things that were completely inappropriate in a new kind of way . . . It certainly did have an effect on me, because I started to look at clothes and think.'[42] Petri's influences were grounded in an urban gay culture, perhaps most notably in the contact he made between the model and the audience, which Frank Mort believes drew on the visual contact involved in gay men's 'cruising' for casual sex.[43] Variations of the buffalo look were circulating in London during the mid-1980s, and there was a two-way influence between Petri's stylised shoots and the young gay urbanites of London's Soho. The styles that Petri was citing were similar to those of the gay rockabilly. They comprised (an almost typically gay 'uniform' of) Levi 501 jeans, Doctor Marten shoes or boots, white socks and a black American MA1 flight jacket, topped off with a flat-top haircut or a fifties-style quiff. For John this look coincided with the arrival of House[44] and hip-hop music from America, and the popularity of minimalist design:

'about 1986 House music happened and that just seemed to change everything . . . House seemed to be what was happening in London and therefore seemed to be attractive, and the way I dressed was I suppose how I perceived people in London were dressing. At first it was all things like black polo necks, black jeans . . . or any colour polo neck, basically . . . DMs, DM shoes rather, like, turn-ups on your jeans so you could see people's socks. People have described it as very minimal: I suppose it was that end of the eighties matt black kind of look. Very clean, and I suppose it was almost the opposite of New Romantics flamboyancy and going over the top with the way you dress and wearing tons of make-up and having big hair, big backcombed black hair crimped to death – and all of a sudden you go to the opposite extreme and – well, I certainly had hair that was very short around the back and the sides and on the top too'.[45]

i-D magazine noted the 'nightclubbin' disguise – blond crop, MA-1 jacket, BodyMap leggings'[46] that was seen in and around London's Soho both at night and during the day. This 'mattblack' Buffalo look became almost a uniform for the fashionable (male, female, gay and straight) Soho set. As Andrew noted: 'there is a certain image, a very sort of Soho look. When I walk around I find it very difficult to tell who's gay and who's not . . . But when somebody comes along with that look – the flat-top, the black jacket and the DM shoes, or whatever – I think they might be gay, but not necessarily. You do sort of look at each other a lot.'[47] To add an element of individuality to the 'uniform' an almost punk DIY element was introduced as people added badges, buttons, safety-pins and other found items to their clothes: 'When garments like denim and MA-1 flying jackets became too popular' *i-D* magazine reported in June 1987, 'an artistic burst of customizing soon turns them from a uniform back into a unique outfit'.[48] Jonny Slut began customising his clothes as he became aware of hip-hop music, mirroring the sampling he heard in the music: 'I guess that coincided with my shaving my head and growing a eight-inch orange unicorn point on the front of my head and wearing an Ariel automatic [soap powder] box on the back. I guess it was a magpie thing. I was just adorning myself with whatever was around I guess. It was just wearing what felt good and natural as well, it was kind of . . . it was never about copying anything. It was just about what was around and what felt right, nothing more than that.'[49] (See Figure 20.)

With the increasing visibility of gay men in British society it was almost inevitable that gay images would appear in the press. The greater vocality of the gay community (particularly around issues such as AIDS and Section 28) led to increased appearance in magazine articles and on television, and not just in negative portrayals. This was particularly noticeable in the new style magazines that were published in the 1980s. As was stated earlier, Ray Petri had drawn upon and re-influenced an urban gay style with his Buffalo photo shoots for the *Face*. The magazine made a more obvious reference to the place of gay men in Britain in its 1986 fashion feature 'New England', where, amongst its representations of the diversity of Britain's population, it printed a photograph of a young gay man dressed in blue jeans and baseball cap, captioned 'Boystown'.[50] Aware of their gay readerships, *i-D* and *Blitz* along with the *Face* featured articles, features and photographs that would appeal to this market. *i-D* included gay men in its street reportage-style approach of photographing people on the streets, and asking questions based on the month's theme, such as 'the earth', 'cool' and 'red hot'. *Arena*, launched in autumn 1986 as a men's style magazine, continued to present gay imagery. Using many of the same photographers, stylists and models as the *Face*, an explicitly homoerotic style developed, consciously or unconsciously aimed at and appealing to a gay audience. In presenting such images *Arena* was inviting heterosexual men to view gay-inspired images and to question the assumptions of the male gaze. Michael Bronski has established that the trend for using homoerotic imagery in mass advertising had appeared, in the United States, in the mid-1970s. He identifies two specific types, with firms roots in gay sensibility: the virile, tough, yet sensitive man (not unlike Petri's Buffalo boys) – the Marlboro Man; and the more European, well-dressed, precisely poised and graceful man, the direct descendant of Wilde's and Coward's aesthete. Bronski highlights the importance of these images, in that they 'offered a compromise for the advertising [and publishing?] world because they enticed mainstream buyers without turning off homosexuals. Gay people perceived the gay images, and thus the ads spoke to them.'[51] This is the same process that was taking place in the British style magazines of the eighties.

The skinhead and rockabilly served to offer gay men a masculine mode of dress, which, while drawing on a heterosexual subcultural image, quickly became incorporated into the accepted gay wardrobe. The prevalence of masculine dress choices amongst gay men still continues, and its gay associations are summed up in the comments made by a group of boys who, when asked on *Skin Complex* what they thought of skinheads, replied 'They look like poofs.'[52]

Notes

1. This was an argument that was also levelled at the gay S/M scene, particularly by feminists and radical lesbians, who argued that it resorted to male dominance over females and that the 'passive' or submissive partner was inherently enacting a feminised role. See the essays in Robin Ruth Linden *et al.* (eds) (1982), *Against Sadomasochism: A Radical Feminist Analysis*, San Francisco.

2. An examination of photographs in gay magazines such as *Gay Times,* taken at gay pubs and clubs at this time, will show the prevalence of the clone, especially outside London.

3. Bill Short (1987), 'Social Trends at Heaven's Pyramid', *Gay Times*, September, p. 53.

4. Jean Baudrillard (1983), *Simulacra and Simulations*, New York, p. 12. Punk had woken up a lot of young people to the possibilities of experimenting with dress and subcultural styles. For accounts and descriptions of the 'explosion' of subcultural 'tribes' in the wake of punk see Ted Polhemus (1994), *Streetstyle: From Sidewalk to Catwalk*, London and Amy de la Haye and Cathie Dingwall (1996), *Surfers, Soulies, Skinheads and Skaters: Subcultural Style from the Forties to the Nineties*, London.

5. The fifties retro look had first appeared in the mid-1970s; see Chapter 11 for its influence on punk.

6. Dick Hebdige (1987 [1979]), *Subculture: The Meaning of Style*, London, p. 82

7. Cole interview with Richard, 19 August 1998.

8. Cole interview with Joe Pop, 19 May 1997.

9. Ray Weller recalled one such item of clothing that became the desirable jacket for gay rockabillies: 'I can remember one of the favourite things that I used to like to wear was a blue jacket. I don't know what they're called, but it was one of those cloth jackets that had a collar: it was dark blue and yellow and had some sort of logo, a fifties college or something on the front, numbers across the back, and it had a split hood, which was detachable, but you always wore it with the hood. I used to

love wearing that, and you used to see that look about with jeans and all that. I can remember being told by a rockabilly who was kind of a real rockabilly, for want of a better word, rather than a pretend one, that no real rockabilly would wear that, because split hoods were only worn in the fifties by American girls, never by boys, and that was not even that they thought about it at the time, but that it just wasn't a man's item of clothes. But it had become quite a kind of sexy item for gay rockabillies at the time; but I'm not sure how many people realised that they had got it the wrong way round, it was actually a feminine item that they had turned into a masculine stereotype': Cole interview with Ray Weller, 26 June 1997.

10. Cole interview with Jonathan Jackson, 26 June 1997.

11. For a more detailed analysis of these adverts see Frank Mort (1996), *Cultures of Consumption: Masculinities and Social Space in Late Twentieth-Century Britain*, London, pp.108–13.

12. Pickles (1984), *Queens*, London, p. 99.

13. George Marshall (1991), *Spirit of '69: A Skinhead Bible*, Dunoon, Scotland, p. 35.

14. Stuart Hall and Tony Jefferson (eds) (1976), *Resistance Through Rituals*, London, p. 56.

15. Murray Healy (1996), *Gay Skins: Class, Masculinity and Queer Appropriation*, London.

16. Cole interview with Peter Robins, 4 August 1997.

17. Quoted in Healy, *Gay Skins*, p. 156.

18. *Jeremy*, vol. 1, no. 7.

19. Ian Walker (1980), 'Skinheads, the Cult of Trouble', *New Society* 26 June, p. 346.

20. Mike Dow (1985), 'Skins: 2', *Out*, April, p. 21.

21. See Chapter 8.

22. 'Skin and Bona: Interviews with Gay Skinheads', *Square Peg*, no.12, 1986, p. 15.

23. Jamie Gough (1989), 'Theories of Sexual Identity and the Masculinisation of the Gay Man', in Simon Shepherd and Mick Wallis (eds), *Coming on Strong: Gay Politics and Culture*, London, p. 119.

24. Doctor Marten's, television programme for Channel 4.

25. Jamie Crofts, quoted in Healy, *Gay Skins*, p.106. 'Gay men all over town (and around the country) trimmed, shaped and refitted the shaggy casualness that was the real essence of the original straight image . . . What emerged was a deliberate new style which does not say, "I am a straight construction worker" but rather "I am a post-liberation gay man": Andrew Kopkind (1979), 'Dressing Up', *Village Voice*, 30 April, p. 34.

26. Quoted in 'Skin and Bona: Interviews with Gay Skinheads', p. 15.

27. Ibid., p. 14.

28. 'Skin Complex', for Channel 4's gay magazine programme 'Out', July 1992.

29. Quoted in 'Skin and Bona: Interviews with Gay Skinheads', p. 14.

30. Marshall, *Spirit of '69*, p. 104.

31. Quoted in 'Skin and Bona: Interviews with Gay Skinheads', p. 14.

32. See 'Skin and Bona: Interviews with Gay Skinheads' and Healy, *Gay Skins*. Isaac Julien and Kobena Mercer argued that 'while some feminists have begun to take on issues of race and racism in the women's movement, white gay men retain a deafening silence on race', citing the rise of gay skinheads as an example of this racism: Isaac Julien and Kobena Mercer (1987), 'True Confessions', in Rowena Chapman and Jonathan Rutherford (eds), *Male Order: Unwrapping Masculinity*, London, p. 132. Black and Asian gay men on 'Skin Complex' also emphasised the threatening nature of gay skinheads, because 'you can't separate dress from politics: people will see a skinhead' (quoted on 'Skin Complex', Channel 4 'Out', July 1992).

33. Quoted in Healy, *Gay Skins*, p. 106.

34. Cole interview with Richard, 19 August 1998. This mirrors many men's decision to become clones. Joe Pop told of a similar realisation after having spent years dressing as a punk: 'Let's put it this way: it took me a long time to work out you get more sex if you didn't wear quite so much make-up' (Cole interview with Joe Pop, 19 May 1997).

35. Mike Dow (1985), 'Skins: 2', *Out*, April, p. 20.

36. Sue Tilley (1997), *Leigh Bowery: The Life and Times of an Icon*, London, pp. 33, 39.

37. Quoted in Healy, *Gay Skins*, p. 167.

38. One of my respondents recalled writing in his diary his pleasure upon first seeing Bronski Beat, as they presented an image of non-effeminate gay men, and how his friends couldn't believe Bronski Beat were gay, when they had been quick to label pop groups such as Duran Duran, Soft Cell and Culture Club. Murray Healy also quotes a man who attributes the popularity of the look to Jimmy Somerville: Healy, *Gay Skins*, p. 196.

39. It is worth noting that Levi's jeans and Doctor Marten boots were among the items that were included in many of the lists of 'design classics that appeared in the 1980s. See Deyan Sudjic (1985), *Cult Objects: The Complete Guide to Having it All*, London; and Stephen Bailey, Philippe Garner and Deyan Sudjic (1986), *Twentieth-Century Style and Design*, London.

40. Michelangelo Signorile (1990), *Outweek*, November 28. For other American images of this see Molly McGarry and Fred Wasserman (eds) (1998), *Becoming Visible*, New York and Susan Stryker and Jim Van Buskirk (eds) (1996), *Gay by the Bay*, San Francisco.

41. Quoted in 'Nature Boy', The *Face*, November 1989, no. 14, p. 60.

42. Cole interview with Bill Wilson, 10 August 1999.

43. Mort, *Cultures of Consumption*, pp. 71–2.

44. For an account of the gay element of House music see Anthony Thomas (1995), 'The House the Kids Built: The Black Gay Imprint on American Dance Music', in Corey K. Creekmuir and Alexander Doty (eds), *Out in Culture: Gay, Lesbian and Queer Essays on Popular Culture'*, London.

45. Cole interview with John, 7 June 1997.

46. Simon Witter (1987), 'BPM/AM', *i-D*, no. 49, July, p. 98.

47. Quoted in Mort, *Cultures of Consumption*, p. 184.

48. 'The Appropriators', *i-D*, no. 48, June 1987, p. 53.

49. Cole interview with Johnny Slut, 11 August 1998.

50. 'New England', *The Face*, August 1986, no. 76, p. 48.

51. Michael Bronski (1984), 'Culture Clash: The Making of Gay Sensibility', Boston, pp.186–7.

52. 'Skin Complex', on 'Out', Channel 4.

14

Are You a Fag? 'Cos You Look Like a Fag!

The history of gay men's dress has been marked by a vacillation between masculine and feminine. Throughout the twentieth century (and certainly before gay liberation) many gay men relied upon an effeminate image to project and reflect their sexuality. Scientific and cultural thinking had advanced the view that male homosexuality was a reflection of a female soul trapped in a male body. This led both to effeminacy's becoming the culturally accepted meaning of homosexuality and to a stereotype of homosexuality. Writing in 1965 J. L. Simmons believed that stereotypes grew from two points 'Stereotypes are variable: at one extreme they may be myths invented from superstition and misinformation; at the other verified scientific generalizations. They may be rigid prejudgments immune to reality testing or they may be tentative appraisals with the built in notion that their validity and applicability to all class members is problematic.'[1] In the absence of any other information the effeminate stereotype became a template for many gay men's expression of their sexuality. Esther Newton argues that this is part of the 'camp/theatrical' gay sensibility, and was most visible amongst the upper and lower classes.[2] Histories of homosexual subcultures have indicated that effeminacy and cross-dressing acted as signifiers to men in search of same-sex sexual relations, and this continued to provide a means to sexual encounters for some men into the 1980s. Boy George, for example, admitted that ''frocking up' was 'always a way of laying straight men . . . I don't think they would have let me do that if I hadn't been dressed up. Partly they admired my bravery for looking the way I did, partly it was because I was like a surrogate woman –that somehow made it okay for them.'[3] The adoption of the outward, visible markers of effeminacy, make-up, coloured hair, feminine or women's clothes took considerable bravery, as it was not only socially stigmatised but often illegal.[4]

Effeminate stereotypes offered a visible means of identification. For some they offered a means of self-identification through disassociation. For gay men who did not feel that they were effeminate such visible markers were unappealing. Many endeavoured to divorce themselves from effeminate gay men and strove to present a masculine image. This was especially significant amongst the more 'restrained' middle classes, and drew on what Jeff Escoffier defines as the 'egalitarian/authentic' gay perspective or sensibility.[5] This saw expression in the writings of the sociologist Edward Carpenter and of Walt Whitman, and advocated a 'masculine' love, an extension of male friendship grounded in the belief that it was possible for two *men* to love one another (without one's being a pseudo-woman). This notion of homosexual masculinity developed over the century. Many pre-liberation accounts note gay men referring to themselves in opposition to 'normal', i.e. straight, men: even though they did not perceive themselves as women, many did not regard themselves as 'real' men. Such men, however, were at pains to 'appear', at least in a non-gay or mixed situation. Martin Levine identifies this strategy as 'passing'. Discussing cinema, Vito Russo noted how gay sensibility was born out of a need for invisibility:

> A gay sensibility can be many things; it can be present even when there is no sign of homosexuality, open or covert . . . Gay sensibility is largely a product of oppression, of the necessity to hide so well for so long. It is a ghetto sensibility born of the need to develop and use a second sight that will translate silently what the world sees and what the actuality may be.[6]

Some men overcompensated and became 'male impersonators'.[7] For some men involvement in established masculine subcultures such as bikers led to the formulation of new identities and means of expression and sexual fulfilment, seen most notably in the rise of leather bars in the 1960s and 1970s. The desire to disengage from the popular stereotype of gay men as effeminate after gay liberation led to the adoption of overtly 'macho' styles of dress. Jamie Gough describes this as 'an attempt by gay men to make themselves more respectable. Empirically this is dubious in that the styles adopted do not actually look "normal": even a clone outfit does not look "normal" and, far from being a disguise, advertises you as gay.'[8] Eventually, the development of the 'butch' clone led to its becoming the new stereotype of homosexuality. Mark Simpson believes that in light of this, the clone was 'less of a liberated identity than a collision of reaction and compensation'.[9] The appearance of a series of masculinised post-clone identities for gay men has ironically given rise to a new identity, although this is not by its very nature one that is defined by an obvious dress choice, but more by an anti-choice, that is, a desire not to dress in any style that is perceived as gay. One man writing to the *Chicago Tribune* stressed that 'Most gay males are indistinguishable from straight males',[10] echoing the argument of the more conservative gay rights groups, that homosexuals are no different from heterosexuals, except in their sexual desire. Simpson sees this as a far more active choice, that many men are consciously 'acting straight': '[This] is not always just a reaction to stereotypes and stigma, but often represents a desire to "pass", to be taken for a heterosexual; the spirit of the closet'.[11] There is a relation here to Quentin Crisp's theory of a 'great dark man', in which a gay man desires a 'real' [i.e. heterosexual] man; but the moment that real man has a sexual relationship with another man he is no longer a 'real' man.[12] The straight-acting gay man of the 1990s accepts that he is gay, but according to Simpson, desires acceptance by straight society and tries to achieve this by copying straight behaviour:

> the ultimate tragedy of the SA [Straight Acting] gay man [is] He desires above all the acceptance of straight men (the 'general public' in his mind is composed almost exclusively of straight men) and hopes against hope that his hyper-het behaviour will achieve this. By exaggerating his 'masculinity' he hopes to woo the straight man and convince him that not all queers are queer.[13]

Writing in 1981, James Chesebro and Kenneth Klenk believed that 'the gay male who is known both as gay and masculine challenges the sensibilities of heterosexual males far more than the effeminate gay male'. Research, they stated, had proved that 'effeminate gay males are more tolerated and less aggressed against than more masculine gay males'.[14] This conforms to earlier theories that gay men had a place in society as long as they fitted the role of 'minstrel'.

Masculinised or feminised identities were an issue that had long been discussed amongst homosexual groups and communities (as well as by observers of those groups). The association with the female was one that many gay men did not question, but accepted as their lot, and advanced and reinforced. Writing of the group of male prostitutes he got to know in London's Soho in the 1930s, Quentin Crisp described their effeminate appearance and behaviour (combing each other's hair and swapping make-up), and noted that 'It never occurred to any of us to try to be more loveable'.[15] Alan Sinfield concludes that this is indicative of the way in which social codes 'feed back into psychic realities'.[16]

As the century progressed gay men did question their identities and the markers and definitions that society put on them. The members of the Gay Liberation Front, and particularly the radical drag queens, questioned assumptions (and presumptions) about male and female roles and masculine and feminine appearances. By the late 1980s, after nearly two decades of gay liberation, new questions were being asked about sexual identity, which gave rise to new 'queer' theories and politics. Such new theories allowed for a fluidity of identity, and presented a medium for (the discussion of) a breakdown of the rigidity of definitions. In discussing dress as a marker of identity, post-modern society allows the choosing or projection of a self-selected identity. However, Judith Butler noted that 'it remains politically necessary to lay claim to "female", "queer", "Gay" and "lesbian" precisely because of the way these terms, as it were, lay their claim on us prior to our knowing'.[17] Ted Polhemus has proposed a 'supermarket of style' theory in relation to subcultural dress, in which the participants can pick and choose elements of styles and identities that can reveal, mask or proffer a commentary on any aspect of personal identity that they may wish to present.[18] Murray Healy has noted that 'the realm of fashion and style is a highly appropriate, maybe even the only, site for successfully disrupting identities in a postmodern society'.[19]

The visibility of gay men and an increase in gay rights campaigning were experienced from the early 1980s, as a result of AIDS, the lack of governments' interest in the plight of gay men affected by the disease, and the introduction of 'anti-gay' legislation (such as Section 28 in the UK). Many young gay men had grown up in the years after the first waves of gay liberation and were now benefiting from the social visibility and (in some locations admittedly limited) acceptance of gay men. The rise in commercial gay venues and services and the existence of gay 'villages' attracted and welcomed gay men, allowing them to develop their identities in a relatively 'safe' space. Accompanied by the increased interest in fashion and grooming amongst men, both homo- and heterosexual, this had an enormous impact upon gay men's dress during the late 1980s and 1990s. The rise of the 'New Man',[20] a sensitive, almost feminist, well-groomed, dress-conscious straight man, coupled with the preponderance of masculine dress images for gay men, has led to what many feel is a difficulty in defining gay dress: 'It is difficult to spot a queen, now that straight boys all look like gay boys', one man claimed –a sentiment echoed by many others.

The adoption of gay images that had begun with the almost unconscious appropriation of gay clothing in the 1960s became a significant trend during the 1980s with the newly perceived marketability of a 'gay lifestyle' through the press. Michael Bracewell recognised that 'as mainstream attitudes towards homosexuality have become more liberal so too has the spectrum of gay iconography opened up to a broader, straight audience, many of whom have been jealous of the glamour of gay clothes'.[21] John Clarke's 'diffusion' theory, where 'a particular style is dislocated from the context and group which generated it, and taken up with a stress on those elements which make it "a commercial proposition", especially their novelty', is relevant here.[22] The adoption of gay imagery can also be linked to the commercialisation of gay 'villages' (such as the Castro in San Francisco, Old Compton Street in London and the Canal Street area of Manchester) and the (perceived) heterosexualisation of such spaces once they have proved successful and appealing to 'straight' society.[23]

Often inspired by club culture, or at least utilising clubs as a site for demonstrations of identity, many gay men (and particularly younger gay men) experimented with different styles of dress and images on an almost seasonal basis in order to retain a fashionability or style that set them apart from straight men. Toby Young believed that 'the pleasure we take from being *à la mode* consists in knowing about something which others do not',[24] something gay men were often at pains to attain. The seasonal adoption of specific brands or types of clothing, such as Schott flying jackets or Dolce and Gabana vests (tanktops), has helped gay men distinguish themselves from their straight counterparts. One particular example from 1993 was the popularity of the kilt amongst fashionable urban gay men in both Britain and America. The *New York Times* reported on the 'deluge of skirts' visible at the annual gay pride parade, noting that it was not the 'marchers in costume, but the young men watching the parade'[25] who were wearing the kilts. This adoption of skirts was not, however, a new form of drag or cross-dressing, it was very much a reflection of the masculine ideal, 'the mating of the masculine, century-old kilt and the muscular bodies of a new generation', the *New York Times* noted.[26] Gay men's appropriation of the kilt had very little to do with a sense of Scottish nationalism, Marion Hume pointed out in *The Independent* (though it did coincide with a revival in the wearing of the kilt among Scottish men).[27] Gay men who were wearing kilts were adding them to the masculinised gay wardrobe that had drawn on utilitarian working clothes. Keith Hepple (who was, '100 per cent gay and zero percent Scottish') said the kilt, 'feels good when you walk and it looks great with heavy socks and work boots',[28] and the *New York Times* observed that 'most of the kilts were short to show sculpted leg muscles and were balanced with a heavy workboot'.[29] By the next summer the popularity of the kilt was beginning to wane, only to be replaced by another traditional men's version of the skirt, the sarong. Once again, this item of clothing was combined with staple items of the gay wardrobe, the ribbed tanktop, to reveal a muscular frame, frequently enhanced by tattoos or body piercings.

That gay men in both New York and London were wearing an item of clothing at the same time was a reflection of the homogenisation of gay culture. Many of the predominant ideas and images were American-based, partly as a result of the international dominance of American culture after the Second World War. Americanisation of gay culture had begun in the early 1970s when European gay men had travelled to the United States, taking advantage of cheap transatlantic flights, and had been exposed to the highly developed and visible gay communities in major cities, such as New York, San Francisco and Los Angeles. The most obvious example of the import of American gay imagery was the clone, which quickly became the staple gay style for gay men throughout Europe. The title of Robert Altman's 1982 book, *The Homosexualization of America: The Americanization of the Homosexual* reflects this process. The process of homogenisation (or Americanisation) has continued, and is evident in the styles of dress worn in large commercial gay clubs and in images in the gay press and of gay men in the mainstream press. The influence of American imagery is even evident among gay men in countries such as Cuba, where the legal climate means that it is difficult to be openly gay and America is officially shunned. The gay men that I met when I was there on holiday in 1997 were desperate to obtain American items of clothing such as Levi's jeans and Nike training shoes. They had also developed a style of dress and body shape that was hugely influenced by American gay club culture –pumped up biceps and 'pecs', short hair, tight T-shirts and Levi's jeans.[30]

Travel had provided a means of developing a gay style prior to the 1970s. During the Second World War many gay men (and lesbians) experienced their first taste of organised gay culture, as they were posted to or passed through cities such as San Francisco, New York and London, as the historian Alan Bérubé has noted: 'A growing population of displaced young men and women on the move learned to think of themselves as gay, locate gay nightspots, met each other, formed relationships, used a new language, followed new codes of behaviour [including dress], and carved out places for themselves in the world as gay men and lesbians.'[31] After the war many chose to settle in these more accepting urban environments rather than returning to their homes. The founding of gay-friendly holiday resorts, such as Cherry Grove on Fire Island, offered destinations at which gay men (and lesbians) could behave and dress in a less constrained fashion. Stephen Cole recalled that '[Men] dressed up [for dinner] in a sort of South of France way . . . a pretty shirt and nice trousers and sandals and maybe a scarf. No jackets or anything like that.'[32] In a similar way the 1950s had seen an increase in travel to Europe. Resorts such as Capri and Cannes had attracted British gay men (those who could afford it), partly because of the more liberal attitudes they experienced there.[33] There gay men had been exposed to a less formal clothing convention, and this precipitated the development of new identifiably gay dress styles, and later as a consequence new forms of heterosexual male dress.

Gay men have long experimented with notions of acceptability in behaviour and dress. The twentieth century has seen a movement in the (straight) public's perceptions of gay men and also in the positioning of gay men's self-identity. Codes of behaviour and styles of presentation that were utilised by gay men have developed and been cast aside as social attitudes and legal positions have altered. Stereotypes that were formed have been challenged, broken down and replaced by new ones. David Forrest observed that the young gay man 'appears to have moved away from seeing himself and being seen by others, as a "gender invert", a "feminine" soul in a "male" body, and towards seeing himself and being seen as a complete (that is, "real") man'.[34] Michael Bracewell argued in 1993 that the final decade of the century is one in which 'the codes have become confused, and fashion, it seems has become one vast grey area, in which readings of style are either informed or indifferent. There is no longer any "us and them", in fashion terms; what remains are more simple notions of style which adapt to the sexuality of the individual.'[35] While Bracewell is right in noting that there has been a breakdown of the gay and non-gay 'us and them', fashion and dress choice are still used by many to differentiate themselves, sometimes as individuals, sometimes as members of a group and sometimes as both.

Many gay men no longer feel the need to define their identity through their choice of dress, while others are making conscious efforts to reinforce a communal identity through behaviour and locations for living and working and dress. One fact that does remain is gay men's interest in clothing; but even that is no longer homogenous, as Andrew Holleran has observed:

> The homosexual world . . . [is] as eclectic as life in New York: In any crowd walking down Saint Marks Place, young men in business suits carrying attaché cases, skinheads with great prongs of hair radiating from their scalps, fifties haircuts on Elvis Presley profiles, boys who want to look like Japanese art students in Paris, men with the long hair and pony tails I last saw in the sixties, and –a small fraction of what used to be the cutting edge –museum-quality clones in mustaches and jeans.[36]

Notes

1. J. L. Simmons (1965), 'Public Stereotypes of Deviants', *Social Problems*, no. 13, pp. 223–32.

2. Esther Newton (1993), *Cherry Grove, Fire Island: Sixty Years in America's First Gay and Lesbian Town*, Boston, p. 85; see also Esther Newton (1972), *Mother Camp: Female Impersonators in America*. Englewood Cliffs, NJ and George Chauncey

(1994), *Gay New York: Gender, Urban Culture and the Making of the Gay Male World, 1890–1940*, New York.

3. Kris Kirk (1988), 'Coming Clean: Boy George', *Gay Times*, no. 112, p. 30.

4. One of the most momentous events in gay history –the Stonewall riots –has been credited to effeminate queens (and 'butch' lesbians), who were brave enough to stand up to police harassment and fight back.

5. See Newton, *Cherry Grove*, p. 85 and Note 29.

6. Vito Russo (1987), *The Celluloid Closet: Homosexuality in the Movies*, New York, p. 92.

7. See Rodney Garland (1995), *The Heart in Exile*, Brighton, p.159 and Mark Simpson (1994), *Male Impersonators: Men Performing Masculinity*, London.

8. Gough, Jamie (1989), 'Theories of Sexual Identity and the Masculinisation of the Gay Man', in Simon Shepherd and Mick Wallis (eds), *Coming on Strong: Gay Politics and Culture*, London, p.131.

9. Mark Simpson (1992), 'Male Impersonators', *Gay Times*, August, p. 52.

10. Ann Landers (1992), 'Flamboyant Few Hurting Gay Cause', *Chicago Tribune*, 12 October, p. 3.

11. Simpson, 'Male Impersonators', p. 52.

12. Cole interview with Quentin Crisp, 2 October 1998.

13. Mark Simpson (1992), 'Male Impersonators', *Gay Times*, August, p. 53.

14. James Chesebro and Kenneth Klenk (1981), 'Gay Masculinity in the Gay Disco', in James Chesebro (ed.), *Gayspeak: Gay Male and Lesbian Communication*, New York, p.101.

15. Quentin Crisp (1985), *The Naked Civil Servant*, London, p.28.

16. Alan Sinfield (1994), *The Wilde Century*, London, p. 46.

17. Judith Butler (1993), *Bodies That Matter*, London, p.193.

18. See Ted Polhemus (1994), *Streetstyle: From Sidewalk to Catwalk*, London.

19. Murray Healy (1996), *Gay Skins: Class, Masculinity and Queer Appropriation*, London, p. 184.

20. This term has often been viewed as media hype; but there was an increased interest in fashion and grooming amongst straight men during the eighties and nineties, evidenced by the number of men's grooming magazines and their reiteration of the heterosexuality of their readers and desire to distance themselves from taints of homosexuality or homoeroticism. See Frank Mort (1996), *Cultures of Consumption* and Paul Jobling (1999), *Fashion Spreads: Word and Image in Fashion Photography Since 1980*, Oxford and Washington DC.

21. Michael Bracewell (1993), 'Dress Codes', *The Guardian*, 25 September, p. 41.

22. John Clarke (1976), 'Style' in S. Hall and T. Jefferson (eds), *Resistance Through Rituals*, London, p.188.

23. In his keynote paper at the 1999 Design History Conference, Chris Reed discussed the identification of the 'gay ghetto' in Chicago by the City authorities, through the erection of markers, 'Art Deco pylons' based on the rainbow flag. He presented both positive and negative responses from the gay communities and the

'straight' press, and noted how the area had become a commercialised playground rather than a gay-populated residential area. Chris Reed, 'Designs For A Gay Home-land: Marking Chicago's "Boys Town"', Keynote Paper at *Home and Away*, Design History Conference at Nottingham Trent University, September 1999.

24. Toby Young (1986), 'The Fashion Victims', *New Society*, 14 March, p. 456.

25. 'Men in Skirts', *The New York Times*, 4 July 1993, p. 3.

26. The dress historian Valerie Steele has claimed that the kilt is acceptable for men, in that it is '*not* a female skirt' but a sort of national dress. Valerie Steele (1989), 'Appearance and Identity', in C. Kidwell and Valerie Steele (eds), *Men and Women: Dressing the Part*, Washington DC, p. 9.

27. Marion Hume (1993), 'The Gay Gordons, Toms, Harrys and Jean-Pauls', *The Independent*, 7 December, p. 21.

28. Ibid.

29. 'Men in Skirts', *The New York Times*, 4 July 1993, p. 3.

30. They had also developed a signifying code based on a particular style of boot (with a metal strip around the heel) that I was assured was a definite sign of a man's homosexuality. What is significant is the similarity of this form of semi-secret identification to those utilised by gay men in Britain and the USA in earlier decades of the century described earlier in this book.

31. Alan Bérubé (1990), *Coming Out Under Fire: The History and Gay Men and Women in World War Two*, New York, p. 117.

32. Quoted in Newton, *Cherry Grove*, p. 69.

33. Denis Shorrock frequently went to Cannes on holiday in the late fifties and early sixties and developed his 'individual, piss elegant' style of dress from observing men he met and by buying clothes in Cannes: Cole interview with Denis Shorrock, 11 August 1997.

34. David Forrest (1993), 'Gay Male Identity', in Andrea Cornwall and Nancy Lindisfarent (eds), *Dislocating Masculinity*, London.

35. Bracewell, 'Dress Codes', p. 41.

36. Andrew Holleran (1988), *Ground Zero*, New York, p. 49.

Bibliography

Ackerley, J. R. (1960), *We Think the World of You*, London

Aguelles, L. and Rich, B. R. (1989), 'Homosexuality, Homophobia and Revolution: Notes Toward an Understanding of the Cuban Lesbian and Gay Male Experience', in M. B. Duberman, M. Vicinus and G. Chauncey Jr (eds), *Hidden From History: Reclaiming the Gay and Lesbian Past*, London

Alcorn, K. (1992), 'Queer and Now', *Gay Times*, May

Aldrich, R. and Wotherspoon, G. (eds) (1998), *Gay and Lesbian Perspectives IV: Essays in Australian Culture*, Sydney

Alfred, R. (1982), 'Will the Real Clone Please Stand Out?', *Advocate*, 18 March

Altman, D., (1982) *The Homosexualization of America: The Americanization of the Homosexual*, New York

——, Vance, C., Vicinus, M. *et al.* (1989), *Homosexuality, Which Homosexuality?*, London

Als, H. (1998), 'Cruel Story of Youth', in R. Violette (ed.), *Leigh Bowery*, London

Anomaly (1948), *The Invert and his Social Adjustment*, London

Anonymous (1958), *A Room in Chelsea Square*, London

Ashley, S. (1964), 'The "Other" Homosexuals', *One*, vol. XII, no. 2

Bailey, S., Garner, P. and Sudjic, D. (1986), *Twentieth-Century Style and Design*, London

Baker, R. (1978), 'Times They Were A-Changing', *Gay News*, no. 5

Barnard, M. (1996), *Fashion as Communication*, London and New York

Barnes, R. (1979), *Mods!*, London

Barr, J. (1982 [1950]), *Quatrefoil*, Boston

Bartlett, N. (1988), *Who Was That Man?*, London

Baudrillard, J. (1983), *Simulacra and Simulations*, New York

Beardemphl, W. E.(1967), 'Drag – Is It Drab, Despicable, Divine?', *Vector*, May

Beaver, H. (1981), 'Homosexual Signs (in Memory of Roland Barthes)' *Critical Inquiry*, Autumn

Bell, D. and Valentine, G. (1995), 'The Sexed Self: Strategies of Performance, Sites of Resistance' in S. Pile and N. Thrift (eds), *Mapping the Subject: Geographies of Cultural Transformation*, London and New York

Bernard, M. (1996), *Fashion as Communication*, London and New York

Bérubé, A. (1990), *Coming Out Under Fire: The History of Gay Men and Women in World War Two*, New York

Birch, I. (1981), *The Book With No Name*, London

Blachford, G. (1981), 'Male Dominance and the Gay World', in K. Plummer (ed.), *The Making of the Modern Homosexual*, London

Block, A. (1982), 'The Confessions of a Gay Rocker', *The Advocate*, 15 April

Boy George with Bright, S. (1995), *Take it Like a Man*, New York

Bracewell, M. (1993), 'Dress Codes', *The Guardian*, 25 September

Brake, M. (1985), *Comparative Youth Culture*, London

Bray, A. (1982), *Homosexuality in Renaissance England*, London

Brighton Ourstory Project (1992), *Daring Hearts: Lesbian and Gay Lives of 50s and 60s Brighton*, Brighton

——, (1995), 'Anyone Who Had a Heart', *Gay Times*, August

Bristow, J. (1989), 'Being Gay: Politics, Identity, Pleasure', *New Formations*, no. 9

Brompton, S. (1984), *Chameleon: The Boy George Story*, London

Bronski, M. (1984), 'Culture Clash: The Making of Gay Sensibility', Boston

——, (1991), 'A Dream is a Wish Your Heart Makes: Notes on the Materialization of Sexual Fantasy', in M. Thompson (ed.), *Leatherfolk: Radical Sex, People, Politics and Practice*, Boston, MA.

Brooke, J. (1950), *Orchid Trilogy*, London

Burke, T. (1969), 'The New Homosexuality', *Esquire*, no. 72

Burston, P. (1992), 'The Death of Queer Politics', *Gay Times*, August

—— (ed.) (1995) *A Queer Romance: Lesbians, Gay Men and Popular Culture*, London

Burton, P. (1985), *Parallel Lives*, London

——, (1995), 'The Way We Wore', in idem, *Amongst the Aliens: Some Aspects of Gay Life*, Brighton

Butler, J. (1990), *Gender Trouble: Feminism and the Subversion of Identity*, London

——, (1991), 'Imitation and Gender Insubordination', in D. Fuss, *Inside/Out – Lesbian Theories, Gay Theories*, London

——, (1993), *Bodies That Matter*, London

Califa, P. (1994), 'Beyond Leather: Expanding the Realms of the Senses to Latex', *Advocate*, no. 395

Cant, B. (ed.) (1993), *Footsteps and Witnesses: Lesbian and Gay Lifestories from Scotland*, Edinburgh

—— and Hemmings, S. (eds) (1988), *Radical Records: Thirty Years of Lesbian and Gay History*, London

Carlson, L. (1968), 'Leather: Open Forum', in *Vector*, June

Carpenter, E. (1906), *Love's Coming of Age*, London

Carpenter, H. (1979), *The Brideshead Generation: Evelyn Waugh and his Friends*, London

Chauncey, G. (1994), *Gay New York: Gender, Urban Culture and the Making of the Gay Male World, 1890–1940*, New York

Chenoune, F. (1993), *A History of Men's Fashion*, Paris

Chesebro, J. and Klenk, K. (1981), 'Gay Masculinity in the Gay Disco', in J. Chesebro (ed.), *Gayspeak: Gay Male and Lesbian Communication*, New York

Clarke, J. (1976), 'Style' in S. Hall and T. Jefferson (eds), *Resistance Through Rituals*, London

——, (1976), 'The Skinheads and the Magical Recovery of Working Class Community', in S. Hall and T. Jefferson (eds), *Resistance Through Rituals*, London

Cohen, A. (1976), 'The Delinquency Subculture', in R. Giallombardo (ed.), *Juvenile Delinquency*, New York

Cohen, D. (1992), 'Puncture Culture', *Him*, no. 60

—— and Dyer, R. (1980), 'The Politics of Gay Culture', in Gay Left Collective (eds), *Homosexuality: Power and Politics*, London

Cohen, P. (1972), 'Subcultural Conflict and Working Class Community', *W.P.C.S.*, 2, Birmingham

Cohn, N. (1971), *Today There Are No Gentlemen: The Changes in Englishmen's Clothes Since the War*, London

Cole, S. (1997), 'Corsair Slacks and Bondi Bathers: Vince Man's Shop and the Beginnings of Carnaby Street Fashions', *Things*, no. 6

Collard, J. (1994), 'No Style on Queer Street?', *Attitude*, October

Comstock, T. G. (1892), 'Alice Mitchell of Memphis', *New York Medical Times*, no. 20

Copley, A. (1989), *Sexual Moralities in France, 1780–1980: New Ideas on the Family, Divorce and Homosexuality*, London

Cory, D. W. (1951), *The Homosexual in America: A Subjective Approach*, New York

——, (1953), 'Can Homosexuals Be Recognized?', *One*, no. 1, September

—— and LeRoy, J. P. (1963), *The Homosexual and His Society: A View from Within*, New York

County, J. with Smith, R. (1995), *Man Enough to be a Woman*, London

Craik, J. (1994), *The Face of Fashion: Cultural Studies in Fashion*, London

Crane, L. (1963), 'How to Spot a Possible Homo', *Daily Mirror*, 28 April

Crisp, Q. (1985 [1977]), *The Naked Civil Servant*, London

Curry, D. (1993), 'Decorating the Body Politic', *New Formations*, no. 19

David, H. (1997), *On Queer Street: A Social History of British Homosexuality 1895–1995*, London

Davis, F. (1992), *Fashion, Culture, Identity*, Chicago

Davis, M. D. and Kennedy, E. L. (1993), *Boots of Leather, Slippers of Gold: The History of a Lesbian Community*, New York and London

Davis, N. (1975), 'Meditations on Drag', *Vector*, May

de la Haye, A., and Dingwall, C. (1996), *Surfers, Soulies, Skinheads and Skaters: Subcultural Style from the Forties to the Nineties*, London

Dellamora, R. (1990), *Masculine Desire*, Chapel Hill, NC

D'Emilio, J. (1981), 'Gay Politics, Gay Community: San Francisco's Experience', *Socialist Review*, no. 11

——, (1983), *Sexual Politics, Sexual Communities: The Making of a Homosexual Minority in the United States, 1940–1970*, Chicago

de Ortega Maxey, W. (1959), 'The Homosexual and the Beat Generation', *One*, Vol. VII, No. 7

Diaman, T. (1970), 'The Search for the Total Man', *Come Out*, December – January

Dow, M. (1985), 'Skins: 2', *Out*, April

Duberman, M. (1994), *Stonewall*, New York

——, Vicinus, M. and Chauncey, G. Jr (eds) (1989), *Hidden From History: Reclaiming the Gay and Lesbian Past*, London

Dyer, R. (1994), 'Fashioning Change: Gay Men's Style' in E. Healey and A. Mason (eds), *Stonewall 25: The Making of the Lesbian and Gay Community in Britain*, London

Eco, U. (1973), 'Social Life as a Sign System', in D. Robert (ed.), *Structuralism: The Wolfson College Lectures 1972*, New York

Ellis, H. (1936), *Sexual Inversion, Studies in the Psychology of Sex*, vol. 2, part 2 New York

Ellmann, R. (1987), *Oscar Wilde*, London

Evans, C. and Thornton, M. (1989), *Women and Fashion: A New Look*, London

Finlayson, I. (1990), *Denim*, Norwich

Finlayson, I. T. (1973), 'The Shifting Erogenous Zone', *Gay News*, no. 28

Fischer, H. (1977), *Gay Semiotics*, San Francisco

Forbes, D. (1984), 'Jim Holmes', *Advocate*, no. 395, 29 May

Ford, C. and Tyler, P. (1933), *The Young and Evil*, New York

Forrest, D. (1993), 'Gay Male Identity', in A. Cornwall and N. Lindisfarent (eds), *Dislocating Masculinity*, London

Foucault, M. (1978), *The History of Sexuality, vol. 1, An Introduction*, trans. Robert Hurley, New York

Fout, J. (1992), *Male Homosexuals, Lesbians and Homosexuality in Germany: From the Kaiserreich Through the Third Reich, 1871–1945*, Chicago and London

Freeman, G. (1969 [1961]), *The Leather Boys*, London

Fritscher, J. (1990), *Some Dance to Remember*, Stamford, CT

Garber, E. (1982), ''Tain't Nobody's Business: Homosexuality in Harlem in the 1920s', *Advocate*, May

Gardiner, J. (1992), *A Class Apart: The Private Pictures of Montague Glover*, London

Gardner, C. W. (1894), *The Doctor and the Devil; or the Midnight Adventures of Dr Parkhurst*, New York

Garland, R. (1995), *The Heart in Exile*, Brighton

Gearing, N. (1997), *Emerging Tribe: Gay Culture in New Zealand in the 1990s*, Auckland and London

Gever, M., Parmer, P. and Greyson, J. (eds) (1993), *Queer Looks*, London

Gidlow, E. (1980), 'Memoirs', *Feminist Studies*, no. 6

Goffman, E. (1959), *The Presentation of Self in Everyday Life*, New York

Goldstein, R. (1975), 'S&M: The Dark Side of Gay Liberation', *Village Voice*, 7 July

Gott, T. (ed.) (1995), *Don't Leave Me This Way: Art in the Age of AIDS*, London

Gough, J. (1989), 'Theories of Sexual Identity and the Masculinisation of the Gay Man', in S. Shepherd and M. Wallis (eds), *Coming on Strong: Gay Politics and Culture*, London

Grau, G. (ed.) (1995), *Hidden Holocaust?: Gay and Lesbian Persecution in Germany 1933–45*, trans. P. Camiller, London

Greenidge, T. (1930), *Degenerate Oxford?*, London

Gross, L. (1991), 'Out of the Mainstream: Sexual Minorities and the Mass Media', *Journal of Homosexuality*, no. 21(1/2)

Hall Carpenter Archives Gay Men's Oral History Group (1989), *Walking After Midnight: Gay Men's Life Stories*, London

Hall, S. (1977) 'Culture, the Media and the "Ideological Effect"', in J. Curran, M. Gurevitch and J. Wollacott (eds.), *Mass Communication and Society*, London

Hall, S. (ed.) (1980), *Culture, Media, Language: Working Papers in Cultural Studies, 1972–1979*, London

—— and Jefferson, T. (eds) (1976), *Resistance Through Rituals*, London

Harris, D. (1997), *The Rise and Fall of Gay Culture*, New York

Harris, F. (1918), *Oscar Wilde*, New York

Harvey, J. (1995), *Men in Black*, London

Hatton, K. (1964), 'The Mods', *Sunday Times Magazine*, 2 August

Healy, M. (1996), *Gay Skins: Class, Masculinity and Queer Appropriation*, London

Hebdige, D. (1987 [1979]), *Subculture: The Meaning of Style*, London

Helmer, W. J. (1963), 'New York's "Middle-class" Homosexuals', *Harpers*, vol. 226, March

Henley, C. (1982), *The Butch Manual: The Current Drag and How To Do It*, New York

Henry, G. W. (1941), *Sex Variants*, New York

Henry, T. (1989), *Break All Rules: Punk Rock and the Making of a Style*, Ann Arbor, MI and London

Herlihy, J. L. (1970 [1965]), *Midnight Cowboy*, London

Heylin, C. (1993), *From the Velvets to the Voidoids*, London

Higgins, P. (ed.) (1993), *A Queer Reader*, London

Hinsch, B. (1990), *Passions of the Cut Sleeve: The Male Homosexual Tradition in China*, Berkeley and Los Angeles, CA

Hix, C. (1979), Looking Good: A Guide for Men, London

Hoffman, M. (1968), *The Gay World: Male Homosexuality and the Social Creation of Evil*, New York

Holleran, A. (1980 [1978]), *Dancer from the Dance: Nights in the City in Gay New York*, London

——, (1982), 'The Petrification of Clonestyle', in *Christopher Street*, no. 69

——, (1988), *Ground Zero*, New York

Hooven, F. V. III (1995), *Beefcake: The Muscle Magazines of America 1950–1970*, Cologne

Horsfall, A. (1988), 'Battling for Wolfenden', in B. Cant and S. Hemmings (eds), *Radical Records: Thirty Years of Lesbian and Gay History*, London

Howes, K. (1994), *Broadcasting It*, London

—— and Wall, A. (1978), 'Punk, Wot's in it for Us?', *Gay News*, no. 136

Hughes, C. H. (1992), 'An Organization of Colored Erotopaths', 1893, reproduced in J. N. Katz, *Gay American History: Lesbians and Gay Men in the USA*, New York

Hume, M. (1993), 'The Gay Gordons, Toms, Harrys and Jean-Pauls', *The Independent*, 7 December

Humphreys, L. (1971), 'New Styles in Homosexual Manliness', *Trans-action*, vol. 8, no 5 & 6

Humphreys, M. (1985), 'Gay Machismo', in A. Metcalf and M. Humphreys (eds), *The Sexuality of Men*, London

Ireland, D. (1988–9), 'Gays in Eastern Europe', in *Peace and Democracy News*, Winter

Isaacs, G. and McKendrick, B. (1992), *Male Homosexuality in South Africa: Identity Formation, Culture and Crisis*, Cape Town and Oxford

Jackson, P. A. (1989), *Male Homosexuality in Thailand: An Interpretation of Contemporary Thai Sources*, Elmhurst, NY

Jarman, D. (1992), *At Your Own Risk*, London

Jivani, A. (1997), *It's Not Unusual: A History of Lesbian and Gay Britain in the Twentieth Century*, London

Jobling, P. (1999), *Fashion Spreads: Word and Image in Fashion Photography Since 1980*, Oxford and Washington DC

Johnson, C. A. (1986), 'Inside Gay Africa', *The New York Native*, 3 March

Johnson, H. (1994), *A Bone in My Flute*, London

Julien, I. and Mercer, K. (1987), 'True Confessions', in R. Chapman and J. Rutherford (eds), *Male Order: Unwrapping Masculinity*, London

Karlinsky, S. (1989), 'Russia's Gay Literature and Culture: The Impact of the October Revolution' in M. B. Duberman, M. Vicinus and G. Chauncey Jr (eds), *Hidden From History: Reclaiming the Gay and Lesbian Past*, London

Katsiaficas, G. (1987), *The Imagination of the New Left: A Global Analysis of 1968*, Boston

Katz, J. N. (1992), *Gay American History: Lesbians and Gay Men in the USA*, New York

Kennedy, E. L. (1995), 'Telling Tales: Oral History and the Construction of Pre-Stonewall Lesbian History', *Radical History Review*, no. 62

Kennilworth, B. (1933), *Goldie*, New York

Kettelhack, G. (ed.) (1984), *The Wit and Wisdom of Quentin Crisp*, New York

Khan, S. (1937), *Mentality of Homosexuality*, Boston

Kiernan, J. (1916), 'Classification of Homosexuality', *Urological and Cutaneous Review*, no. 20

Kirby, A. (1959), 'Some Folkways of the Dune People', *One*, vol. VII, no. 10

Kirk, K. (1988), 'Coming Clean: Boy George', *Gay Times*, no. 112

—— and Heath, E. (1984), *Men in Frocks*, London

Kleinberg, S. (1978), 'Where Have All the Sissies Gone?', *Christopher Street*, March

Kopkind, A. (1979), 'Dressing Up', *Village Voice*, 30 April

Landers, A. (1992), 'Flamboyant Few Hurting Gay Cause', *Chicago Tribune*, 12 October

Laver, J. (1977), *A Concise History of Costume*, London

Legman, G. (1941), 'The Language of Homosexuality: An American Glossary' in G. W. Henry, *Sex Variants*, New York, vol. 2

Levine, M. P. (1998), *Gay Macho: The Life and Death of the Homosexual Clone*, New York and London

Linden, R. R. *et al.* (eds) (1982), *Against Sadomasochism: A Radical Feminist Analysis*, San Francisco

Loughery, J. (1998), *The Other Side of Silence: Men's Lives and Gay Identities: A Twentieth Century History*, New York

Lukey, R. J. (1970), 'Homosexuality in Menswear', *Menswear*, February

McDowell, C. (1992), *Dressed to Kill: Sex, Power and Clothes*, London

McGarry, M. and Wasserman, F. (1998), *Becoming Visible: An Illustrated History of Lesbian And Gay Life in Twentieth-Century America*, New York

MacInnes, C. (1959), *Absolute Beginners*, London

McNeil, L. and McCain, G. (eds) (1996), *Please Kill Me: The Uncensored Oral History of Punk*, London

Magister, T. (1991), 'One Among Many: The Seduction and Training of a Leatherman', in M. Thompson (ed.), *Leatherfolk: Radical Sex, People, Politics and Practice*, Boston

Mains, G. (1984), *Urban Aboriginals: A Celebration of Leathersexuality*, San Francisco

Manning, T. (1996), 'Gay Culture: Who Needs It?', in M. Simpson (ed.), *Anti-Gay*, London

Marcus, E. (1992), *Making History: The Struggle for Gay and Lesbian Equal Rights, 1945–1990*, New York

Margin, J. D. (1955), 'The Margin of Masculinity', *One*, vol. III, no. 5

Marshall, G. (1991), *Spirit of '69: A Skinhead Bible*, Dunoon, Scotland

Marshall, J. (1981), 'Pansies, Perverts and Macho Men: Changing Conceptions of Male Homosexuality', in K. Plummer (ed.), *The Making of the Modern Homosexual*, London

Maupin, A. (1988), *Tales of the City*, London

Melly, G. (1970), *Revolt Into Style: Pop Arts Since the 50s and 60s*, Oxford

Mercer, M. (1991), *Gothic Rock*, Birmingham

Miller, N. (1992), *Out in the World: Gay and Lesbian Life from Buenos Aires to Bangkok*, New York

——, (1995) *Out of the Past: Gay and Lesbian History from 1869 to the Present*, London

Moore-Gilbert, B. (ed.) (1994), *The Arts in the Seventies: Cultural Closure*, London

Mort, F. (1988), 'Boys' Own? Masculinity, Style and Popular Culture' in Chapman, R. and Rutherford, J. (eds) *Male Order: Unwrapping Masculinity*, London

——, (1996), *Cultures of Consumption: Masculinities and Social Space in Late Twentieth-Century Britain*, London

Nardi, P. M., Sanders, D. and Marmor, J. (1994), *Growing Up Before Stonewall: Life Stories of Some Gay Men*, London

National Lesbian and Gay Survey (1993), *Proust, Cole Porter, Michelangelo, Marc Almond and Me: Writings by Gay Men on their Lives and Lifestyles*, London

Nehring, N. (1993), *Flowers in the Dustbin: Culture, Anarchy and Postwar England*, Ann Arbor, MI

Nestle, J. (1987), *A Restricted Country: Essays and Short Stories*, London

Newton, E. (1972), *Mother Camp: Female Impersonators in America*, Englewood Cliffs, NJ

——, (1993), *Cherry Grove, Fire Island: Sixty Years in America's First Gay and Lesbian Town*, Boston

Niles, B. (1991), *Strange Brother*, London

Nixon, S. (1992), 'Have You Got the Look? Masculinities and Shopping Spectacle', in R. Shields, *Lifestyle Shopping: The Subject of Consumption*, London

Nochlin, L. (1976), *Realism*, London

Norton, R. (1992), *Mother Clap's Molly House: The Gay Subculture in England 1700–1830*, London

Oosterhuis, H (ed.) (1991), *Homosexuality and Male Bonding in Pre-Nazi Germany: The Youth Movement, the Gay Movement and Male Bonding Before Hitler's Rise (Original Manuscripts from Der Eigene, the First Gay Journal in the World)*, trans. H. Kennedy, New York and London

Parker, S. (1984), 'Cardiff and South Wales', *Him*, no. 65

Pearce, F. (1973), 'How to be Immoral and Ill, Pathetic and Dangerous, All at the Same Time: Mass Media and the Homosexual', in S. Cohen and J. Young (eds), *The Manufacture of News: Social Problems, Deviance and the Mass Media*, London

Picano, F. (1996), *The Lure*, New York

Pickles (1984), *Queens*, London

Plummer, D. (1965), *Queer People: The Truth About Homosexuals in Britain*, New York

Polhemus, T. (1988), *Body Styles*, Luton

——, (1994), *Streetstyle: From Sidewalk to Catwalk*, London

——, (1996) and Randall, H., *The Customized Body*, London and New York

Porter, K. and Weeks, J. (eds) (1991), *Between the Acts: Lives of Homosexual Men 1885–1967*, London

Potter, Dr L. F. (1933), *Strange Loves: A Study in Sexual Abnormalities*, New York

Preston, J. (1991), 'What Happened?', in M. Thompson (ed.), *Leatherfolk: Radical Sex, People, Politics and Practice*, Boston

Radcliffe, M. (1994), 'The Incredible Bulk', *Independent*, 4 August

Reade, B. (1970), *Sexual Heretics*, London

Rechy, J. (1964), *City of Night*, New York

——, (1984), *Numbers*, New York

Reed, T. (1984), 'Reclaiming Effeminacy – A Starting Point?', *Square Peg*, no. 5

Renault, M. (1959), *The Charioteer*, London

Reynolds, S. (1983), *Punch*, April

Rouse, E. (1989), *Understanding Fashion*, Oxford

Rupaul (1995), *Lettin' It All Hang Out: An Autobiography*, London

Russell, I. (ed.) (1983), *Jeb and Dash: A Diary of a Gay Life 1918–1945*, Boston and London

Russo, V. (1987), *The Celluloid Closet: Homosexuality in the Movies*, New York

St Clair, S. (1976), 'Fashion's New Game: Follow the Gay Leader', *Advocate*, March

Savage, J. (1988), 'The Enemy Within: Sex, Rock and Identity', in Simon Frith (ed.), *Facing the Music: Essays on Pop, Rock and Culture*, London

——, (1990), 'Tainted Love: The Influence of Male Homosexuality and Sexual Divergence on Pop Music and Culture Since The War', in A. Tomlinson (ed.), *Consumption, Identity and Style: Marketing, Meanings and the Packaging of Pleasure*, London

——, (1991), *England's Dreaming: Punk Rock and the Sex Pistols*, London

Schuyf, J. (1993), '"Trousers with Flies!!" The Clothing and Subculture of Lesbians', *Textile History*, 24 (1)

Sedgwick, E. K. (1985), *Between Men*, New York

——, (1993), 'Queer Performativity: Henry James's *The Art of the Novel*', in *GLQ*, no. 1

Shepherd, G. (1987), 'Rank, Gender and Homosexuality: Mombasa as a Key to Understanding Sexual Options', in P. Caplan (ed.), *The Cultural Construction of Sexuality*, London

Short, B. (1987), 'Social Trends at Heaven's Pyramid', *Gay Times*, September

Signorile, M. (1990), *Outweek*, 28 November

——, (1997), *Life Outside*, New York

Simmel, G. (1957 [1904]), 'Fashion', *International Quarterly*, reprinted in *American Journal of Sociology*, no. 62, May

Simmons, J. L. (1965), 'Public Stereotypes of Deviants', *Social Problems*, no. 13

Simpson, M. (1992), 'Male Impersonators', *Gay Times*, August

——, (1994), *Male Impersonators: Men Performing Masculinity*, London

Simpson, M. (ed.) (1996), *Anti-Gay*, London

Sinfield, A. (1994), *The Wilde Century*, London

——, (1998), *Gay and After*, London

Smith, R. (1999), 'Oh No Love You're Not Alone', *Gay Times*, no. 250, July

Sontag, S. (1969), 'Notes on Camp', in *Against Interpretation*, New York

Sparrow, P. (1970), 'Tattooing and Sex: How Much Do You Reveal About Yourself?', *Vector*, August

Spencer, C. (1995), *Homosexuality: A History*, London

Stabiner, K. (1982), 'Tapping the Homosexual Market', *The New York Times Magazine*, 2 May

Steakley, J. (1975), *The Homosexual Emancipation Movement in Germany*, New York

Stearn, J. (1962), *The Sixth Man*, New York

Steele, V. (1989), 'Clothing and Sexuality' and 'Appearance and Identity', in C. Kidwell and V. Steele (eds), *Men and Women: Dressing the Part*, Washington DC

Steward, S. M. (1991), 'Dr. Kinsey Takes a Peek at S/M: A Reminiscence', in M. Thompson (ed.) *Leatherfolk: Radical Sex, People, Politics and Practice*, Boston, MA

Stimpson, C. R. (1982), 'The Beat Generation and the Trials of Homosexual Liberation', *Salmagundi*, no. 58–59

Stryker, S. and Van Buskirk, J. (1996), *Gay by the Bay*, San Francisco

Sudjic, D. (1985), *Cult Objects: The Complete Guide to Having It All*, London

Talsman, W. (1966 [1958]), *The Gaudy Image*, London

Taylor, I. and Wall, D. (1976), 'Beyond the Skinheads', in G. Mungham and G. Pearson (eds), *Working Class Youth Culture*, London

Tellier, A. (1948), *Twilight Men*, New York

Thomas, A. (1995), 'The House the Kids Built: The Black Gay Imprint on American Dance Music', in C. K. Creekmuir and A. Doty (eds), *Out in Culture: Gay, Lesbian and Queer Essays on Popular Culture*, London

Thompson, M. (ed.) (1991), *Leatherfolk: Radical Sex, People, Politics and Practice*, Boston, MA

Tilley, S. (1997), *Leigh Bowery: The Life and Times of an Icon*, London

Townsend, L. (1983), *The Leatherman's Handbook II*, New York

Trevison, J. S. (1986), *Perverts in Paradise*, London

Trumbach, R. (1989), 'Gender and the Homosexual Role in Modern Western Culture: The 18th and 19th Centuries Compared' in, D. Altman, C. Vance, M. Vicinus *et al.*, *Homosexuality, Which Homosexuality?*, London

Tseelon, E. (1982), 'Is the Presented Self Sincere?, Goffman, Impression Management and the Postmodern Self', *Theory, Culture and Society*, no. 9

Tucker, S. (1991), 'The Hanged Man', in M. Thompson (ed.), *Leatherfolk: Radical Sex, People, Politics and Practice*, Boston, MA

Tuller, D. (1991), 'Gay Activism in Eastern Europe', *The Advocate*, 18 June

Vale, V. and Juno, A. (1989), *Modern Primitives: An Investigation of Contemporary Adornment and Ritual*, San Francisco

van Naerssen, A. X. (ed.) (1987), *Gay Life in Dutch Society*, New York

Vermorel, F. (1997), 'The Godparents of Punk' in *NE Trains* magazine

——, (1997), *Fashion and Perversity: A Life of Vivienne Westwood and the Sixties Laid Bare*, London

Vickers, H. (1955), *Cecil Beaton*, London

Viegener, M. (1993), 'The Only Haircut That Makes Sense Anymore: Queer Subculture and Gay Resistance', in M. Gever, P. Parmer and J. Greyson (eds), *Queer Looks*, London

Walker, I. (1980), 'Skinheads, the Cult of Trouble', *New Society* 26 June

Ware, C. (1935), *Greenwich Village, 1920–1930* New York

Warner, M. (1993), *Fear of a Queer Planet: Queer Politics and Social Theory*, Minneapolis, MN

Warren, C. A. B. (1974), *Identity and Community in the Gay World*. New York

Warren, P. N. (1979 [1974]), *The Front Runner*, New York

Watanabe, T. and Iwata, J. (1989), *The Love of the Samurai: A Thousand Years of Japanese Homosexuality*, London

Watts, C. (1995), 'AIDS and the Body', *Rouge*, no. 21

Waugh, E. (1985), *Brideshead Revisited*, London

Weeks, J. (1989), 'Inverts, Perverts, and Mary-Annes: Male Prostitution and the Regulation of Homosexuality in England in the Nineteenth and Early Twentieth Centuries', in M. B. Duberman, M. Vicinus and G. Chauncey Jr. (eds), *Hidden From History: Reclaiming the Gay and Lesbian Past*, London

——, (1990), *Coming Out: Homosexual Politics in Britain from the Nineteenth Century to the Present*, London

——, (1990), *Sex, Politics and Society*, London

Welch, P. (1964), 'Homosexuality in America', *Life*, 26 June

Werther, R. (1922), *The Female Impersonators*, New York

West, D. J. (1977), *Homosexuality Re-Examined*, Minneapolis, MN

Whipplasch, L. (1968), 'Why Leather? or "What's a Nice Boy Like Me Doing Tied to a Stake Like This?"', *Vector*, June

White, E. (1986), *States of Desire: Travels in Gay America*, London

Whittington, G. (1969), 'Fashion . . . The Male's Emergence', *Vector*, April

Wilson, A. (1952), *Hemlock and After*, London

Wilson, E. (1985), *Adorned in Dreams: Fashion and Modernity*, London

Winn, G. (1967), *The Infirm Glory*, London

Witter, S. (1987), 'BPM/AM', *i-D*, no. 49, July

Wojcik, D. (1995), *Punk and Neo Tribal Body Art*, Jackson, MS

Wotherspoon, G. (1991), *'City of the Plain': History of a Gay Sub-Culture*, Sydney

Young, A. (1981), *Gays Under the Cuban Revolution*, San Francisco

Young, T. (1986), 'The Fashion Victims', *New Society*, 14 March

Index